D0886419

PRISON LIFE WRITING

LIFE WRITING SERIES

Series editors: Marlene Kadar, York University; Sonja Boon, Memorial University

Wilfrid Laurier University Press's Life Writing series celebrates life writing as both genre and critical practice. As a home for innovative scholarship in theory and critical practice, the series embraces a range of theoretical and methodological approaches, from literary criticism and theory to autoethnography and beyond, and encourages intersectional approaches attentive to the complex interrelationships between gender, class, race, ethnicity, sexuality, ability, and more. In its commitment to life writing as genre, the series incorporates a range of life writing practices and welcomes creative scholarship and hybrid forms. The Life Writing series recognizes the diversity of languages, and the effects of such languages on life writing practices within the Canadian context, including the languages of migration and translation. As such, the series invites contributions from voices and communities who have been under- or misrepresented in scholarly work.

PRISON
LIFE
WRITING

CONVERSION AND THE
LITERARY ROOTS OF THE
U.S. PRISON SYSTEM

SIMON ROLSTON

WLU PRESS
WILFRID LAURIER
UNIVERSITY PRESS

Inspiring Lives.

This book has been published with the help of a grant from the Canadian Federation for the Humanities and Social Sciences, through the Awards to Scholarly Publications Program, using funds provided by the Social Sciences and Humanities Research Council of Canada. Wilfrid Laurier University Press acknowledges the support of the Canada Council for the Arts for our publishing program. We acknowledge the financial support of the Government of Canada. Funding provided by the Government of Ontario and the Ontario Arts Council. This work was supported by the Research Support Fund.

Library and Archives Canada Cataloguing in Publication

Title: Prison life writing : conversion and the literary roots of the U.S. prison system / Simon Rolston.

Other titles: Conversion and the literary roots of the U.S. prison system | Conversion and the literary roots of the United States prison system

Names: Rolston, Simon, 1977- author.

Series: Life writing series.

Description: Series statement: Life writing series | Includes bibliographical references and index.

Identifiers: Canadiana (print) 20200412434 | Canadiana (ebook) 2020041318X | ISBN 9781771125178 (softcover) | ISBN 9781771125185 (EPUB) | ISBN 9781771125192 (PDF)

Subjects: LCSH: Prisoners' writings, American—History and criticism. | LCSH: Prisoners—United States—Biography—History and criticism. | LCSH: Prisoners in literature. | LCSH: Prisons in literature. | LCSH: Conversion in literature. | LCSH: Prisons—United States.

Classification: LCC PS153.P74 R65 2021 | DDC 810.9/9206927—dc23

Cover photo and design, and interior design by Michel Vrana.

© 2021 Wilfrid Laurier University Press
Waterloo, Ontario, Canada
www.wlupress.wlu.ca

This book is printed on FSC®-certified paper. It contains recycled materials, and other controlled sources, is processed chlorine free, and is manufactured using biogas energy.

Printed in Canada

Every reasonable effort has been made to acquire permission for copyright material used in this text, and to acknowledge all such indebtedness accurately. Any errors and omissions called to the publisher's attention will be corrected in future printings.

No part of this publication may be reproduced, stored in a retrieval system, or transmitted, in any form or by any means, without the prior written consent of the publisher or a licence from the Canadian Copyright Licensing Agency (Access Copyright). For an Access Copyright licence, visit http://www.accesscopyright.ca or call toll free to 1-800-893-5777.

CONTENTS

ACKNOWLEDGMENTS

YEARS AGO, I WAS TEACHING A CLASS ON *The Autobiography of Malcolm X* to imprisoned students at Auburn Correctional Facility in Upstate New York, and I was describing how Norfolk Prison, when Malcolm X was incarcerated there in the late 1940s, was known for its innovative rehabilitation programming – when a hand at the back of the class shot up. "It's kinda still like that," said the man as he lowered his hand. For several minutes, he detailed the inner workings of the prison, and he explained that, while it was certainly not the social experiment of the postwar period, it retained some semblance of its former focus on rehabilitation. I asked him how he knew so much about the prison, and he answered, "Because I did time there."

This moment illustrates how my expertise is based on the experiences of others: what I know about the prison system, what I write about in this book, is indebted to incarcerated and formerly incarcerated men and women who taught me about experiences that I thankfully never had. I am therefore extremely grateful to the aforementioned imprisoned men at Auburn (who attended Stephanie DeGooyer's class as part of the Cornell Prison Education Program, where I was a guest speaker), the imprisoned men who participated in Ed Griffin's writing class at Matsqui Institution in BC, who shared their writing with me and who graciously read some of my early work about prison literature, and the imprisoned men and women at Edmonton Institution and Fork Saskatchewan Correctional Center, who discussed their experiences of reading with me. If this book is dedicated to anyone, it is to imprisoned people. And, of course, this book owes a particular debt to those incarcerated people who managed to write about their lives.

I would also like to thank the teachers at the University of British Columbia who guided my Social Sciences and Humanities Research Council-funded doctoral research, which was the starting point for this book. I particularly want to thank Michael Zeitlin, Susanna Egan, and Glenn Deer, who supported and encouraged me through the initial stages of my work.

Many people read early versions of this book, and their feedback was invaluable: Deena Rymhs, Peter Caster, Sean McAlister, Moberly Luger, Jared Morrow, and Eddie Curran, to name just a few people, critiqued my work and helped give my ideas coherence at different stages of this project. Thanks, also, to Dan Berger, who graciously met me for coffee one wet day in Seattle and helped me work through a tangle of problems that I encountered while completing a first draft.

I am grateful to everyone at Wilfrid Laurier University Press, especially to Siobhan McMenemy, and to the reviewers of this manuscript, whose comments helped make this a better book. Thank you, also, to the many reviewers who provided feedback on passages that were originally published elsewhere. Some content from this book's introduction and Chapter 1 was previously published as "Conversion: Life Writing and the Story of the American Prison," in *Critical Survey* 23, no. 3 (2011): 103–18. Some of Chapter 2 was published in the following articles: "'His Enemy's Language': African American Prison Life Writing, the Literary Forms of Institutional Power, and George Jackson's *Soledad Brother*," in *Imprisonment, Institutionality, and the Literary World*, edited by Claire Westall and Michelle Kelly (Abingdon: Routledge, 2020); and "Bad: Prison Life Writing, African American Narrative Strategies, and *The Autobiography of James Carr*," in *MELUS: Multi-Ethnic Literature of the US* 38, no. 4 (2013): 191–215. And a portion of Chapter 3 was previously published as "White Boy: Prison Life Writing and the Rhetoric of White Male Victimhood in T.J. Parsell's *Fish* and Jack Henry Abbott's *In the Belly of the Beast*," in *American Studies* 55, no. 4 (2017): 187–206. I am grateful to these publications for accepting my work and for permitting me to republish the aforementioned material.

ACKNOWLEDGMENTS

Finally, a big thanks to my family, who are always enthusiastic about my work, especially to my boys, Fynn and Solomon Rolston, whose joy of living, boundless creativity, and intellectual curiosity I so admire.

AUTOBIOGRAPHY AND THE PROBLEM WITH RESISTANCE

THE CONVERSION NARRATIVE IN PRISON DISCOURSE AND US PRISON LIFE WRITING

Them fools say you can become anything when it's over.
Told 'em straight up, ain't nothing to resurrect
after prison.
—Reginald Dwayne Betts, "Ghazal"

WHEN I WAS NINETEEN, I WAS INCARCERATED AT THE SANTA BARBARA County Jail for four days as a result of a scuffle with local police officers. After overcoming my initial, shocked realization that I was behind bars, I learned how imprisoned people passed the time: they told stories about their lives. Years later, with these stories on my mind, I conducted a study of reading practices in a jail and prison in Alberta, Canada. There, imprisoned men and women suggested books that I should read in order to understand what incarceration was like. The overwhelming majority of those books were life writings. Both my jail time in Santa Barbara and my visits to jails and prisons as a researcher in Alberta (and later similar visits to prisons in Vancouver and New York) demonstrated to me that incarcerated people place great stock in life narratives – a conclusion confirmed in the prison literature genre, which is largely comprised of autobiographies and memoirs.

So I was surprised to discover that life writing as a genre was largely overlooked in the scholarship about US prisons. There have been numerous monographs about prison writing and the role of the prison in American culture, beginning with H. Bruce Franklin's *The Victim as Criminal and Artist* (1978), which is largely credited with launching the study of American prison writing as a research field. More recently, there have been numerous book-length studies of US prison writing, including Auli Ek's *Race and Masculinity in Contemporary American Prison Narratives* (2005), Jason Haslam's *Fitting Sentences: Identity in Nineteenth- and Twentieth-Century Prison Narratives* (2005), Dylan Rodríguez's *Forced Passages: Imprisoned Radical Intellectuals and the U.S. Prison Regime* (2006), Peter Caster's *Prisons, Race, and Masculinity in Twentieth-Century U.S. Literature and Film* (2008), Caleb Smith's *The Prison and the American Imagination* (2009), and Joy James's anthologies, which interweave scholarly analyses of the prison and prison culture with the critical work of "imprisoned intellectuals."[1] There have also been many excellent collections of prison writing (Franklin, Chevigny, and Blunk and Levasseur, to name a few).[2] But there are no book-length studies of American prison *life* writing even though it is the most common form of writing in prisons and, I should add, the genre most likely to be read by the wider public.

Prison life writing: I use the term throughout this book, so let me briefly explain what it means and how I intend to use it. "Life writing" is an umbrella term that denotes (mostly) non-fiction literature that focuses, in some fashion, on real people's life experiences. It includes subgenres like autobiography, biography, memoir, letters, and diaries.[3] This book focuses primarily on autobiography and memoir – life writing where the author and the narrator are the same. Autobiography tends to be more focused on the story of the person who is the "I" of the narrative and whose name graces the book's cover (although sometimes autobiographies are written with collaborators or amanuenses); memoir, by comparison, typically focuses more attention on the lives of the people around the narrative subject. The former is more interior, the latter more exterior, in focus.[4] *Prison* life writing broadly refers to life writing written by incarcerated or formerly incarcerated people whose stories focus in some fashion on their experiences in carceral institutions.

Perhaps because there has been no sustained consideration of prison life writing as a genre, scholars, educators, and activists consistently misidentify American prison life writing as "resistance literature," which presumes that the genre has an ideological cohesion that is not entirely accurate.[5] That presumption is faulty. For example, Caren Kaplan claims that "the act of writing itself resists the rationale of the prison and the state power it represents," and Tara T. Green writes that prison life writing (and she is specifically discussing George Jackson's *Soledad Brother*) "challenges the system designed to render prisoners voiceless and powerless."[6] Similarly, Auli Ek claims that "prison narratives counteract the established logic of imprisonment," and Sandra Young argues that "autobiography provides a model ... to counter-write that which is forcibly imprinted through the 'vocabulary' of imprisonment."[7]

The autobiographical writings of imprisoned people are sometimes defined as counter-texts – or what Ioan Davies in *Writers in Prison* (1990) calls "anti-texts" – because they can provide the imprisoned or formerly imprisoned person with an alternative forum for truth-telling –alternative, that is, to the courtroom.[8] Paul Gready employs this paradigm when he writes that while "prisoners ha[ve] little or no control over the manner in which they [a]re captured and fixed in official writing, other written forms[,] [such as] the writing of autobiographical accounts, provid[e] a way of regaining control."[9] In this formulation, autobiography becomes what Leigh Gilmore calls an "alternative hearing."[10] Although these analyses of prison life writing are valid, they are incomplete: their focus on writing as resistance overlooks how even the most militantly resistant works of prison life writing are saturated with the organizational and disciplinary features of institutional power. In prison life writing, the *prison* is writing too.

Reading prison life writing as resistance literature all too often represents life writing as a liberatory practice and the prison as an oppressive and restrictive institution. Again, while this is sometimes true, it is only part of the story. For one thing, life writing is an important component of the prison's disciplinary and ideological work: prison staff use life writing as a form of surveillance (in incarcerated people's files or through the work of prison censors), social control (in parole hearings), and rehabilitation (in writing classes or therapy), for example. In myriad ways, the prison is constantly requiring incarcerated people to confess. These confessions are sometimes like penal variants of what Ebony Coletu calls "biographic mediations," that is, "structured request[s] for personal information that facilitat[e] institutional decision-making," although the prison's requests for self-disclosure are often accompanied by threats of violence, be they direct (punitive solitary confinement) or indirect (the refusal of parole). In other words, although prisons discourage certain forms of life writing, they encourage and even insist on others.[11] Rather than simply "rendering prisoners voiceless and powerless," as Green writes, prisons often use life writing to channel imprisoned voices into established discourses.

The prison system thus shares with life writing an interest in the psychological and biographical components of an incarcerated person's identity. Warren Spaulding of Massachusetts, one of the most influential Progressive Era prison reformers, wrote that the incarcerated person's "past character and conduct, surroundings, associates, and tendencies ... what family the offender has; whether he works regularly and supports those dependent upon him, whether he has habits which lead him into criminal ways," are all significant factors for the criminal justice system as it seeks to define the appropriate way to punish and correct them.[12] From the Progressive Era court-appointed probation officer to the Treatment Era parole board, criminal justice officials have always relied on elements of biography and autobiography as important tools for surveillance and control.

But this is not simply a matter of prison life writing and prison surveillance having parallel interests: these interests converge in incarcerated people's written works whenever they write about themselves. As Spaulding suggests, when incarcerated people tell their stories, they do so within what Erving Goffman calls "total institutions" that want to know about their lives and through that knowledge *determine* their lives.[13] Autobiography, a genre premised on the revelation of personal information, risks magnifying the surveillance capacities of prison and criminal justice officials. Imprisoned people cannot simply tell all, reveal all, because confessions have disciplinary and legal consequences for them as well as for any other incarcerated people they write about in their work. Curiously, even formerly incarcerated people writing about their incarceration are not immune to the influence of the prison, although the impact of the prison on their work is typically more diffuse and abstract, sometimes linked to broader anxieties that formerly incarcerated people might have about their precarity in a society that sees them as alien and dangerous. Essentially, my point is this: prison life writing is not inherently resistant; instead, even for formerly incarcerated people writing after they have been released, it remains highly contested territory.

To presume that prison life writing is necessarily resistant to institutional power risks overlooking the ideological *and* aesthetic complexities of that writing. As I have been suggesting, the relationship that is posited between self (*autos*), life (*bios*), and writing (*graphe*) in autobiography involves institutional discourse in ways that are fundamentally different from other literary forms.[14] To navigate the role of the prison in their lives and work, incarcerated people make surprising innovations that redefine what can and what cannot be said in autobiographical discourse; in this way, they challenge how we think about life writing and institutional power. Reading prison life writing as though institutional discourse is not imminent to it, coercing it, sometimes even structuring and defining it, misses how incarcerated people experiment with literary form in order to accommodate or contest these powerful discursive forces.

In this book, I explore the complicated tensions of power and resistance in prison life writing by focusing on the conversion narrative, which maps a life writer's fall, conversion, and social reintegration. Although largely unmentioned in the prison writing scholarship, the conversion narrative appears in prison life writing so frequently that it virtually dominates the genre (except, notably, in imprisoned women's life writings, which I will address in a moment). Conversions are common in a variety of autobiographical modes employed by imprisoned people, but they are especially common in published monographs, which are the primary focus of this book.

Moreover, I argue that the conversion narrative is also a metanarrative of the US prison system: since the first penitentiary experiment at the end of the eighteenth century, theories of rehabilitation have employed the conversion narrative to conceptualize how the prison changes someone from a criminal to a citizen.[15] Thus, prison life writing and prison discourse share a vocabulary. Exploring this vocabulary, this shared narrative territory, complicates scholars' presumptions about prison, rehabilitation, power, resistance, and even literature. It also maps prison life writing's generic boundaries, including how those boundaries are moved or transgressed in incarcerated people's autobiographical work, and it clarifies the genre's aesthetic connections to diverse literary and aesthetic categories, from religious practices to African American folk traditions, as well as to non-literary discourses, such as criminology, penology, and psychology. Ultimately, by exploring incarcerated people's autobiographies and memoirs that adhere to but also break from the traditions of the prison life writing genre, I take stock of an important literary field whose features have yet to be fully understood.

LIVES OF REINVENTION: A BRIEF INTRODUCTION TO THE CONVERSION NARRATIVE IN AMERICAN PRISON LIFE WRITING

Since this book views prison life writing largely through the lens of the conversion narrative, which I suggest is a defining feature of the genre, I first want to describe what the conversion narrative is and explain how it typically works in prison life writing. The conversion narrative, according to autobiography theorists Sidonie Smith and Julia Watson, "develops through a linear pattern – descent into darkness, struggle, moment of crisis, conversion to new beliefs and worldview, and consolidation of a new communal identity."[16] In the American tradition, conversion narratives have a largely Christian pedigree with roots in Puritan New England in the early seventeenth century.[17] Secular writers in the eighteenth century then adopted the conversion narrative as a way to articulate dramatic but non-spiritual self-transformations in their life writings. In *Sacred Estrangements* (1993), Peter A. Dorsey explains that the secular use of the religious conversion narrative really began when Rousseau adapted the form of Augustine of Hippo's *Confessions* (398) to write his 1782 autobiography of the same name:

> For Augustine, God was the only source of grace, who in a radical act of transformation gave meaning and value to an individual's life. For Rousseau, conversion, though an experiential reality, had variable consequences. It could change one's ideas, define one's personality, merge one with a community, or draw one into isolation. Less than an absolute good, conversion simply became a means by which one perceived the world.[18]

After Rousseau, writes Dorsey, the conversion narrative became a way to represent "any radical change or new insight," and he suggests that many of its features underpin modern autobiography.[19]

That said, the conversion narrative has several important characteristics that distinguish it from similar forms of life writing.[20] Chief among them is the trope of the bifurcated self, or the motif of rebirth. Crucial to both religious and secular expressions of the conversion experience is a complete change from one way of being to another, which is usually described as a division of selfhood: an old (sinful or unenlightened) self is separated from a new (repentant or enlightened) self – what Evangelical Christians describe as a process of being "born again." William James, in *The Varieties of Religious Experience* (1902), describes this as "a complete division ... established in the twinkling of an eye between the old life and the new."[21] Although there are many iterations of the conversion narrative, some with more baroque morphologies than others, all conversion narratives hinge on this metaphor, which divides a past from a present self or identity – a division that, as I will show, is especially appealing to incarcerated people interested in shucking off the vestiges of their criminality once released but also to the criminal justice system, with its rehabilitative philosophy of judgment, punishment, renewal, and social reintegration.

Although the conversion narrative is a literary paradigm, it has also served uniquely non-literary functions in American life. Most obviously, within faith communities, conversion has a long history of helping people understand, articulate, and make shareable the experience of divine intervention. But some communities have also used the conversion narrative to ensure social cohesion, even social control. As I will discuss in Chapter 1, during the colonial period, the Puritans relied on the conversion narrative to ensure social unity and define community hierarchies. Similarly, in the twentieth century, members of Alcoholics Anonymous work to change their lives through a twelve-step conversion narrative, which helps them maintain their sobriety but also establish their position, their belonging, as part of a community of recovering alcoholics. These practices show how the conversion narrative shuttles back and forth between the literary and the social, how it helps articulate the individual experience while also providing a socially determined framework within which that individual experience can be expressed – and, perhaps in some cases, normalized, disciplined, even coerced.

Let me further explain how the conversion narrative works, what constitutes its defining features, and why it matters for incarcerated people and the US prison system. I will do so through a reading of *The Autobiography of Malcolm X*, which is undoubtedly the most famous book in the American prison life writing archive.[22] Now, it might seem strange that *The Autobiography of Malcolm X* is a cornerstone of the prison life writing tradition, given that it is an as-told-to narrative that was written well after Malcolm X was released from prison, and that his prison experience is limited largely to two chapters, "Satan" and "Saved." First, there is a long tradition of autobiographies written with amanuenses (fugitive slave narratives, for example, but also many prison narratives). While these collaborative life narratives might seem to push against the boundaries of what we would consider autobiography, and while some theorists have questioned the applicability of the term "autobiography" to collaborative life narratives that involve discrepancies of power and agency when a storyteller (such as an enslaved or imprisoned person) has significantly less power than an editor or amanuensis, collaborative life narratives are certainly conventional variants of the life writing genre.[23]

Second, although Malcolm X's autobiography mostly takes place outside prison, the prison is central to the most significant change in Malcolm's life, and his repeated invocation of his imprisonment in the rest of the autobiography and in his speeches indicates that we should see the prison as playing a central role in the book's narrative arc – hence, why we should read it within the prison life writing genre. Finally, and importantly, *The Autobiography of Malcolm X* is repeatedly invoked in the life writings of other imprisoned and formerly imprisoned people, including many of the people discussed in this book (from George Jackson and Eldridge Cleaver to Shaka Senghor and Assata Shakur). This often happens with canonicity: later writers explicitly or implicitly acknowledge a debt to, or identify a shared literary territory with, important predecessors within a particular genre. Many prison life writings name-check Malcolm X's autobiography because it is one of the genre's *ur*-texts.

The Autobiography of Malcolm X is a book about change – multiple changes, in fact. Malcolm X undergoes a series of dramatic self-transformations throughout his life and before his untimely death in 1965 – so many that he describes his life as "a chronology of ... changes," which Manning Marable references in the subtitle of his acclaimed 2011 biography, *Malcolm X: A Life of Reinvention*.[24] However, Malcolm's first conversion while he was imprisoned is perhaps his most dramatic and is certainly his best-known. Sentenced to eight to ten years for larceny, breaking and entering, and the illegal possession of a firearm (an uncommonly lengthy sentence at the time, which Malcolm justifiably claims had more to do with his being with two white women accomplices than with his crimes), he is sent to Massachusetts' Charleston State Prison and later to Concord Prison. Eventually, he is transferred to Norfolk Prison Colony, which he describes as "an experimental rehabilitation jail."[25]

At Norfolk, Malcolm experiences a dramatic conversion that he likens to the biblical story of Paul's conversion on the road to Damascus.[26] In explaining his conversion, he repeatedly uses the trope of rebirth that, as I have said, is a defining feature of the genre. For example, at one point, he writes, "I still marvel at how swiftly my previous life's thinking pattern slid away from me, like snow off a roof. It is as though someone else I knew had lived by hustling and crime. I would start to catch myself thinking in a remote way of my earlier self as another person."[27] Here, his past self is distinguished from an emergent identity: "my previous life"; "as though *someone else* I knew had lived by hustling and crime"; "thinking ... of *my earlier self* as *another person*." This metaphor of an "earlier self," and the narrative pattern of which this metaphorical transformation is a part, is also enshrined in Malcolm's name changes throughout his autobiography.[28] Born Malcolm Little, he takes the name Detroit Red while living as a street hustler, drug dealer, and thief. Once imprisoned, and due in part to his foul mood and shock of red hair (his mood was partly due to his sudden and forced drug withdrawal in prison), he is called Satan by the other incarcerated people, a moniker that also attests to his fallen condition according to the conversion teleology. (Could one fall lower than Hell?) After his conversion, which occurs at the lowest point in his life (what Alcoholics Anonymous calls "rock bottom"), he takes the name Malcolm X, which memorializes his dramatic rebirth but also acknowledges the new community, the Nation of Islam, that helps sustain his post-conversion, communal identity. This pattern, where an incarcerated person undergoes a conversion experience behind bars that transforms them in some fashion from a criminal to a citizen, is a defining feature of prison life writing.

Why Malcolm X undergoes his conversion is especially important since it illuminates some of the ideological entanglements of the genre that I will be focusing on throughout this book. Obviously, as most people familiar with his story know, Malcolm converts because of his then-nascent religious beliefs. In prison, he learns from his siblings about the Nation of Islam, a home-grown African American Islamic organization, and he initiates a correspondence with the group's leader, Elijiah Muhammad, that eventually culminates in his conversion.

But the prison's rehabilitation programming plays a defining role in his self-transformation too. At the same time that he learns about the Nation of Islam, he accelerates his studies, famously copying out the entire dictionary to improve his vocabulary and spending countless hours reading in the prison library and in his cell. "I was the nearest thing to a hermit in the Norfolk Prison Colony," he writes.[29] Rather than simply the work of an autodidact, however, this intensive education was a requisite component of the Norfolk program. As Malcolm noted, Norfolk (now called the Massachusetts Correctional Institute at Norfolk) was an "experimental" institution, an exemplar of emergent prison reform efforts during the "Treatment Era" (1945–76). Putting into practice new penological theories that reframed prisons as asylums or schools, Norfolk sought to reform rather than punish its incarcerated charges. It did so in part by focusing strongly on education, one component of which was a well-stocked prison library. In studying so intensely, Malcolm was hardly resisting the prison system, given that Norfolk encouraged and even required its incarcerated people to conduct precisely the kind of work that he was doing. "As you can imagine," Malcolm explains, "especially in a prison where there was heavy emphasis on rehabilitation, an inmate was smiled upon if he demonstrated an unusually intense interest in books."[30]

Of course, Malcolm used this educational system for ends quite different from those the prison officials intended. Officials at Norfolk were eventually quite eager to oust him from their program and force him to return to spend the last year of his sentence in the general population at Charleston Prison, presumably because of his outspoken beliefs about race, which he had acquired through his correspondences with Elijah Muhammad but also through his studies in his cell and in the prison library.[31] And yet, the role of the prison in his conversion, its implication in the experience that transformed his life, points to the peculiar and unexpected ways that competing discourses merge uneasily in prison life writing, making it difficult to see the genre as solely on one side of a Manichaean divide between a powerless writer and a powerful institution.

More often than not, conversions in prison life writing feature prison education, especially experiences of reading and writing, as producing transformative effects. When Malcolm X writes, "Prison enabled me to study far more intensively than I would have if my life had gone differently and I had attended some college," when he asks, "Where else but in prison could I have attacked my ignorance by being able to study intensely sometimes as much as fifteen hours a day?" he redefines a place of punishment as a place of education, a prison as a college, in a way that speaks to the centrality of the prison-as-college trope in the wider prison life writing genre.[32] Of course, few incarcerated people have the luxury of studying for "fifteen hours a day," and most prisons are brutal, understaffed, and underresourced. In *Soul on Ice*, for instance, Eldridge Cleaver writes, "I want to devote my time to reading and writing, with everything else secondary, but I can't do that in prison. I have to keep my eyes open at all times or I won't make it. There is always some madness going on, and whether you like it or not you're involved."[33] Certainly, most prisons are not experimental rehabilitative institutions like Norfolk, with its extensive library, guest speakers from academia, and blue-ribbon debating team. Most prisons are oppressive, violent, and inhospitable places.

Yet despite the usual inhospitality of prisons to learning and personal betterment – and despite the (sometimes quite radical) differences between specific prisons, between prison regimes in different states, and between prisons in different regions around the country (most notably, between southern agricultural prisons like Parchman and Angola and industrial prisons in the north and west) – incarcerated people (including Eldridge Cleaver) repeatedly foreground in their life writings that they have been transformed through reading and writing, that they have been educated in prisons, and that this education has made them dramatically different and usually more socially amenable to life on the outside as a result. Consider how this passage, from Caryl Chessman's *Cell 2455* (1954), bundles together the conversion narrative, education, and rehabilitation:

> The long years lived in this crucible called Death
> Row have carried me beyond bitterness, beyond
> hate, beyond savage animal violence. Death Row
> has compelled me to study ... to accept disciplines
> I never would have accepted otherwise and to gain

a penetrating insight into all phases of this problem of crime that I am determined to translate into worthwhile contributions ... This book ... signals the beginning for me of a journey back from outer darkness.[34]

Like Malcolm X, Chessman defines his cell as an ideal location for "study." As a result of his education and the imposed isolation of death row, Chessman is "carried" beyond a state of extreme anti-sociality to a state where he accepts new values, even to the point where he becomes a kind of self-made criminologist, undertaking a transformative process from "darkness" presumably to light, from "savage animal[ity]" to humanity, from criminality to citizenship.

Or consider a more recent example of the same phenomenon, this one from the preface to Stanley "Tookie" Williams's *Blue Rage, Black Redemption: A Memoir*: "In the past, redemption was an alien concept to me. But from 1988 until 1994, while I lived in solitary confinement, I embarked on a transitional path toward redemption. I underwent years of education, soul-searching, edification, spiritual cultivation, and fighting to transcend my inner demons."[35] Here, the preface to Williams's memoir boils down, condenses, his story to features of a conversion narrative that repeatedly appear in prison life writing: most notably, by invoking "redemption" and transcendence through "years of education" in solitary confinement.

Clearly, then, the conversion narrative I have identified in *The Autobiography of Malcolm X* preceded Malcolm X (e.g., in Chessman's *Cell 2455*) and is repeated with surprising clarity in later examples of the prison life writing genre (e.g., in Williams's *Blue Rage, Black Redemption*). To understand prison life writing, we would do well to start with this narrative pattern. But given that conversion has also historically performed a social role, either to ensure group cohesion or to serve as a form of normalization and discipline, the prevalence of this narrative feature in prison life writing suggests that it is doing more than functioning as a mould an imprisoned writer can use to make shareable a life-changing experience. The mould itself is freighted with a history, invested with an ideology.

As I have suggested, the prison, too, has historically been conceptualized in terms of conversion. Since the first penitentiary experiment at the close of the eighteenth century, where solitary confinement cells were built into an existing Philadelphia jail to test whether such conditions might change convicted people, prison reformers and prison officials have repeatedly invoked the conversion narrative when conceptualizing how an incarcerated person might be dramatically transformed through the magic of prison discipline and prison architecture. Although education had always been part of prisons in some ancillary way, it became progressively more important to theories of rehabilitation after the Civil War and in the early twentieth century, and it was made integral to the prison system after the Second World War.[36] For prison officials, education was an important tool for producing the conversions, reforms, and rehabilitations they were looking for in their incarcerated charges. When a late nineteenth-century prison reformer named Zebulon Brockway described the prison where he was warden as less a prison than a "college on the hill," he was invoking a metaphor that would reappear with increasing frequency in the prison system, especially in the postwar period.[37]

What I argue in the pages that follow is that this story about an incarcerated person's conversion or rehabilitation behind bars, this narrative where an imprisoned person's identity is reshaped through a transformative educational experience, provides a linkage between two presumptively oppositional discourses: the discourse of the prison and prison life writing. When incarcerated or formerly incarcerated people like Malcolm X, Eldridge Cleaver, George Jackson, James Carr, Jack Henry Abbott, Stanley "Tookie" Williams, Shaka Senghor, or Joe Loya undergo a conversion as a result of education, that experience is happening in an institution that, rhetorically at least, *requires* such an experience from them.[38]

Malcolm X's conversion in prison usefully illustrates other components of the prison life writing genre, including how the conversion narrative helps incarcerated people reach a reading public that might otherwise be reluctant to read their work. Malcolm's conversion, which produces a division between a criminal past and a non-criminal present, allows him to reflect on his crimes even while distancing himself from them, a dialectic that is fundamentally important to much prison life writing. (This division is hardly absolute, however. Malcolm famously draws on his old self after his conversion, even using techniques he learned as a hustler while a Nation of Islam preacher.)[39] Through the conversion narrative, incarcerated people can describe their criminal past, even revel in it for the entertainment of readers whose interest in criminal narratives is often prurient and voyeuristic; at the same time, they can articulate how they are fundamentally different people – that is, how they are now rehabilitated, reformed, and trustworthy.[40]

Trustworthiness is paramount in life writing. Philippe Lejeune and others have shown that life writing requires a relationship between a reader and an author that is different from that of other literary forms. Central to autobiography is an unspoken contractual agreement between the writer and the reader – what Lejeune calls the "autobiographical pact" – and part of that agreement is that what the autobiographer writes is as true as he or she can remember it.[41] Imprisoned people who have been convicted of crimes are invariably viewed by readers as untrustworthy, even unworthy of readers' attention. It follows that readers are hesitant to enter into autobiography's figurative contract with someone whom they are unable or unwilling to trust. The conversion narrative's metaphor of rebirth, which dramatizes how the criminal (and untrustworthy) elements of a person's character are firmly in the past (even at the very moment that that person is discussing, and identifying with, their past), is one tool that imprisoned people can use to demonstrate that they can be trusted by skeptical readers.

Moreover, the conversion narrative is an established way for incarcerated people to confess through literature and receive absolution in the public sphere, so incarcerated people who use the conversion narrative are meeting the genre expectations of their readers, who are thus more likely to see those confessions as true, since they fit an established paradigm for truth-telling. In other words, by using the conversion narrative, incarcerated people seek to "achieve as proximate a relation as possible to what constitutes truth" in the interlocking discourses around imprisonment.[42] Certainly, this is one reason for the abundance of conversion narratives in the prison life writing archive. Publishers who are reluctant to consider work by convicted criminals – because of ethical or legal concerns or simply because prisons and the criminal justice system have raised barriers that make the everyday work of publishing difficult – are more likely to look approvingly on prison life writings that meet their expectations of what prison life writing looks like.[43] Again, though, the maintenance of the prison life writing genre by readers, publishers, writers, academics, and literary critics – a "communications circuit" between different writerly and readerly positions inside and outside prison – must also account for the role of the prison in circulating and legitimating a similar story about crime, punishment, redemption, and social inclusion.[44] The fact that different and frequently antagonistic discourses are consistently telling the same story about imprisonment suggests there is some unexamined ideological work being done within prison discourse and prison life writing that is worth exploring – and that is the project of this book.

Of course, there are memoirs or autobiographies written by imprisoned people that do not conform to the conversion narrative. Perhaps most notably, women's prison life writings rarely feature conversion narratives, which is partly due to the ideological project of women's institutions, which have exerted different pressures on the writings of incarcerated women. Historically, women's prisons have not encouraged or coerced women to transcend their status as criminals through conversion so as to join the public sphere as citizens. Instead, women's prisons, which evolved into separate institutions in the late nineteenth century, somewhat predictably sought to force wayward women into the domestic sphere, to make them "angels in the house," often by trying to transform their sexuality.

Similarly, the wider discourse about women in prison, which has been mostly *about* rather than *by* incarcerated women, since life writings by incarcerated woman have been rare (surely also the result of a culture that generally privileges men's writings), provides little space for women to adopt the conversion narrative. So, while the conversion narrative has been virtually (and sometimes literally) obligatory in the life writings of incarcerated men, it has held little sway over the life writings of incarcerated women. Although women's prison life writings share many features with men's prison life writings (which I will discuss), and while gender is certainly not the only marker of difference in prisons (differences of class and race are also considered throughout this book, for example), the near wholesale absence of the conversion narrative in women's published monographs, in contrast to its omnipresence in imprisoned men's life writings, indicates how the segregation of institutions according to sex has its corollary in narrative, in terms of the available paradigms for telling stories.

PRISON LIFE WRITING FROM THE TREATMENT ERA TO MASS INCARCERATION

After the Second World War, prison writing, and prison life writing more specifically, became intelligible as a genre. As H. Bruce Franklin writes in *The Victim as Criminal and Artist*, postwar prison writing "constitutes an unprecedented phenomenon. The quantity itself is so vast that it makes for the first qualitative distinction: this is a coherent *body* of literature, not just works by individual criminals and prisoners."[45] Dylan Rodríguez quite rightly argues that genre-making is problematic when it comes to writing in prison because, for one thing, "prison" becomes a marker of an imprisoned author's status rather than anything to do with what that author writes.[46] As Paul St. John explains in "Behind the Mirror's Face," an essay cited at length in Rodríguez's chapter on prison writing and "radical prison praxis," "*Prison writing is literally forced upon the writer, who, incidentally, has been stripped of just about everything else*" (St. John's emphasis). But the fact that the "*writer in prison is never simply free to write*," as St. John puts it, is precisely why identifying and analyzing genre is so important here (St. John's emphasis).[47] In this book, "prison life writing" is a designation that recognizes the conventions that have inevitably developed around the life writing of imprisoned people, the "horizon of expectations against which" any work written by incarcerated or formerly incarcerated people "is read."[48] But the term also acknowledges how those conventions are constrained by, even at times produced by, the institution.

Also, I should note that, although I use the term prison life writing throughout this book since it underscores how the prison plays a role in the production of the genre, I try to avoid terms like "prisoner" or "ex-convict" throughout this work wherever possible, favouring instead "incarcerated" or "formerly incarcerated" person (although, for clarity's sake, I will continue to use the term "political prisoner"). While I prefer the neatness of "prisoner" and ex-convict," and while many incarcerated people often use these terms themselves, I find that terms like "incarcerated people" or "formerly incarcerated" person better emphasize the humanity of incarcerated women and men, by not subsuming their identities under the nomenclature of the institution.

The development of prison life writing as a coherent genre after the Second World War accounts for this book's focus on life writing from the postwar period until today. This book's first chapter historicizes the conversion narrative and shows how it appears in the discourse of the US prison system from the nineteenth-century penitentiaries to the Treatment Era prisons. The subsequent chapters address important historical, political, institutional, and literary developments over the roughly seventy years since the Second World War. For instance, Chapter 2 discusses how prison discourse took root in prison life writing during the Treatment Era of the late 1960s and early 1970s. Chapter 3 focuses largely on prison life writing at the close of the Treatment Era that helped foster a turn toward a more punitive prison policy at the end of the 1970s. Chapter 4 considers prison life writing written during the long period of mass incarceration that is still with us today. Finally, Chapter 5 considers women's prison life writings written after the Treatment Era and during the period of mass incarceration, when women's incarceration rates began to rise dramatically.

This book's trajectory thus starts with the birth of the prison at the close of the eighteenth century and reaches forward from there to the current crisis of "mass incarceration" – a term that refers to the high rates of imprisonment beginning in the late 1970s and that are still with us today, and that have egregiously affected (and continue to affect) African American communities (although scholars like Elizabeth Hinton and Anne E. Parsons have argued that we should consider the rise of mass incarceration as having started even earlier).[49] Although this book addresses a wide swath of prison history, its discussion pivots from prison history to prison life writing during the Treatment Era because of the expansiveness of the prison's rehabilitative ideology and the concomitant upswell of prison life writing during this period. During the Treatment Era, prison discourse was quite literally forced into prison life writing.

Moreover, the legacy of the Treatment Era continues to be felt today. For one thing, incarcerated people in the present era like Shaka Senghor often perceive their life writing as in conversation with writers of the earlier period, like Malcolm X and George Jackson.[50] And the turn to prison education in recent years has resurrected the rhetoric of conversion-through-education that reached its apogee during the Treatment Era, when writers, teachers, and post-secondary students entered prisons in large numbers to take part in rehabilitation programming. For example, Jean Trounstine, in *Shakespeare behind Bars: The Power of Drama in a Women's Prison*, argues that "art has the power to redeem lives."[51] Trounstine and Robert P. Waxler run the Changing Lives through Literature Program, which describes itself as a form of alternative sentencing; their program nominally reproduces the rhetoric of change so central to prison conversion.[52] Joseph Bruchac, in *The Light from Another Country: Poetry from American Prisons*, writes that "working with writers in prison has ... been an object lesson in the power of poetry to reach and even change human lives."[53] Boston University claims on its website that its prison outreach program has the "power" to "elevate, nurture, and transform," to "change a life."[54] Certainly, these programs have made a difference for many imprisoned people. But their rhetoric, the promise that reading changes *lives* (and the presumption that those lives need to be changed in the first place), also reproduces the conversion paradigm that dominated similar prison education programs during the Treatment Era.

This book will be addressing the political, ideological, and aesthetic qualities of prison life writing, but it begins with prison history. In Chapter 1, "From the Penitentiary to the Treatment Era: Conversion and the Story of the US Prison," I trace how the conversion narrative evolved in the discourse of the US prison system from the first penitentiaries at the close of the eighteenth century to the prisons that housed men like Malcolm X in the mid-twentieth century. I argue that the conversion narrative, which played a major role in US culture at the inception of the modern prison, helped early prison reformers conceptualize how their new architectural system might make citizens out of criminals.

But I also show how the conversion narrative predates the prison in the US criminal justice system. Colonial-era criminals about to be hanged for capital crimes were encouraged to convert before their death, often in front of a large crowd at the scaffold.

At the close of the eighteenth century, when capital punishment was abolished for many crimes and replaced with incarceration, the popular narratives of death and resurrection were transferred to the penitentiary. Before prisons existed, criminals confessed, converted, were washed of their sins, and then executed and dispatched to heaven; after capital punishment was abolished for many crimes, criminals were converted into citizens in the penitentiary, ostensibly to be washed of their sins so that they could be returned to the community.

Having examined the history of the conversion narrative in US criminal justice, I explain how this story of conversion behind bars – what I call the *prison conversion narrative* – after the Second World War became a largely secular story about conversion through education. That shift had an impact on prison life writing. I close this chapter by showing how Treatment Era legal, legislative, and bureaucratic methods helped force the prison conversion narrative – or key elements of it – into prison life writing. In complicated and unpredictable ways, prison discourse was braided into incarcerated people's autobiographical acts. Ultimately, this chapter provides a necessary backstory to contemporary prison life writing, explaining how the genre came to be invested with the structuring power of prison discourse.

In Chapter 2, "The Treatment Era: African American Prison Life Writing and the Prison Conversion Narrative in George Jackson's *Soledad Brother* and James Carr's *Bad*," I illustrate how the prison – including prison policies and methods, penal philosophy, institutional discourse, and, by extension, the prison conversion narrative – influences incarcerated people's autobiographical work. To demonstrate that the prison has a productive effect (rather than a merely restrictive one) on incarcerated people's life writings, even in work that openly challenges the prison's legitimacy, this chapter focuses on George Jackson's *Soledad Brother* (1970) and James Carr's *Bad: The Autobiography of James Carr* (1975). Jackson and Carr were friends who served time together during the Treatment Era.

Their autobiographies are, in different but complementary ways, militantly resistant to the prison system; they are also illustrative of African American prison life writing published after the death of Malcolm X and in the age of Black Power, the Black Panthers, and what Eric Cummins calls the "radical prison movement."[55]

But their work also points to how life writing during the Treatment Era was entangled in the prison's surveillance and disciplinary functions. Because of Treatment Era policies and sentencing laws, George Jackson's epistolary autobiography exhibits a tension between acquiescence and militancy, between rehabilitation and revolution, that has gone virtually unexamined because most studies of *Soledad Brother* take for granted that his book constitutes an unalloyed challenge to the prison system.[56] I suggest that exploring the role of the prison in his book – including how the prison censor shapes Jackson's letters, how the parole board determines Jackson as a narrative subject, how the prison's rehabilitative and educational programs and services informed Jackson's growing self-awareness, and, by extension, how the prison conversion narrative underpins his evolution over the course of his letters – illustrates how the prison is productive rather than simply restrictive, as well as how and why prison discourse is imminent to prison life writing.

This is not to suggest that Jackson was somehow less revolutionary – far from it. Instead, emphasizing the role of the prison in producing *Soledad Brother* sharpens our view of what revolutionary writing looks like. I show how Jackson employs a technique that I call *corruption* in order to (mis)use the prison conversion narrative: he redefines his rehabilitation, especially his prison education, as a revolutionary act that uses the prison's materials – its books and libraries, its metaphors and conversion narrative – against the institution, indeed against capitalist, white supremacist America. Like incarcerated people who retool objects in prison to serve different purposes (for example, by turning a toothbrush into a knife), Jackson repurposes – that is, he *corrupts* – this institutional discourse so that it serves revolutionary ends. By excavating the role of the prison in *Soledad Brother*, then, I reveal the political tactics and literary aesthetics that are engaged when an imprisoned writer like George Jackson writes about his life. Like many other imprisoned radicals of the period, Jackson uses the narrative form of the institution in order to articulate very different content: the revolutionary ideology that informed the prison resistance movement and the wider social justice activism of the period.

James Carr's *Bad* features many of the same tensions between contestation and compliance that we find in Jackson's *Soledad Brother*, and Carr, like Jackson, similarly corrupts the prison conversion narrative, redefining it in revolutionary terms. But Carr's autobiography ultimately rejects the symbolic role of the imprisoned black militant that defines Jackson and his work and defined much prison life writing during this period. Rather than represent himself as a black revolutionary, Carr makes a peculiar aesthetic decision: he hybridizes the prison life writing genre with African American folk storytelling traditions in order to represent himself as a violent, hyper-sexual folk anti-hero, a character type that is common in prison culture but that rarely appears as a speaking autobiographical subject in life writing. As I will show, Carr's persona breaks rules: representing same-sex desire in prison but also glorifying prison rape and celebrating unrepentant brutality and murder, his book is transgressive but also deeply unethical, as likely to challenge the systems of power that victimize African American communities as it is to victimize the disempowered.

Carr's *Bad* breaks the rules of prison life writing and gives voice to a disturbing figure in African American prison literature and prison culture. By examining how Carr's *Bad* is transgressive, I illuminate some of the ways that prison life writing is policed and what such policing seeks to repress; I identify the often unspoken rules governing what can be said and who can speak within its discursive boundaries; and I reveal the kinds of aesthetic innovations that are required of incarcerated people who want to find new ways to bring prison life into autobiographical discourse. Carr's book is important precisely because it is deeply problematic and unethical: it represents those incarcerated people whose voices rarely find their way into prison life writing but who are, while disturbing, nonetheless part of prison culture.

In Chapter 3, "From the Treatment Era to the Monster Factory: Carl Panzram's and Jack Henry Abbott's Anticonversion Narratives and the Dawn of Mass Incarceration," I consider how Carl Panzram's (and Thomas E. Gaddis and James O. Long's) *Killer: A Journal of Murder* and Jack Henry Abbott's *In the Belly of the Beast* invert the terms of the prison conversion narrative, producing what I call an *anticonversion narrative*.[57] In the anticonversion narrative, the prison changes incarcerated people into what George Jackson in *Soledad Brother* calls "monsters."[58] I apply Jackson's gothic metaphor to Panzram's and Abbott's life writings to show how *formerly* incarcerated people living in an indeterminate world between freedom and exile are "monstrous" because they do not and often cannot belong – a categorical instability that is often resolved only after formerly incarcerated people are returned to prison. Monstrosity thus consolidates the social, juridical, psychological, and affective indeterminacies of post-prison life, a world of invisible laws, spectral constraints, and legal hauntings that is perhaps best seen through a gothic lens. Prisons have always been recognized as gothic spaces. My use of the gothic is different: I show how, for a formerly incarcerated person, *normal* life is a gothic world.[59]

Killer and *In the Belly of the Beast* grapple in vastly different ways with the role of the prison, however. *Killer* is a multivocal text, composed of Panzram's writings (including a short autobiography and a series of letters that Panzram sent to a guard he had befriended named Henry Lesser), and Gaddis and Long's biographical, historical, and contextual work, which narrativizes Panzram's story. I argue that Gaddis and Long's narrative, which is informed by and cites numerous criminologists and psychologists who became interested in Panzram before and after his execution for murder, redefines Panzram's work as a case study rather than as prison life writing. This subtle but important genre-switching has profound consequences: it removes Panzram's agency, his capacity to speak, even his function as an author (only Gaddis and Long are listed as authors on the book's cover) and instead identifies him as an object of analysis who paradoxically legitimates the criminal justice system at the very moment that he is critiquing it. Far from a passive analysand, however, Panzram, in some of his later letters that are published in *Killer*, actively challenges the criminological and psychological methods applied to him – methods that work to identify him as a case study – thus initiating a struggle over the meaning of his work within the text itself. This in turn illustrates how discourses of power are invested in prison life writing and play an important role in the way people perceive incarcerated people's work, as well as how incarcerated people negotiate with these forces within their life writings.

Jack Henry Abbott's epistolary autobiography *In the Belly of the Beast* is a literary descendant of Panzram's work: Abbott dedicates his book to Panzram (along with several other people); also, he uses an anticonversion narrative that dissects the emotional, psychological, and social dissolution inflicted by long-term imprisonment and thereby complicates the common presumption that education and literature are emancipatory. However, Abbott also dedicates his book to George Jackson, and he braids his anticonversion narrative with an adaptation of Jackson's revolutionary narrative in a way that is revealing for its resulting efforts to manage race and belonging. In particular, because Jackson's revolutionary writings influence Abbott's work, constitute a relevant pedigree for his thinking, and provide a framework for understanding his resistance to the prison system, Abbott is forced to confront his own racial identity, his whiteness.

In rethinking his whiteness, however, Abbott distances himself from white identity even while paradoxically acknowledging his complicity with it. In other words, he tries but fails to make his whiteness translucent, to make his racial identity disappear, within a prison system that is rapidly becoming more black and brown. As a result, *In the Belly of the Beast* illustrates how whiteness in prison, like whiteness elsewhere in American society, seeks invisibility, becomes colour-blind, and asserts its own victimhood precisely when it is called upon to be accountable. Finally, *In the Belly of the Beast*, and the media response to the book after Abbott went on trial for murder, is particularly significant for helping us understand the role that life writing played in justifying, or appearing to justify, a wholesale rejection of Treatment Era policies, including rehabilitative mandates and education programs, toward the end of the 1970s, which ushered in a new era of mass incarceration. Abbott's epistolary memoir, including what I have been calling his monstrosity, reflected but also helped instigate a massive cultural shift toward a "carceral state," which in this book refers to the post-1980s expansion of prisons, jails, and detention centres across the United States and the wide array of private and public "technologies" that have grown up around brick-and-mortar carceral institutions, such as bail bonds, for-profit businesses that provide prisons and jails with health or food services, and electronic monitoring systems.[60]

In Chapter 4, "Life Writing in the Contemporary Carceral State: *Writing My Wrongs*, *A Place to Stand*, and the Making of a 'Better Human Being,'" I explain why the prison conversion narrative has had a resurgence in recent years (if it ever went away), and I show how contemporary prison life writing uses but also departs from the prison life writing of previous decades. I focus on two acclaimed works from the early twenty-first century: Jimmy Santiago Baca's *A Place to Stand: The Making of a Poet* (2001) and Shaka Senghor's *Writing My Wrongs: Life, Death, and Redemption in an American Prison* (2013). Baca's writings fit within the tradition of what B.V. Olguín calls the "pinto picaresque," and *A Place to Stand* forms an essential part of Chicana/o prison life writing.[61] Similarly, *Writing My Wrongs* is part of, and self-consciously draws on, a long tradition of African American prison life writing, including *The Autobiography of Malcolm X* and George Jackson's *Soledad Brother*.[62] However, inasmuch as Baca's and Senghor's books resonate with these traditions, they also depart from them in ways that are revealing for what they say about the ideological work of the prison conversion narrative, the meaning of rehabilitation and prison education, and the future of prison life writing.

In particular, I argue that both books use the prison conversion narrative because its metaphor of rebirth, which produces a past and present self, inoculates Baca and Senghor from the criminality of their past even while allowing them to represent that past. I suggested earlier that this is a common technique in the prison life writing genre. But *how* these formerly incarcerated people are inoculated from their past criminality has troubling ideological consequences. In *A Place to Stand*, Baca's conversion turns on a human/primitive binary that unintentionally revives the problematic trope of the atavistic criminal, a figure that has historically served to dehumanize incarcerated people.

By contrast, in *Writing My Wrongs*, Senghor monetizes his prison experiences, trading on what I call *carceral capital*, which fetishizes imprisonment and legitimates capitalist individualism as a necessary response to mass incarceration instead of addressing capitalism's role in making mass incarceration possible (as earlier writers like George Jackson have done). *A Place to Stand* and *Writing My Wrongs* help illustrate an interesting disconnect that has developed between prison ideology and prison life writing since the end of the Treatment Era in the late 1970s. Although contemporary prisons have largely rejected the rehabilitative mandate of earlier periods, choosing instead to focus on the effective containment and control of incarcerated people in an era when prisons have been expanding at an unprecedented rate, the shelves of the prison life writing archive are heavy with works by incarcerated people like Baca and Senghor who have undergone conversions, and who have essentially rehabilitated themselves, usually through education, particularly through reading and writing.

Chapter 5, "'Love Is Contraband in Hell': Women's Prisons, Life Writing, and Discourses of Sexuality in *Assata* and *An American Radical*," considers women's prison life writing in the years after the Treatment Era ended, during the period of mass incarceration, when women's incarceration rates increased, seemingly exponentially, and several important women political prisoners, including Assata Shakur and Susan Rosenberg, published their life writings. Shakur and Rosenberg's life writings were published at different but telling periods during the rise of mass incarceration: Shakur's *Assata: An Autobiography* in 1987, when women's incarceration rates were beginning to rise, and Rosenberg's *An American Radical: Political Prisoner in My Own Country* in 2011, after women's incarceration rates had reached some of the highest ever recorded.[63] *Assata* and *An American Radical* are important books because, among other important issues, they address the intersections of racism, sexism, and homophobia in US women's prisons; they struggle with what it means to be a political prisoner in America; and they contend with the legacies of radical, revolutionary movements in the United States that used force in the service of political struggles.

What neither book does is follow a conversion narrative. Yet despite being published more than twenty years apart, both books demonstrate that, while most life writings by imprisoned women do not use the conversion narrative, women's prison life writings still grapple with institutional discourses – notably, discourses of sexuality. Women's prisons were constructed around narratives of domesticity, and those narratives were often responses to discourses about dangerous women's sexualities – stories about fallen women, eugenicist narratives of contagion, and accounts about venereal disease and prostitution. Historically, women's prisons have been developed around discourses of sexuality that are freighted with the vocabulary of masculine authority and feminine subservience. In Chapter 5, then, I consider the centrality of sexual discourses to women's prisons, and I explore how those discourses arise in (and are contested by) the life writings of incarcerated and formerly incarcerated women, specifically those of Assata Shakur and Susan Rosenberg.

Moreover, through *Assata* and *An American Radical*, I show how women's prisons use sexual violence to ensure women's subservience to patriarchal authority, thus repeating narratives about patriarchal power and men's access to women's bodies found elsewhere in American society, from the male-dominated workplace to the patriarchal home. However, Shakur's and Rosenberg's autobiographies also demonstrate how imprisoned women often use sexuality as a means to resist the prison system's authority over them. For example, Assata Shakur has sex with a male co-defendant in jail while awaiting trial, and she eventually becomes pregnant while incarcerated. Here, Shakur represents sex as an act of resistance in a way that I suggest undercuts what Patricia Hill Collins calls "controlling images" about black women's sexuality and black motherhood – images that have historically served to criminalize African American women. Shakur's representation of her pregnancy as a revolutionary act also redefines the meaning of family, thus illuminating lines of community in a way that chimes with the work of Angela Davis, who defines the political prisoner as ineluctably part of a collective – a feature of imprisoned women's life writings that is also at work in Susan Rosenberg's autobiography.

Like *Assata*, Susan Rosenberg's *An American Radical* represents how the prison uses sexual violence as a discourse of power. Rosenberg points to how the law camouflages the institution's use of sexuality to assert its authority over women's bodies and identities, which I argue shares conceptual territory with the "unmaking of the world" that Elaine Scarry sees in other performances of state violence, especially torture. But Rosenberg contrasts the prison's sexual violence with loving, same-sex relationships that I suggest redefine the meaning of belonging, family, and home within the patriarchal domestic space of the prison. Sexuality as an expression of love or community is quite different from how sex is represented in men's prison life writings, which is almost invariably as a violent expression of power and dominance. Yet I caution that these gendered representations of sexuality come to us through a genre that has specific rules around what can and what cannot be represented in discourse. These gendered differences may say as much about what is and what is not sayable in prison life writing as it does about the material conditions of incarcerated people.

In this book's conclusion, I consider how we *read* prison life writings. I suggest that the prison conversion narrative is seductive for readers because it legitimates our belief in the healing and transformative power of literature. Certainly, reading and writing can change people. But this narrative tends to individualize rehabilitation in a way that obscures how structural inequalities and the US criminal justice system often make positive social reintegration incredibly difficult even for those formerly imprisoned writers whose lives are exemplary. Moreover, readers often tend to extend stories of dramatic self-transformation into the realm of policy, presuming that such stories could be reproduced in real people's lives if only prisons were given enough resources, which I suggest risks legitimating the prison system at a moment when its function in American society is increasingly being questioned.

I close with a discussion of Susan Burton and Cari Lynn's *Becoming Ms. Burton: From Prison to Recovery to Leading the Fight for Incarcerated Women* because Burton's book is a conversion narrative that seems to adhere to a kind of entrepreneurial, bootstraps tradition that is common in the life writings of imprisoned men, especially in recent years. But at the same time, *Becoming Ms. Burton* complicates this tradition by placing Burton's story among a mosaic of experiences of other incarcerated and formerly incarcerated women – experiences that make it difficult to read Burton's memoir as one of individual uplift, personal rehabilitation, or transcendence without also recognizing the massive institutional failure that makes such a story virtually impossible in the lives of most incarcerated women and men. *Becoming Ms. Burton* demonstrates how we can read a story of personal transformation without seeing it as exemplary of the prison experience. In particular, Burton's memoir suggests how we can read the life writings of incarcerated and formerly incarcerated people relationally rather than individually. We can read for the myriad ways that extraordinary stories of conversion are also stories about communities of people who help make reintegration, fighting an unfair criminal justice system, radical transformation, or simply returning to normal life a possibility for men and women who have been under the control of the US prison system.

Obviously, with the exception of Chapter 1 and the Conclusion, each chapter in this book considers two life writings by different authors: one book that is generally well-known in studies of prison writing (George Jackson's *Soledad Brother*, Jack Henry Abbott's *In the Belly of the Beast*, Assata Shakur's *Assata*, and Jimmy Santiago Baca's *A Place to Stand*), and one book that is generally less well-known but nonetheless important for what it says about the genre, its historical period, and the relationship between prison discourse and prison life writing (James Carr's *Bad*, Carl Panzram's *Killer: A Journal of Murder*, Susan Rosenberg's *An American Radical*, and Shakha Senghor's *Writing My Wrongs*).

I have chosen these books because they are exemplary texts: they are unique, but they also interlock with prison discourse in ways that I suggest are representative of what happens in other works by imprisoned men and women. Focusing on one book that is to some degree canonical within the prison writing genre (whose author's work is anthologized in H. Bruce Franklin's *Prison Writings in 20th Century America*, for instance), and one book that I suggest is important to the genre yet rarely (if ever) discussed in popular writings about the field or in the academic criticism, enables me to show how the features of prison life writing that I discuss cross a wide spectrum of works by imprisoned and formerly imprisoned people.

In its most general terms, *Prison Life Writing* takes stock of the genre and inaugurates a discussion about it. More specifically, by focusing on the conversion narrative, this book identifies the complicated vectors of power that intersect in prison life writing; it also demonstrates how the interpretive paradigm typically applied to resistance literature all too often fails to address the ideological complexities of incarcerated people's work. Recognizing these complexities helps illuminate the aesthetic innovations of imprisoned writers, whose work is frequently relegated to the status of minor literature, to a kind of folk- or outsider-art that is incorrectly presumed to lend little beyond historical value to our understanding of American literature. In this book, I hope to demonstrate that prison life writing is more than a touchstone for studies of prisons or crime; it is more than a useful footnote to histories of the US prison system; it is more than activism and political work: it is also a rich and multivalent art form.

Additionally, I demonstrate that prison life writing is actively involved in the cultural and political work that reinforces or destabilizes prisons and the vocabularies of power that sustain them. Years ago, I received a response from a peer reviewer who claimed that the article about prison life writing I had submitted for review was interesting; but that same reviewer could not understand why reading prison life writing mattered. In this book, I hope to make that clear.

Finally, although there are many valid arguments for the importance of prison life writing to the much broader canon of American literature, including the sheer quality of the work, one important reason for reading this material is the degree to which Americans, especially African Americans, have been forced into contact with prisons and auxiliary forms of incarceration during the historical period this book is covering. As Heather Ann Thompson writes, there is little doubt that the incredible numbers of incarcerated men and women "both reflected and shaped the history of postwar America" – and, I would add, the literary traditions of America.[64]

Since 1973, the US incarceration rate has risen by roughly 500 percent; 2.2 million people are currently locked in US jails and prisons, which is, by any measure, an astounding number.[65] Moreover, as Marie Gottschalk writes in *The Prison and the Gallows: The Politics of Mass Incarceration in America* (2006), the "reach of the U.S. penal state extends far beyond the 2.2 million men and women who are now serving time in prison or jail in America. On any given day, nearly seven million people are under the supervision of the correctional system, including jail, prison, parole, probation, and other community service sanctions."[66] This expansive system, the carceral state, maps onto and feeds off mass incarceration. Michelle Alexander calls the increased scope of the criminal justice system the "New Jim Crow," since mass incarceration, as well as "the larger web of laws rules, policies, and customs that control those labelled criminals both in and out of prison" – which is a system that makes criminals "an *undercaste* – a lower caste of individuals who are permanently barred by law and custom from mainstream society" – specifically targets African Americans, thereby reproducing the exclusionary logic of (the old) Jim Crow segregation system.[67]

So, prison life writing is important because it represents the collective lived experiences of mass incarceration, a system that impacts the lives of many Americans, especially, to an alarming degree, African Americans, but also Latinx, other people of colour, poor whites, and members of LGBTQ communities (who are statistically overrepresented in US prisons but at dramatically higher risk of mistreatment and violence compared to cisgender incarcerated people).[68] Additionally, to understand the scope of American literature, which has historically been a literature formed and tested at the margins, regenerated by the powerful at the frontiers and redefined by the powerless at the periphery, one must take stock of literary developments from the legal and cultural boundaries of the country. This is particularly important for African American prison life writing, which speaks from a uniquely frightening position within what may be the civil rights issue of our time.

CONVERSION AND THE STORY OF THE US PRISON

IN MAY 2007, PARIS HILTON – A-LIST CELEBRITY, SOCIALITE, AND heiress to the Hilton empire – was sentenced to forty-five days in jail for violating the terms of her probation in a drinking-and-driving case. Immediately after her conviction, her lawyers managed to get her sentence reduced to twenty-three days, of which Hilton served three before being sent home because of an unspecified medical condition, with permission to serve the remainder of her time under house arrest. Several days later, and in part because of public outcry, Hilton was admitted once again to Los Angeles County Jail to serve out her sentence behind bars. After her readmission to jail, Hilton's stance suddenly changed and she decided not to appeal her sentence. In her first jailhouse interview, which she conducted with Barbara Walters, Hilton revealed that her imprisonment was, in fact, a blessing. She had undergone a radical self-evaluation and transformation in her cell. "I'm not the same person I was," she explained. "God has released me ... I have been thinking that I want to do different things when I am out of here. I have become much more spiritual. God has given me this new chance." Hilton had fallen, but through her days of enforced isolation she had found God and been transformed. No longer "the same person," she had been reborn and was ready to be accepted back into the fold of the community.[1]

Despite its gaudy artificiality, Hilton's supposed spiritual awakening conforms to a classic narrative structure: the prison conversion narrative, which maps the conversion paradigm of fall, struggle, crisis, and self-transformation onto a person's incarceration. By defining her brief jail term according to the parameters of the conversion narrative, Hilton exaggerates the contours of a tradition in the US carceral system that has, over the past two hundred years, become a form of common sense. Although there was predictable public skepticism over the timeliness of her sudden transformation, no one questioned whether the conversion narrative was an appropriate template for how incarceration should be experienced and shared. For Hilton and her audience, the conversion narrative was a current, recognizable, even necessary script for explaining her time behind bars. Hilton's interview and the ensuing debate about her conversion suggest that the conversion narrative seems "of little consequence," as H. Bruce Franklin describes it, only because it has become a normalized part of the discourse about incarceration in America.[2] Perhaps as a result, the influence of the conversion narrative on prison writing and the American imaginary is easy to miss.

Although the conversion narrative has been largely overlooked in studies of prison writing, incarcerated or formerly incarcerated people frequently employ the tropes and metaphors of conversion, or reproduce the conversion narrative, to describe their prison experiences. Like Paris Hilton, some incarcerated people define incarceration as a site of religious transformation. While radically different, and, I should stress, far removed from Hilton's performance, the aforementioned autobiographies of Malcolm X and Stanley "Tookie" Williams define incarceration as a site of personal transformation and spiritual renewal.[3] However, as I have shown, religious conversion is central to these books but so is education: these men are changed through practices of reading and writing at the same time that they are changed by God.

Setting aside the sheer ridiculousness and opportunism of Paris Hilton's self-transformation, what differentiates her conversion from the conversion narratives that tend to dominate the contemporary prison life writing genre is this: conversions in prison life writing tend to be the result of educational experiences. For example, Piri Thomas's *Down These Mean Streets* (1967), Nathan McCall's *Makes Me Wanna Holler* (1994), and Joe Loya's *The Man Who Outgrew His Prison Cell: Confessions of a Bank Robber* (2004) all define prison as a site of radical, secular self-transformation that accords with the general paradigm of the religious conversion narrative.[4] And while these secular conversions are the result of many factors, they are all stories of men transformed as a result of the liberal arts.

Liberation through the liberal arts: this is at the core of the contemporary prison conversion narrative, which features reading and writing as having an alchemical effect on incarcerated people's identities. Because conversion narratives abound in prison writing and in popular depictions of imprisonment, the tropes of rebirth or resocialization through education in prison take on the status of truth, policing how prison and post-prison life enters into discourse. It is, however, a truth at odds with the majority of incarcerated people's experiences. Prison populations have notoriously low education and literacy rates, and while there are some regional differences, prison education programs are few and far between, making dramatic changes through education unlikely.

Moreover, in general, conversion, through education or otherwise, is often less common than recidivism. Most incarcerated people are rearrested, convicted of a crime, and often returned to prison within three years of their release.[5] (The reasons for recidivism are, of course, much too complex to be covered here.) While we should in no way discount the validity of the conversion experiences of men and women who are or have been incarcerated in America, it is important to address the disparity between the popularity of narratives of conversion and the statistical reality lived by the majority of American incarcerated people. Since rates of recidivism suggest that incarcerated people are not undergoing dramatic conversions behind bars, why has this narrative of change endured for so long? Why is the conversion narrative a normalized way to experience (or to narrativize the experience of) incarceration? What ideological work does the conversion narrative perform?

One reason why the conversion narrative continues to have currency in prison life writing is because it is also produced in the discourse of the prison system, thus constituting what Joy James might call a "(neo)slave narrative" of the "master-state."[6] Of course, there are fundamental differences between the first penitentiaries developed at the dawn of the nineteenth century, the reformatories of the post-bellum period, and the "correctional" institutions of the postwar Treatment Era. However, over the roughly two centuries that prisons have been in operation, the various reformers, administrators, and defenders of these institutions have consistently resorted to the rhetoric of conversion to explain how these institutions were supposed to change criminals into citizens. Hilton's performance of a sudden jailhouse conversion thus invokes a powerful metanarrative that accords with a major premise of the US carceral system: that incarceration does more than confine and punish criminals; it can change their behaviour, even their identities.

In this chapter, I show how the prison conversion narrative is knitted into the discourse of the US prison system. First, I briefly sketch the role of the conversion narrative in American culture. I emphasize how conversion has an extra-literary history: it represents someone's dramatic self-transformation in a literary work, of course, but it also serves as a map, what Puritans called a "'guid[e] to godliness,'" that outlines pre- and pro-scribed behaviour within particular communities.[7] Unlike other literary forms, the conversion narrative can slide back and forth between a mode of self-expression and one of social control. Its appearance in the prison is thus not so much an anomaly as it is a natural extension of its historical function, which is to change individual behaviour so that it conforms to social expectations.

After providing some contextual history for conversions in America, I trace the evolving role of the conversion narrative in

American prison discourse. I am not arguing that the prison was built according to some conversion narrative blueprint. The US prison system has multiple roots, including Enlightenment philosophy, Quaker spiritual practices, the Protestant belief in the moral value of work – even theories about the effects of climate, diet, and disease on the "moral faculties."[8] Instead, in this chapter, I am interested in the role the conversion narrative plays in prison *discourse* – that is, in the collection of statements, utterances, writings, and texts consolidated around the prison that seek to articulate what the prison is for and how it is supposed to work. This discourse constitutes a kind of vocabulary for discussing incarceration in America – a lexicon that determines what can and what cannot be said about the institution as well as who can and who cannot speak about it. I am mostly figuring this as an institutional discourse, comprised of the writings of prison reformers and prison officials as well as those with links to the criminal justice system, such as penologists and criminologists. Prison discourse is thus distinguishable from popular culture and prison life writing; however, this kind of generic barrier is invariably porous – as I will show in the following chapters, prison discourse is in dialogue with other discursive fields as well. Of course, it is the overlap between prison discourse and prison life writing that is the focus of this book.

Beginning with the early penitentiary, prison discourse repeatedly invoked the terms of the conversion narrative to conceptualize how the institution changed imprisoned people. Moreover, after the Civil War, prison reformers and prison officials increasingly linked education – especially reading and writing – with rehabilitation (a process that has its roots in the antebellum period with Social Gospel ministers and activists, who stocked prison libraries with religious tracts). So by the time prison life writing cohered into a genre after the Second World War, education had long been a central plank of the prison system's rehabilitative philosophy. Conversion, rehabilitation, education, reading and writing: these terms were bundled together during the postwar period in prison discourse, with the result that the conversion-through-education narratives that so dominate prison life writing are in a complicated dialogue with this discursive tradition. This shared discursive territory suggests one reason why prison life writing repeatedly features conversion narratives, but it also raises new questions about *how* prison life writings make use of this ideologically freighted literary and institutional material – questions I seek to answer in the following chapters.

REDEMPTION AS NORMALIZATION: THE CONVERSION NARRATIVE IN AMERICA

The centrality of the conversion narrative in the US prison system should come as no surprise, given that it has always been a powerful metaphor in American culture, one that enables self-expression but also conformity. In the seventeenth century, Puritan settlers understood the conversion narrative as fundamental to their social, political, and religious lives. They believed that only a select few would be chosen by God for heaven in the afterlife. They demonstrated the authenticity of their "election" through public confessions, which had to adhere to a sanctioned plot that church leaders could recognize and legitimate – what Edmund S. Morgan calls a "morphology of conversion."[9] If a convert's confession fit the established criteria, if it adhered to the kind of conversion they saw as authentic, the convert was admitted to a "gathered church" – a church "that restricted their membership to professed believers" – which was at the centre of Puritan religious but also social, political, and economic power in the community.[10] The Puritan conversion narrative sought to record the intervention of the divine into a believer's life in such a way that it fit an established mould and thus justified the power structure of the Puritan community. In other words, conversion was a profoundly individual, spiritual experience that, when articulated within specific narrative conventions so as to meet the genre expectations of a community of powerful listeners, was also a political and social act that reinforced real positions of power in early colonial communities.[11] The conversion narrative was thus both a literary genre and a disciplinary technology.

Puritan conversion formed the backbone of early captivity narratives. These were accounts of Puritan (and later, also non-Puritan but primarily white) men, women, and children who had been seized by Indigenous nations, had later returned home through force, trade, or escape, and had written about their experiences, sometimes with the guidance of clergy. The most famous of these life narratives, *The Narrative of the Captivity and the Restoration of Mrs. Mary Rowlandson* (1682), details Mary Rowlandson's capture by Wampanoag Indians and is plotted according to a series of "Removes" that take her farther away from her small Puritan community and deeper into the alien world of the Wampanoag.[12] Like other Puritan authors of captivity narratives, Rowlandson understands her captivity as a test of her faith. Her experience is framed according to a conversion narrative, which identifies her path from confinement to freedom as a conversion from darkness to light, from a "howling wilderness" to the realization of God's grace.

Again, though, there is a tension here between the genre's capacity to enable Rowlandson to tell her story – it functions, perhaps, as a trauma narrative to help her find a vocabulary for an otherwise unspeakable experience – and its capacity to organize her story so as to legitimate the ideology of the church, including the primacy of conversion as an imprimatur of divine election, and thus the divine right of those church elect whose conversions attested to their authority in the community. Eventually, Rowlandson's story became a bestseller in Colonial New England.[13] Indeed, the captivity narrative, the first home-grown American genre – one that would encompass a wide variety of writings about settler experiences of Indian captivity – would become an international sensation and play a formative role in American life writing.[14]

The influence of the captivity narrative is especially notable in the African American life writing tradition, beginning with slave narratives. Abolitionists and escaped slaves who wanted enslaved people's stories to reach and influence a wide audience often resorted to the ever-popular captivity narrative, with its conversion framework, for a template.[15] Thus, the fugitive slave narrative genre is replete with stories of escaped slaves whose paths from slavery to freedom are plotted according to the conversion narrative paradigm. In the most widely read slave narrative, *Narrative of the Life of Frederick Douglass, An American Slave* (1845), the eponymous Douglass writes, "You have seen how a man was made a slave; you shall see how a slave was made a man."[16] Here, Douglass presents the conversion narrative as a rebirth from slavery to manhood. As Douglass writes, explicitly invoking the religious vocabulary so familiar to the conversion narratives of earlier Puritan writers, "It was a glorious resurrection, from the tomb of slavery, to the heaven of freedom."[17]

However, the tension between individual expression and normalization encountered in earlier conversion narratives arises in slave narratives as well: escaped slaves' voices were sometimes silenced or muted by white editors and amanuenses. This posed significant problems for black writers or speakers, whose control over their own stories was thereby weakened. White editors or amanuenses not only recorded but also often dramatically shaped the work that found its way into print. John Sekora writes:

> Not black recollection, but white interrogation brings order to the [slave's] narration. For eighteenth-century [slave] narratives the self that emerges is a pre-existing form, deriving largely from evangelical Christianity. For the abolitionist period, the self is a type of the antislavery witness. In each instance the meaning, relation, and wholeness of the story are given before the narrative begins; they are imposed rather than chosen.[18]

Sekora argues that slave narratives reflected white editors' desire to publish a specific *kind* of narrative – one that reproduced evangelical values and legitimated the abolitionist movement. This mattered more to them than presenting black narrators' actual truth. As with Puritan conversion narratives and captivity narratives, albeit with quite different equations of power, slave narratives reflect a tension between the narrator-protagonists' freedom to tell their story and an imposed standardization.

The conversion narrative, which white editors often used to encase black stories so as to make them more marketable to white readers, functioned as an ideological groove into which an enslaved writer's story could be slotted. As William Andrews explains, white "editors ... solicited these stories because they conformed or were conformable to cultural myths and literary traditions of an already established audience appeal, such as an Indian captivity or evangelical conversion narratives ... Black self-portraits were cropped and framed according to the standards of an alien culture."[19] Cropping and framing in order to ensure conformity: this further illustrates how the literary history of the conversion narrative is about more than stories of personal self-transformation; conversion narratives are also highly ideological documents that serve diverse, even contradictory interests. They have a history of being enmeshed in especially acute problems of power and control.

Conversion narratives were also central to many American faith communities when the country was in its infancy. Thus, for many Americans, the conversion narrative constituted a familiar blueprint for representing, and enacting, identity reformation. Besides playing a central role in the captivity narratives and slave narratives that circulated among American readers in the country's early history, conversion narratives also played a defining role in the evangelical tradition that burned over the country in the First (beginning in the 1730s) and Second (beginning in the 1790s) Great Awakenings.[20] Evangelicalism, with its emphasis on often dramatic individual conversions as testaments of faith, influenced American culture as revivals enflamed American towns.

Quakers, who developed the first penitentiary experiment in Philadelphia, had their own conversion tradition. In the genre of the Quaker spiritual journal, adherents explore their relation to the world and their communities through the doctrine of the Inner Light, which holds that divinity is within each individual equally and can be accessed through quiet and prolonged contemplation.[21] Coincidentally, many famous Quaker conversions took place in prisons (most famously in John Bunyan's *Grace Abounding to the Chief of Sinners* [1666]), or they were written there – suggesting, perhaps, an early linkage between conversion and incarceration for those Philadelphia Quakers who sought a vocabulary for explaining the transformative function of the penitentiary system they were creating.[22]

Although conversion continued to play a defining role in American Christian communities, and while conversion also played an important role in other religious traditions, its secularization in the eighteenth century (especially with Rousseau's *Confessions*, as noted in this book's introduction) made it a useful paradigm for representing a range of dramatic, life-changing experiences in later years, especially in the twentieth century, from coming out to addiction recovery. The 12-Step program of Alcoholics Anonymous (A.A.), which has been adopted by myriad self-help groups since that organization was founded in the 1930s, is an especially interesting use of the conversion paradigm because it explicitly seeks to modify the behaviour of the person who follows the program. Recalling the detailed "morphology" of its Puritan antecedents, the 12-Step program features stages of development that lead toward "a spiritual awakening" (Step 12). It requires the acceptance of a non-denominational "higher power" (it can even be a non-religious one) that induces the conversion experience and is invited to remove "defects of character" (Step 3). The conversion experience requires a confession, followed by the ongoing repetition of ritual confessions

(Step 9). Finally, the confession acts as a form of entrance into a new community (here, the community of alcoholics). These stages move from a fall – being completely powerless to addiction – through tortured conscience – the "fearless" inventory of wrongs committed against others followed by the confrontation of past guilt – and, through prayer and meditation, redemption and a new life of sobriety.[23] A.A. members generally see the organization of the raw material of their life experiences into an established narrative as beneficial rather than manipulative. The 12-Step program illustrates how the conversion narrative has remained a powerful tool for identity formation and social conformity ever since it was first diffused in twentieth-century American self-help culture (even if, in this instance, that conformity is welcomed).

Conversion has always been an integral part of American literature – but also, as I have underscored here, American identity formation. Importantly, conversion does more than register someone's dramatic self-transformation from one way of being to another; it is also a technology for inculcating someone into a group, maintaining a sense of communal cohesion, and ensuring ideological consistency. Seeing the conversion narrative as, in part, a method for changing an individual's behaviour so that it conforms with the demands of the community clarifies why it might play such a significant role in the US prison, which is, of course, an architectural system for realigning the behaviour – in fact, the identities – of wayward people so that they conform with the social expectations of their communities, states, and country.

THE PRISON CONVERSION NARRATIVE

Precisely how the conversion narrative became part of the discourse of the US prison is harder to determine, especially since the men who developed the first penitentiary in the country were drawing on a wide variety of sources in order to improve the criminal justice system. One could argue, perhaps, that the penitentiary was a technology for producing in the individual what had happened to the country only a few years earlier. The country had just fought the Revolutionary War, and the nation had itself undergone a kind of conversion: the American Revolution had created an entirely new nation; colonial Britons had become Americans. As J. Hector St. John de Crèvecoeur writes in *Letters from an American Farmer* (1782), "He is an American who, leaving behind him all his ancient prejudices and manners, receives new ones from the new mode of life he has embraced ... Here individuals of all nations are melted into a new race of men, whose labours and posterity will one day cause great changes in the world."[24] Although a national revolution is not the same as an individual conversion, the sense of a complete transformation of national identity that bestows a new form of citizenship on a people – who have become "a new race of men" – is not *unlike* conversion, either. Indeed, from the metaphor of the "new world" to the Declaration of Independence to theories of self-reliance and the American Dream, the grand narratives of American life repeatedly stress dramatic self-transformation as a particularly American model of identity, literary or otherwise. So a criminal justice system that aimed to catalyse such transformations was very much of the moment.

Or perhaps the Quakers, who as I have suggested played an outsized role in developing the first penitentiary experiment, introduced conversion into the system. To be sure, along with a worldwide resource of Enlightenment-era theories of crime and punishment, the Pennsylvania Quakers drew on models of identity formation reproduced in the conversion narrative to conceive of the first penitentiary experiment at Philadelphia's Walnut Street jail in 1790. Walnut Street was the first application of "the Pennsylvania system" (or "separate system"), as it was called, which enforced total isolation. This system was dramatically expanded thirty years later with the construction of the imposing, castle-like Eastern State Penitentiary. Drawing on the Quaker doctrine of Inner Light – the belief that divinity existed within each individual – the Pennsylvania system employed solitary confinement to force incarcerated people into a state of penitence (hence the term "penitentiary"). Alone in their cells, separated from the moral contagion of other criminals, incarcerated people were expected to turn inward: to reflect, find the inner divine, and repent.[25] The magical space of the solitary prison cell was supposed to manufacture resurrections; incarcerated people were supposed to emerge, Lazarus-like, from the tomb of their cell into the light of the American Republic; they were to be new people, ready to uphold the values of their community.

Yet, although the late eighteenth century was rife with conversions, revolutions, and transformations, which helped promote the idea that American identity was something plastic and mouldable, and while Quakers employed the logic of conversion to conceptualize how solitary confinement might affect someone's identity, the conversion narrative was *already* part of the US criminal justice system. Conversion narratives played a major role in colonial American rituals of punishment. In Puritan New England, executions were staged events, and audiences who observed executions repeatedly watched criminals act out the same performance before their deaths – a performance that followed the script of the conversion narrative. Condemned criminals were counselled by clergy to confess to the sinful nature of their lives of crime, and these confessions were often performed before an audience at the gallows. After their confessions, the condemned were redeemed, ready to be accepted into heaven as changed men and women.

Some of these confessions, along with commentary by clergy about those confessions, came to be published, thus constituting an early genre of criminal literature.[26] One such execution sermon, "Death the Certain Wages of Sin to the Impenitent" (1701), which details the execution of Esther Rogers and relates her final confession, asks its readers to understand Rogers's execution this way:

> Here is One in the Congregation at this time, of
> whom it may be thus spoken, That she is a Dead

> Woman; not only that she was dead in Trespasses
> & Sins, but is Dead in Law, and by a Sentence of
> Condemnation must be put to Death before another
> Sabbath come about: And yet there is more than a
> possibility through Grace, that she may Live again;
> though not in this World, yet for ever [*sic*] in a bet-
> ter, where she shall neither sin nor sorrow more.[27]

Rogers, who was executed for "murdering her infant begotten in whoredom," as the sermon's lengthy subtitle describes her crime, may have fallen in this world, but her confession and repentance within the Puritan theocratic system had cleansed her sins, and, after her execution, had enabled her to be reborn in heaven. This genre of gallows confessional, which Daniel E. Williams calls the "criminal conversion narrative," links together life writing, law, punishment, conversion, and identity formation – a conceptual bundle that would reappear later in US penitentiaries after they supplemented the gallows as the preferred mode of punishment in the country. Unlike the gallows, however, the US penitentiary was, in theory, a machine for transforming criminals into citizens who could be returned to the community rather than dispatched to heaven.[28]

So, whatever the explicit theories that informed the creation of the new penitentiary system – and those theories were manifold – the effect of this new penitentiary technology was to update and retool the conversion paradigm that had always been crucial to the US criminal justice system. In other words, the new system of punishment was certainly new, but how people *described* that system, how they explained the way it was supposed to function, tapped into a conceptual model that had been part of the old system. For example, compare the framing of Esther Rogers's execution in the late seventeenth century with the description of incarcerated people's rehabilitative experiences by the prison inspectors who audited Eastern State Penitentiary in the early nineteenth century. In an 1842 report, the inspectors explain that incarcerated people are "fallen, debased and convict" but also have "minds capable of improvement": "The inspectors hope that the language 'return, repent, and live,' is heard in the prisoner's solitude; and through that aid *which alone* can produce the change, many a prisoner can regard his cell as the 'beautiful gate of the temple' leading to a happy life, and by a peaceful end, to heaven."[29] As though writing a kind of antebellum corrective to the early eighteenth-century sermon for Esther Rogers's execution, the inspectors explain that the solitude of the prison cell rather than the gallows produces conversion. Rather than a gateway *directly* to heaven provided by a conversion at the scaffold, incarceration enabled a detour to heaven by way of a regenerated life on earth.

Indeed, the Eastern State Penitentiary inspectors frequently perceived the metaphors of conversion in the demeanour of the penitentiary's incarcerated people (at least in their reports). Another inspector's report, republished in George W. Smith's *A Defence of the System of Solitary Confinement of Prisoners Adopted by the State of Pennsylvania* (1833), details the stages of an imprisoned person's rehabilitation in terms redolent of the conversion narrative:

> We mark that at first the prisoner indulges in morose or vindictive feelings, and is guilty of turbulent and malicious conduct; but after a few weeks he adopts a more subdued tone, becomes reasonable, and his countenance indicates a more amiable state of mind; is disposed to talk of his past life as one of misery and folly; begins to think that the barrier between him and good reputation is not impossible; and that there are those in the community, whose prejudices against the condemned are not so strong as to induce the withholding a friendly countenance to his attempt at restoration. In many, the retrospect of life becomes a horrible and loathsome subject of reflection – the sense of shame and

feelings of remorse drives them to some source of
consolation, and the ordinary means of stifling an
actively reproving conscience being denied by reason of their solitariness, the comforts of the Bible
and the peace of religion are eagerly sought for.[30]

Built into the very walls of Eastern's solitary, cellular confinement
system was the tripartite schema of the conversion narrative that
had earlier framed the criminal confessions of people like Esther
Rogers: fall, tortured conscience, and redemption. Here, the incarcerated person, whose crimes identified them as spiritually fallen,
moved through a "guilty" state marked by "morose and vindic-
tive feelings" and "turbulent and malicious conduct"; next, once
they were in a more "amiable" and pliable state, their past life of
"misery and folly" was codified within a moral framework that
reflected their "shame and feelings of remorse"; and finally, compelled through the introspection of solitary confinement to seek
the guidance of the Bible, the imprisoned person progressed to an
ontological state amenable to the requirements of the prison system
and the newly formed American Republic beyond the prison walls.

Again, whereas the gallows confessionals ended with the convert's new identity finding acceptance in heaven, the penitentiary
made possible the criminal's rebirth in American society. As the
inspectors' report suggested, the incarcerated person felt that there
were "those in the community" who were eager to accept him back
into their ranks, who offered a "friendly countenance to his attempt
at restoration" – a key component within the conversion ritual,
since a community of like-minded believers would be essential to
supporting the convert's new communal identity. This imagined
"restoration" reflected the esteemed early prison reformer (and
Declaration of Independence signer) Benjamin Rush's expectation
that formerly incarcerated people would "recover their former connections with society" after their incarceration. In *An Enquiry into
the Effects of Public Punishments upon Criminals and upon Society*,

Rush wrote, "methinks I already hear the inhabitants of our villages and townships counting the years that shall complete the reformation of one of their citizens. I behold them running to meet him on the day of his deliverance. His friends and family bathe his cheeks with tears of joy; and the universal shout of the neighborhood is, 'This our brother was lost, and is found—was dead and is alive.'"[31] Rush identified the social acceptance of the formerly incarcerated person as crucial to the effectiveness of incarceration, imagining this moment as one of exuberance where the family of the prodigal convict along with the members of his community would hurry to embrace him as a newly formed citizen.

Notably, during this early period, Social Gospel ministers circulated through US prisons and stocked prison libraries with religious tracts that promoted conversion. In the penitentiaries, writes Vibeke Lehmann, the "'librarians' were almost all members of the clergy. The main purpose of reading was believed to be strengthening of character, religious devotion, and what we today would call behavior modification."[32] Books that promoted this "behavior modification" included Richard Baxter's *A Call to the Unconverted* (1831), seventy-five copies of which were the sole readings at Mount Pleasant Female Prison in Ossining, New York, in 1844.[33] In a series of essays, Baxter promoted conversion: "scriptural repentance ... that deep and radical change whereby a soul turns from the idols of sin and of self unto God, and devotes every movement of the inner and the outer man, to the captivity of his obedience."[34] The links between conversion and education were made most explicit during the post-bellum period with the work of the new penologists; however, education, including the ostensibly transformative effects of reading and writing, can be seen during this earlier period as well, as ministers promoted conversion through prison libraries in ways that confirmed the ideological work of the wider institution within which imprisoned people were celled.

By the early nineteenth century, with new sentencing guidelines and the creation of several prisons across the country, actual death at the scaffold had become a metaphorical death in the penitentiary. This change from real to metaphorical death was actually the point for the early reformers of the criminal justice system. They generally believed that execution was barbaric and antisocial; the penitentiary was meant to put an end to the bloody, sensational, public executions they viewed as expressions of an antiquated criminal justice system. In *Considerations on the Injustice and Impolicy of Punishing Murder by Death*, Benjamin Rush writes that "capital punishments are the natural offspring of monarchical governments"; by comparison, he continues, "the united states [*sic*] have adopted these peaceful and benevolent forms of government," so it "becomes them therefore to adopt their mild and benevolent principles."[35] Prior to 1764, *real* death in the form of capital punishment had been meted out for a variety of offences, including burglary, treason, rape, sodomy and buggery, and counterfeiting, "as well as for a second conviction of any felony."[36]

With the advent of the penitentiary system, imprisonment replaced execution for many previously capital crimes. Death was not eliminated thereby; rather, it was sublimated into the narrative of the prison, in the form of symbolic death (or "death-in-life," as John Edgar Wideman calls it, signifying on Coleridge's term from *The Rime of the Ancient Mariner*)[37] as well as in "civil death" statutes, which rendered a convicted criminal legally dead. According to Richard Hawkins and Geoffrey P. Alpert in *American Prison Systems: Punishment and Justice* (1989), "[civil death] statutes meant the prisoners had no standing in legal action involving their property, marriage, custody of their children, or other matters outside the prison."[38] Incarcerated people could not enter into contractual agreements and were no longer recognized as subjects by the courts. Although civil death statutes were largely revoked in later years, civil death continues to haunt incarcerated people after their release, for their treatment as social pariahs has been institutionalized through a patchwork of state laws that limit their capacity to function in civil society, essentially revoking the "deliverance" that early prison reformers like Benjamin Rush believed was the ultimate goal of incarceration.[39]

Gustave de Beaumont and Alexis de Tocqueville, in their early inspections of US penitentiaries, describe how the metaphor of death was lived out by incarcerated people in the early penitentiary system: "the silence within those vast walls, which contain so many prisoners, is that of death. We have often trod during night those monotonous and dumb galleries, where a lamp is always burning: we felt as if we traversed catacombs; there were a thousand living beings, and yet it was a desert solitude."[40]

Again, though: unlike death at the scaffold, this "death" was not to be final; instead, it was intended to serve the conversion process.[41] "In this closed cell," writes Michel Foucault, "this temporary sepulchre, the myths of resurrection arise easily enough."[42] Although the ritualistic "death" of the incarcerated person, his live burial within the tombs of the prison, seems to contradict the humanitarian promise of the prison reformers to rehabilitate rather than execute the criminal, the metaphorical work of this practice makes perfect sense when viewed in terms of the conversion narrative, especially when mapped onto the resurrection, as Foucault suggests. The incarcerated person dies symbolically and legally in order to be resurrected as a newly formed citizen. While this regenerative process certainly reproduces Enlightenment principles of social renewal, including enacting the originary drama of the social contract that theorists believed bound the community together (a metaphor that Caleb Smith addresses in *The Prison and the American Imagination*), the metaphors of religious conversion are also unmistakably at work here, serving to conceptualize how this transformative process was to be enacted and understood.

However innovative it was, the Pennsylvania system, with its emphasis on near-complete solitary confinement, never really caught on across the country. There were many reasons for this, not least of which were the reports that solitary confinement induced mental deterioration and increased the risk of suicide attempts.

Colin Dayan notes that this was a concern for Tocqueville, who saw the penitentiary system not within the framework of "Quaker renewal" but rather in terms of "the despair, fear, and personal effacement of Puritan conversion." It may have approximated "the stages on the way to personal regeneration ('the morphology of conversion' that would become prescriptive in the evangelical churches)," Dayan writes, but it did not make room for the "promised rebirth through God's free grace" and thus was likely to "bring about madness" rather than reflection.[43] Still, during the early nineteenth century, debates raged over whether the Pennsylvania system or what was called the "Auburn system" (or "congregate system") was the most effective way to rehabilitate incarcerated people.

The Auburn system, which was developed at New York's Auburn Prison in the 1820s, borrowed much from its Walnut Street-experiment predecessor, particularly with regard to the distinctly Quaker emphasis on separation and silence as preconditions for conversion. Beaumont and Tocqueville's description of the prison as a "tomb" (discussed earlier) is in fact an account of Auburn Prison's silent halls at night. Of the Auburn system, they write that "the idea was not given up, that the solitude, which causes the criminal to reflect, exercises a beneficial influence." The goal of the new congregate system was to mitigate against "the evil effect of total solitude ... by leaving the convicts in their cells during night, and by making them work during the day, in the common work-shops, obliging them at the same time to observe absolute silence."[44]

Also, whereas work was a privilege in the Pennsylvania system, considered less important than solitary reflection in affecting behaviour, hard work was central to an imprisoned person's rehabilitation in the Auburn system. In their notes, Beaumont and Tocqueville cite Auburn and Sing Sing warden Elam Lynds, who writes that

> if you lock up in a cell, a person convicted of a
> crime, you have no control over him: you act only

> upon his body. Instead of this, set him to work, and
> oblige him to do everything he is ordered to do; you
> thus teach him to obey, and give him the habits of
> industry; now I ask, is there anything more power-
> ful than the force of habit? If you have succeeded in
> giving to a person the habits of obedience and labor,
> there is little chance of his ever becoming a thief.[45]

Hard work not only reformed the incarcerated person but also made good fiscal sense. The Protestant work ethic provided the ideological backbone for the growing political demand that penitentiaries reduce their dependence on taxpayer money by increasing the labour-potential of incarcerated people. In fact, the prospect that the Auburn model could be self-sufficient ultimately ensured that it became the accepted standard for prison design for the nation; the less economically sound Pennsylvania model slowly became obsolete.[46]

The abolition of slavery in 1865 changed the scope of US prisons. In the South, the criminal justice system picked up where slavery left off: the transition from slave plantation to prison plantation, from slave chain gang to prison chain gang, indexes the ease with which the southern penal system absorbed the institutional function of slavery. African Americans were routinely incarcerated on spurious charges such as vagrancy. Such charges formed part of what came to be called the "Black Codes," a patchwork of laws across the South that sought to dramatically curtail black people's recently acquired freedoms. Once incarcerated, African Americans were often loaned out to private companies, ostensibly to work off fines as well as additional fees the state had added to cover the costs of their incarceration. This "convict lease system" provided cheap labour to industries like tobacco, mining, and cotton; in this way, incarcerated African Americans were forced to perform some of the labour previously performed by slaves. Southern prisons, unlike northern ones, paid little lip service to notions of conversion or rehabilitation, even for incarcerated white people. Rehabilitation as a program for prisons "was generally confined to the wealthier states of the North until the thirties," writes Williams Banks Taylor in *Down on Parchman Farm: The Great Prison in the Mississippi Delta* (1999). Until the twentieth century, there were hardly any attempts in the southern carceral system to systematize a process for the conversion or reform of imprisoned persons.[47]

The southern carceral system, with its network of chain gangs, labour camps, and agricultural prisons (some, like Angola in Louisiana, even located on former slave plantations), extended the legacy of the slave system into the twentieth century. Although contemporary prisons are not the same as antebellum plantations, there is a disconcerting continuity between the two – and not simply in appearance. As Joy James writes in her introduction to *The New Abolitionists: (Neo)Slave Narratives and Contemporary Prison Writings* (2005),

> racially fashioned enslavement shares similar features with racially fashioned incarceration. Plantations, historically, were penal sites – prisons for the exploitation of agriculture, domestic, and industrial labor and the dehumanization of beings. Prison is the modern day manifestation of the plantation ... Physical, emotional, sexual, and economic exploitation and violence [that were features of the plantation system] are visited upon bodies with equal abandon and lack of restraint in sites disappeared from conventional scrutiny. The old plantation was a prison; and the new prison is a plantation.[48]

James is aware that aligning the prison with the plantation risks obscuring the clear differences between these systems. She points out that scholars like Matthew Mancini in *One Dies, Get Another* and Orlando Patterson in *Slavery and Social Death* argue that slavery is *not* a condition of the post-emancipation carceral system. Yet James's grouping of these two systems is important, for the clear lines of continuity between the plantation and the prison – most notably, the obvious and discomfiting ways that the prison targets African Americans in wildly disproportionate numbers – illustrate how systems like slavery and segregation do not simply disappear; instead, they are often reconfigured in different forms to perpetuate racially based discrepancies of power.

After the Civil War, US prisons, in the North as well as the South, helped entrench white supremacy by targeting communities of colour, especially African American men. When seven million African Americans migrated from South to North during the Great Migration of the early twentieth century, prison populations, which had been majority white, began to undergo a dramatic shift in their racial composition as African American men were incarcerated in increasingly large numbers. Historians have demonstrated that this was no accident but rather a consequence of policy decisions. For example, in *From the War on Poverty to the War on Crime: The Making of Mass Incarceration in America* (2016), Elizabeth Hinton shows how the federal government responded to the advances of the civil rights movement by expanding the carceral state.[49] Naomi Murakawa notes in *The First Civil Right: How Liberals Built Prison America* (2014) that the criminalization of blackness was bipartisan, furthered by Republicans (most notably with the policies of Nixon and Reagan) but also by Democrats (from Truman Democrats to Clinton Democrats, who pursued a "liberal law-and-order agenda").[50] After legislators introduced draconian laws to fight various "wars" on crime and drugs – laws that targeted African American populations – and after the economic shift away from industrial labour in the 1970s that disproportionately impacted black communities, incarceration rates skyrocketed for African Americans.[51] Black communities continue to be disproportionately affected by the 1970s "punitive turn" in US prisons. As William J. Stuntz writes in *The Collapse of American Criminal Justice* (2011), if "present trends continue, one-third of black men with no college education will spend time in prison. Of those who do not finish high school, the figure is 60 percent."[52]

When considering the history of US efforts to introduce prison reforms aimed at rehabilitating incarcerated people – reforms that I argue are consistently described in terms redolent of the conversion narrative – it is worth keeping in mind the racial dynamics of US prisons, given that black men have often been viewed by (white) prison officials as incapable of reform. Ta-Nehisi Coates, the *Atlantic Monthly* national correspondent who has recently helped cultivate public awareness of the expansion of the criminal justice system, writes that "it is impossible to conceive of the Gray Wastes [his term for carceral institutions] without first conceiving of a large swath of its inhabitants as both more than criminal and less than human. These inhabitants, black people, are the preeminent outlaws of the American imagination."[53] Angela Davis suggests that the correlation between the dramatic increase in incarcerated black men since the 1970s and the repudiation of rehabilitative programming in prisons is no coincidence: the "notion that the 'criminals' with which prisons are overcrowded are largely beyond the pale of rehabilitation – that 'nothing works' – is very much connected with the fact that in the contemporary era, the terms 'back' and 'male,' when combined, have become virtually synonymous with 'criminal' in the popular imagination."[54] So, notwithstanding the rhetoric of rehabilitation, reform, and conversion, which may ostensibly be addressed to all incarcerated people, the practical application of such theories is dramatically uneven, especially along racial lines.

"EDUCATION ALONE MAKES THE MAN": CONVERSION, POSTWAR PRISONS, AND THE TREATMENT ERA

So far, I have sketched the history of the US conversion narrative. I have also explained how that narrative appeared in the rhetoric of prison reformers as they tried to explain how their newly built

Jacksonian institutions, which they called penitentiaries, could dramatically change people's identities. Next I consider how the prison conversion narrative has functioned in postwar prison discourse – especially how it has been linked to a belief in the transformative potential of a liberal arts education – in order to explain its relationship to the prison life writing that began to flourish during the same period.

But to understand postwar prison reforms and their effect on prison life writing, we need to return to the post-bellum period, a time when many of these reforms were in their infancy. After the Civil War, a new group of prison reformers sought to transform the Jacksonian prison system. This new generation of reformers saw the existing prison system as unnecessarily brutal, expensive, and ineffectual. Enoch Wines and Theodore Dwight's 1867 *Report on the Prisons and Reformatories of the United States and Canada* inaugurated these efforts. Wines and Dwight produced their report after the New York Prison Association (NYPA) authorized them to tour prisons in the northern states and parts of Canada. Their survey generated a six-hundred-page report as well as seventy volumes of documentation.[55] The recommendations they made were rearticulated three years later at the National Congress on Penitentiary and Reformatory Discipline in Cincinnati, Ohio, where this emerging group of prison professionals gathered to discuss how to reform America's fledgling prison system. The congress lent credence to Wines and Dwight's methodology, defined by Wines as the "scientific study of crime," or the "new penology."[56]

These New Penologists, as they came to be known, envisioned a prison system based on a rehabilitative model that eschewed the violence and deprivation of the earlier system. Although their theories culminated in the construction of some "reformatories," as they called their model prisons, their impact on the prison system was more theoretical than practical – at least until Progressive Era prison reformers interested in renewing efforts at upgrading the prison system essentially retrofitted many of the New Penologists' theories and applied them to prisons in a patchwork of states across the country.[57] Progressive Era reforms were, in turn, updated after the Second World War by another generation of prison reformers. Before the postwar period, then, the history of the prison system largely revolved around efforts at reforming failed prisons. These efforts were invariably based on the rehabilitative ideal – the theory that prisons were supposed to change people rather than simply punish and contain them. Diverse theories about rehabilitation that had been incubating since Wines and Dwight's 1867 report were applied to postwar prisons. Concepts like the indeterminate sentence and the parole board, and especially the importance of education for rehabilitating incarcerated people, would have a dramatic impact on prison life writing.

After the Second World War, the economy was booming, and psychologists and social scientists, with manic optimism, popularized the belief that human behaviour could be treated and changed. In the wake of all this, prisons refocused their resources on the individualized treatment, and rehabilitation, of "offenders." This period, which ended in the mid-1970s, is called "The Treatment Era." The American Prison Association aligned itself with this approach by changing its name to the American *Correctional* Association (ACA) in 1954. Incarcerated people were to be "corrected," according to the ACA's mandate, rather than punished.

Although the postwar prison system was guided by the language of the psychological, medical, and social sciences, and the religious rhetoric of earlier reform movements was largely missing from official guidelines, the metaphors of conversion repeatedly appear in discussions of the rehabilitative ideal during this period. In *Prison within Society: A Reader in Penology*, published in 1968 when the Treatment Era was in full swing, Lawrence E. Hazelrigg writes that the prison is, or should be, a "people-changing" institution so as "to fulfill its integrative function to larger society."[58] Penologists like Hazelrigg argued that prisons were in the business of "changing" imprisoned "people," a metaphor that, once again, reinscribed what William James had called the "complete division" "between the old life and the new" that is the defining metaphor of the conversion narrative. An influential report on prisons, the 1971 Quaker-produced *Struggle for Justice: A Report on Crime and Punishment in America*, underscored how conversion was latent in the new methodologies of rehabilitation. In it, the authors wrote that the concept of rehabilitation, with its focus on the total transformation of "the whole personality" and its rhetoric of "remaking people," was "akin to religious conversion."[59] Likewise, in *American Prison Systems: Punishment and Justice* (1989), Hawkins and Alpert described the rehabilitative ideal as a "control-by-conversion philosophy."[60] At a time when rehabilitation was ostensibly at its most scientific, the old rhetoric of conversion was perhaps most obvious.

Precisely *how* people were to be converted was harder to define in practice for postwar prison reformers. Reformers, social scientists, and eventually prison officials ultimately arrived at two models for rehabilitating offenders: medical, and educational. As I have suggested, like many postwar innovations in US prisons, these models were based on earlier theories initially developed by the New Penologists. For the New Penologists, the "new" prison was no longer just a prison. According to the widely influential New Penologist and superintendent of the experimental Elmira Reformatory, Zebulon Brockway, in a description that was to resonate throughout the twentieth century, the new institution was to be "so little like an ordinary prison and so much like a college or a hospital."[61] Within this new system, incarcerated people were "patients" or "students."[62] During the postwar period, the medical model, which redefined incarcerated people as patients, identified criminality as something that could be treated and changed using treatment methods that varied widely, from drug treatment to counselling or even surgery.[63] But the most common forms of treatment employed "various behavioral or psychiatric methods to break down criminal values ... replacing them with values associated with free society."[64] Group therapy was a commonly used technique to achieve this end, and, perhaps coincidentally, two of the most popular therapeutic programs in prisons were (and continue to be) the conversion-based 12-Step models of Alcoholics Anonymous and Narcotics Anonymous.[65]

Although therapy certainly played an important role in incarcerated people's lives during this period, the educational model had a more enduring impact on prison discourse and popular culture and especially on prison life writing. The educational model took a number of possible forms in prison. Prison classification committees could assign an imprisoned person to vocational instruction, where they could learn a trade like baking, auto mechanics, or printing.[66] Depending on the region, a prison system might offer secondary- or post-secondary-level education courses. In California's prison system, for example, which has historically been a bellwether for changes in prisons in the twentieth century, increased attention to and funding for prison libraries, educational programs, and educational-therapeutic programs like bibliotherapy, coupled with a surge in popular and academic interest in supporting the education of incarcerated people, linked rehabilitation with the rhetoric of self-improvement already associated in the US imaginary with education.[67] Because "remaking people is an educational function," as the authors of *Struggle for Justice* observe, postwar prison reformers emphasized education as an important plank of Treatment Era policies.[68]

In particular, reading and writing were central to the educational efforts of Treatment Era prison education programs. For one thing, incarcerated people who became better readers and writers were more articulate and better poised to communicate to prison officials that they had, in fact, changed. Reading and writing were thus seen as relatively effective tools for rehabilitation in a system that often had difficulty defining what rehabilitation looked like. This is perhaps best articulated in the words of an anonymous Progressive Era prison warden cited in Sullivan and Vogel's "Reachin' Behind Bars":

> All the prisoners who can read understandingly avail themselves of the privilege. The improvement from it is astonishing. Young men who two years ago were taught their first lesson here are now good readers; and it seems as if they had changed entirely in body and mind. They keep themselves now neat and clean, while they formerly were very filthy in their habits. They have better manners, and look more intelligent, more like human beings. Ignorance makes many convicts; education alone makes the man.[69]

Here, reading has an almost magical quality. It not only provides incarcerated people with an education, enabling them to change "entirely in ... mind," but it also has an effect on the "body." So reading, and by extension the education that such reading provides, produces more than changes and conversions: it is a social (and somehow even physical) hygiene, a cleansing, that not only improves thinking and "manners" but is constitutive of becoming "human." Although this rhetoric of education, and especially reading, as a human-making technology might seem like a throwaway turn of phrase, where the warden is merely looking for a useful expression that will articulate the kind of radical change he is seeing in his incarcerated charges, this same metaphor reappears with some frequency to explain the seemingly subhuman qualities associated with criminals (a metaphor whose significance I will explain in Chapter 4) and the edifying and human-making work of education.

Americans have also long believed that students who read the right books absorb the psychological, emotional, and social requirements needed to sustain a democratic society. Francis Allen, in his book about the failure of the rehabilitative ideal in prisons, writes that education was naturally suited to the rehabilitative project since it had citizen-making properties: "It is the American tradition that public schools are a marvelous instrumentality for producing the kind of character that makes a democratic society possible."[70] For incarcerated people, reading and writing provided the necessary skills for participation in a literate society, but they also, ostensibly, developed the softer skills of good citizenship. Teaching incarcerated people to read and write worked well with the transformative claims of the Treatment Era, and stories of incarcerated people who learned to read and write in prison, and who published their own work, multiplied so rapidly during this period that a 1981 *Saturday Night Live* skit, "Prose and Cons," joked that great writers of the future were not educated in universities but made in prisons.

So, US prisons during the Treatment Era were governed by a philosophy that privileged education, and especially reading and writing, as a key conduit for conversion. Prison life writing during this period was responding, in complicated ways, to this discourse since it tended to dominate incarcerated people's lives. Simultaneously, specific prison policies were being implemented that made it essential for incarcerated people to represent themselves as rehabilitated in ways that prison officials would recognize as legitimate – and these policies would play a formative role in prison life writing.

During the Treatment Era, incarcerated people were under enormous pressure from two linked criminal justice policies to represent themselves as rehabilitated: the indeterminate sentence, and the parole board. These policies affected how they represented themselves in their life writings. Initially introduced by the New Penologists, indeterminate sentences were eventually expanded to prisons across the country in the early twentieth century, so that by 1920, most incarcerated people in state institutions were serving indeterminate sentences. By the Treatment Era, the indeterminate sentence was a well-entrenched feature of the prison landscape.[71]

Indeterminate sentences were introduced as a way to provide agency for the incarcerated. Determinate sentencing, where imprisoned people's sentences were fixed, was viewed as inflexible, besides being unfair to those people who had worked to change their lives while imprisoned. With indeterminate sentencing, an imprisoned person received a broad sentence whose duration was ultimately to be decided by a parole board that reviewed their success or failure to rehabilitate while behind bars. Incarcerated people serving indeterminate sentences would be given set minimums and set maximums; these were far enough apart that they could be held until they had proven their reform or until the end of their maximum sentence, whichever was sooner. Before this new system was implemented, a person convicted of forgery might receive a determinate sentence of five years in prison. Under indeterminate sentencing, a conviction for forgery might earn the incarcerated person a sentence of five years to life.

These incredibly broad sentences were quite common at the time. As I will discuss in the next chapter, George Jackson, the author of *Soledad Brother* (1970) and *Blood in my Eye* (1971), received an indeterminate sentence of one year to life in prison for robbery. James Carr, who I will also discuss in the next chapter, received a similar "five-to-life" indeterminate sentence.[72] With the indeterminate sentence in place, incarcerated people had to produce evidence that they had changed if they hoped to be released. Consequently, the ways in which the authorities could be convinced of an imprisoned person's rehabilitation became of primary importance to incarcerated people. If ever there was a technology for producing narratives of rehabilitation in the life writings of the imprisoned, this was certainly it.

The successful demonstration of an imprisoned person's rehabilitation was ultimately based largely on the discursive subject the parole board encountered in their file. "Only the file could be trusted," writes prison writer Malcolm Braly.[73] The prison file is a complicated site of auto/biographical production. Besides being a collective biography, of sorts, since it is written by numerous prison officials about a particular incarcerated person, it is also autobiographical. Incarcerated people often had to contribute different forms of life writing to their file throughout their prison term. For example, George Jackson describes how the newly imprisoned had to "write a confession" as part of their intake process. The confession "is placed right in the front of your jacket [a prison term for their file] under your picture and number." An imprisoned person who failed or refused to write a confession would never be paroled, explains Jackson.[74] Moreover, as I will show in my discussions of Jackson's *Soledad Brother* (Chapter 2) and Carl Panzram's *Killer: A Journal of Murder* (Chapter 3), an incarcerated person's letters, which were read by prison censors before they were mailed to anyone on the outside, were often compiled in an imprisoned person's file too. Incarcerated people also associated themselves with specific programs and activities in order to produce discursive selves in their files that would please the board. In a sense, imprisoned people were in a very real way *life* writing: organizing their days, months, and years so as to produce a narrative in their files that would convince the parole board that they had changed and should be released.

Obviously, the indeterminate sentence placed great power and exegetical authority with the parole board, an official body whose role in the US prison system was, like the indeterminate sentence, initially developed by the New Penologists but largely implemented during the Progressive Era.[75] As most people are aware, parole is a form of conditional release. The term "parole" has its origins in twelfth-century France: as a noun, it meant a kind of promise. In judicial, military, and penal usage, *parole* has its origins more specifically in the French term *parole d'honneur*, that is, "word of honour." A *parole d'honneur* refers not just to a promise but to a weighty, unwritten contract between people, the idea being – as the term developed within the prison system – that an imprisoned person could be released if he or she promised to comply with a set of conditions.[76]

Parole in the criminal justice system was only granted if incarcerated people were able to link their rehabilitation to a paradigmatic narrative, with the parole board ruling on whether they had succeeded. In other words, imprisoned people hoping to be released had to produce in their file a story about their rehabilitation that would match criteria used by the parole board to identify them as genuinely rehabilitated. However, the parole board's expectations were often maddeningly vague. Malcolm Braly describes how incarcerated people obsessively strategized so as to present the most successful demonstrations of their rehabilitation before the Adult Authority (California's name for the parole board): "There was nothing that interested us more and we logged years trying to thrash out a basis on which to predict the Adult Authority. This was our great debate. We knew which programs to try to associate ourselves with and we knew which ploys were now exhausted. We could gauge public pressure and the changing winds of penal philosophy."[77]

Braly shows how incarcerated people serving indeterminate sentences – and that was most of the imprisoned during the Treatment Era – obsessed about the parole board's criteria. No clear model was available to them, and this caused them to anxiously cast about for ways to appeal to the board. At the same time, incarcerated people were well aware that educational programming, and actively demonstrating their involvement in that programing by identifying themselves as enthusiastic readers and writers, was one way they could demonstrate to the board that they had changed and were ready to be returned to society.

The indeterminate sentence and the parole board eventually came to dominate incarcerated people's lives, and thus, not surprisingly, both often feature prominently in prison life writing during the Treatment Era, as I will show in the next chapter. In tandem, they required imprisoned people to demonstrate that they had been rehabilitated before they could be released, and this, coupled with the privileging of educational methods as ways to demonstrate that rehabilitation, is one reason why the prison conversion narrative promoted during the Treatment Era found its way into prison life writing.

"IN THE JAILERS' EYES ... WE ARE 'GIRLS'": WOMEN'S INSTITUTIONS, ENFORCED DOMESTICITY, AND THE MISSING CONVERSION NARRATIVE

Of course, not all prison autobiographies or memoirs adhere to the conversion narrative. Notably, the conversion paradigm that is so ubiquitous in the life writings of incarcerated men rarely appears in women's prison life writings. The near wholesale absence of the conversion narrative in women's prison life writings is mostly the result of a tangle of ideological and institutional factors that make certain narratives available to imprisoned men but unavailable to imprisoned women. Book publishers, the reading public, and prisons have traditionally been invested in stories of incarcerated men who have been changed through their imprisonment to such a degree that they have transcended their lives of crime and entered the public sphere – and have changed enough to participate in the rarified space of literary production as writers or political figures.

For women, by contrast, the available narratives have been quite different. As Angela Davis explains in *Are Prisons Obsolete?*, "male punishment was linked ideologically to penitence and reform. The very forfeiture of rights and liberties implied that with self-reflection, religious study, and work, male convicts could achieve redemption and could recover these rights and liberties. However, since women were not acknowledged as securely in possession of these rights, they were not eligible to participate in this process of redemption."[78] If, as I have been suggesting, prison life writing is deeply affected by prison discourse, then the absence of the conversion narrative as a guiding metaphor in women's prisons likely goes some way toward accounting for its absence in imprisoned women's life writings. But if women were not thought to be capable of the kind of conversion that guided men's institutions, what ideological work did women's prisons perform, and what kind of pressure did these institutions and their attendant discourses exert on incarcerated women's life writings?

Women's prisons, according to Nicole Hahn Rafter in *Partial Justice: Women, Prisons, and Social Control*, evolved out of men's institutions into two different models toward the end of the nineteenth century: "custodial institutions," which were essentially conventional prisons modelled on men's penitentiaries, and "reformatories," which were typically comprised of unwalled, smaller, cottage-style dwellings grouped together on rural grounds.[79] Custodial institutions were usually filled with adult women serving longer sentences for more substantial (but mostly non-violent) crimes. Also, custodial institutions tended to house larger numbers of black women, since black women were policed more aggressively and charged more severely than other women, especially white women. And, just as black men were thought to be unfit for full citizenship, black women were similarly believed to be incapable of reform, in part because, as Hazel Carby writes in "Policing the Black Woman's Body in an Urban Context," they were "characterized as sexually degenerate and, therefore, socially dangerous."[80] Reformatories, for their part, typically housed younger, almost exclusively white women charged with lesser crimes who were thought to be fit for rehabilitation, according to Kali Nicole Gross in "African American Women, Mass Incarceration, and the Politics of Protection."[81]

Although the reformatory movement fizzled out in the 1920s, the ideological work of that system had a significant impact on women's prisons in the twentieth century and even to this day. The reformatory movement was spearheaded by middle-class white women who sought to instil in (often poor or working-class) white women and girls notions of femininity that had, since the emergence of the middle class earlier in the nineteenth century, undergirded the middle class's ideas about itself as a distinct class. These reformers sought to indoctrinate young "fallen women" into what Barbara Welter called the "cult of true womanhood," whose features "could be divided into four cardinal virtues – piety, purity, submissiveness and domesticity. Put them all together," writes Welter, "and they spelled mother, daughter, sister, wife-woman."[82] The features of the cult of true womanhood thus provided the ideological framework for the kind of change that middle-class women reformers sought in their inmates. As Nicole Hahn Rafter writes,

> reformatory designers adopted the late nineteenth-century penology of rehabilitation, but they tailored it to fit what they understood to be women's special nature. To instill vocational skills, they used not prison industries but domestic training. Inmates were taught to cook, clean, and wait on table; at parole, they were sent to middle-class homes to work as servants. Whereas men's reformatories sought to inculcate "manliness," women's reformatories encouraged femininity – sexual restraint, genteel demeanor, and domesticity. When women were disciplined, they might be scolded and sent, like children, to their "rooms." Indeed, the entire regimen was designed to induce a childlike submissiveness.[83]

Predictably, then, women's reformatories were not focused on the same kinds of transformational narratives that guided men's prisons. The prison conversion narrative, with its arc from criminality to citizenship, was withheld from women, who were encouraged to see themselves as irrational and childlike – precisely the kind of subjectivity incapable of performing the requisite duties of full citizenship.

The reformatories' infantilization of women, an offshoot of late nineteenth-century theories of gender that figured women as inherently childlike and dependent on the rational fortitude of men, and the concomitant institutionalization of the cult of domesticity, were both folded into the ideological project of women's prisons in the twentieth century. That project arguably continues to play a role in how women are treated in prison today. For example, in her autobiography, Angela Davis describes how the jails and prisons she observed during her incarceration in the 1970s routinely infantilized incarcerated women: "There were the well-worn cards and games, indispensable props for every jail – things to coat the fact of imprisonment with sugary innocuousness, fostering an imperceptible regression back to childhood. As I had noticed from the parlance at the House of D., in the jailers' eyes, whether we are sixteen or seventy, we are 'girls.' They loved to watch over their child-prisoners happily engrossed in harmless games."

In the same passage, Davis goes on to note "the stubborn presence of the washing machine, clothes dryer and ironing paraphernalia which, discounting the metal tables and backless stools, were the sole furnishings of the day room." She writes that the "'reasoning' behind this was presumably that women, because they are women, lack an essential part of their existence if they are separated from their domestic chores."[84]

Even today, women's prisons across the country frequently offer rehabilitative programs that privilege domestic work, such as courses on cooking and cleaning and home economics. A recent study of the Texas prison system (i.e., the Texas Department of Criminal Justice [TDCJ]) found that while "men have access to an Associate, Associate of Applied Science, Bachelor's, or Master's degree plan, as well as certifications in 21 occupations ... incarcerated women in Texas have access to an Associate degree plan and certifications in two occupations: office administration and culinary arts/hospitality management."[85] Of course, this comes as no surprise: the prison system is reproducing, albeit perhaps in more concentrated forms, the sexism of the country as a whole. But the prison is also an institution that has historically served to produce, often through direct or indirect violence, the kinds of heteronormative gender and sexual roles that help maintain patriarchal power. In other words, while the prison reflects the mores of the culture in which it is located, it also plays a defining role in generating, reifying, and legitimating those roles.

CONCLUSION: THE PRISON CONVERSION NARRATIVE AND PRISON LIFE WRITING

Rehabilitative methods that defined the Treatment Era, like the parole board and the indeterminate sentence, have haunted prison life writing ever since. In their life writings, imprisoned people describe going before the board and detail their efforts at representing themselves as rehabilitated. They discuss taking therapy and vocational courses in order to improve their chances at early release. And they often detail the myriad ways in which their behaviour is observed and recorded by guards, civilian staff, other incarcerated people – even their own family members – and presented before the interpretive gaze of the parole board. As I will show in the chapters that follow, these rehabilitative mechanisms find their way into imprisoned people's life writings in surprising ways, often setting the boundaries for what the incarcerated can and cannot say in their work.

More than anything, however, incarcerated people describe in their life writings how they changed as a result of an educational experience in prison and how that education has made them better, more socially aware, and more socially acceptable people. In other words, they use the prison conversion narrative. Of course, prison life writing that uses the prison conversion narrative, that describes how an imprisoned person undergoes a dramatic self-transformation as a result of their education, is not solely an effect of the prison system's regulating power and discursive authority. As critics like Joy James have suggested, for example, African American prison life writing has a literary genealogy that can be traced to slave narratives – what James calls "(neo)slave narratives."[86] Given that slave narratives often used the conversion paradigm, including identifying how a slave's education catalysed his or her self-transformation (as in the case of Frederick Douglass), the preponderance of conversion narratives in African American prison life writing is likely an extension of this literary tradition

– a tradition that, importantly, registers the deeply problematic connections between the "peculiar institution" of slavery and the carceral institution that is the modern prison system.

But even if the imprisoned are drawing on different literary and cultural traditions when they produce conversion narratives in their life writings, they are also living in total institutions that have a vested interest in producing dramatic transformations in the discursive selves of their imprisoned subjects. And this institutional pressure is important – sometimes even determinative. The system rewards the conversion experience, so it is hard to separate conversions from the institution that requires them.

Now, I am not suggesting that every imprisoned person's conversion is simply an effect of the prison's transformative, coercive, or discursive powers; conversions in prison may be opportunistic, obedient, or subversive, or completely genuine. But whatever their value or legitimacy, incarcerated people's conversions need to be considered in relation to the institution in which they are performed – an institution that, notwithstanding its correlative punitive function (or because of it), itself looks to produce discursive conversions in order to legitimize its own existence. As I will show in the next chapter, however, this in no way means that prison life writing is wholly defined by these institutional pressures or bound by these discursive limitations. Indeed, as I have been arguing, identifying how institutional discourse impinges on prison life writing reveals the ideological but also the aesthetic complexity of a genre that represents the lives of people living in the most peculiar institution in contemporary American life.

THE TREATMENT ERA

AFRICAN AMERICAN PRISON LIFE WRITING AND THE PRISON CONVERSION NARRATIVE IN GEORGE JACKSON'S *SOLEDAD BROTHER* AND JAMES CARR'S *BAD*

SO FAR, I HAVE OUTLINED HOW THE PRISON CONVERSION NARRATIVE evolved in prison discourse, and I have explained how Treatment Era policies like the indeterminate sentence and the parole board generated an atmosphere in which incarcerated people had to represent themselves as rehabilitated. Now I want to show how these policies set limits on prison life writing and helped sculpt the kinds of identities that entered into autobiographical discourse, and I want to explain how these institutional forces helped push the prison conversion narrative into prison life writing during the Treatment Era, which lasted from 1945 to around 1976.

In identifying how institutional power affects imprisoned people's autobiographical works, I am not simply arguing that prison life writing constitutes what David Guest calls a "discourse that enables ... the criminal justice system."[1] Instead, during this period, incarcerated people's life writings often managed to subvert the ideology of the prison system by *exploiting* prison discourse, including the prison conversion narrative and its rhetoric of rehabilitation. In this chapter, then, I consider two autobiographies that were deeply affected by the rehabilitative pressures of the Treatment Era prison system, that were influenced by the indeterminate sentence and the parole board, and that reproduced the prison conversion narrative: *Soledad Brother: The Prison Letters of George Jackson* and *Bad: The Autobiography of James Carr*. These two authors deliberately adapted the prison conversion narrative to serve radically different purposes than those intended by the prison system.

George Jackson and James Carr were friends who served time together in California's prison system throughout the 1960s during the Treatment Era. Jackson and his writings are fairly well-known. He played an important role in the Black Power movement, the Black Panther Party, and the Radical Left in the 1960s and 1970s. His writings and activism, and his dramatic and violent death, helped galvanize the radical prison movement. Lee Bernstein acknowledges his importance by calling the period in the 1970s when imprisoned people became radicalized "the age of Jackson."[2]

James Carr is less well-known and typically appears as a footnote to Jackson's story. Yet Carr's autobiography is, in my estimation, one of the most fascinating and aesthetically complex pieces of contemporary prison life writing. His book is also one of the most disturbing and problematic within that genre. By his own admission, Carr was a dangerous and brutal man while he was incarcerated, and after he was released on parole, he was suspected of multiple acts of violence, including the murder of a suspected police informant. His violence is deeply unethical, but it is also part of what makes his autobiography compelling, for it tests and indeed stretches the limits of what is sayable in prison life writing. Tragically, both Jackson and Carr were killed under circumstances that are similarly controversial (albeit for different reasons and with very different degrees of publicity): Jackson was shot by a guard sharpshooter during an alleged prison escape attempt; Carr was gunned down in his front yard one morning by two Black Panther-affiliated assassins.

The complexities of these two men are carried over into their life writings. Jackson was certainly a revolutionary figure who confronted the prison system in *Soledad Brother*, yet this combative position is not entirely consistent throughout his book. In it, Jackson sometimes resists the prison system, often to the detriment of his own freedoms; but other times, he responds favourably to the prison's rehabilitative demands, thus dramatizing how prison life writing was constrained and policed during the Treatment Era. However, most analyses of Jackson fail to consider the degree to which the prison influenced some of the key features of his book, including his revolutionary identity as it evolved over the course of his letters. For instance, Dylan Rodríguez writes that Jackson "advocates a form of political rupture that defies the possibility of rehabilitation" and that he rejects rehabilitation "as a modality of assimilation into the fabric of an essentially oppressive and white-supremacist civil society."[3] Although this is certainly true, it is not *always* true. It ignores those moments where Jackson does not defy "the possibility of rehabilitation" but instead seeks to represent himself *as rehabilitated* – in precisely the kind of terms that the prison system requires of him if he ever hopes to be released.

Now, I am not suggesting that Jackson's use of the prison's rehabilitation rhetoric is unintentional, an internalization of the prison's disciplinary methodology or rules. This can happen, certainly. For example, as Marilyn Buck explains, imprisoned people sometimes censor themselves, often without fully realizing it: "I censored how I spoke to people, how I interacted," she says. "You begin to censor yourself, so that they [prison staff] can't censor you."[4] By contrast, Jackson's use of the prison's rehabilitation rhetoric is quite deliberate and situational, as well as understandably opportunistic – attuned, that is, to the requirements of the indeterminate sentence and the parole board. Identifying where Jackson adheres to the rehabilitative demands of prison discourse, and how the prison's rhetorical and disciplinary forces impact Jackson's evolving identity in the narrative, helps explain where Jackson's revolutionary identity comes from, including how it emerges out of an engagement with, rather than a rejection of, the prison's discursive characteristics, including the prison conversion narrative.

Jackson's *Soledad Brother* features the now familiar story of an imprisoned person changed through reading and writing that, as I demonstrated in the previous chapter, was promoted in California's

Treatment Era prisons as a clear marker of an incarcerated person's rehabilitation. However, as I will show, Jackson inverts the purpose of prison education: rather than change him from a criminal into a citizen, his prison education radicalizes him, transforming his "black criminal mentality into a black revolutionary mentality."[5] I suggest that this deliberate misuse of the prison conversion narrative so that is serves different purposes emerges organically out of prison culture, where imprisoned people often retool objects so that they serve new and often subversive ends. I call this prison-specific cultural and literary technique *corruption*, a concept that expands on a theory of prison literary production that Jean Genet explains in his introduction to *Soledad Brother*. Ultimately, in order to understand Jackson's revolutionary identity – an identity that, as Lee Bernstein argues, is key to understanding an important moment in prison history, and that, as Joseph E. Peneil shows, is also central to understanding the evolution of Black Power in America – one must address how this identity emerged from him in relation to the pressures of the indeterminate sentence and the analytic power of the parole board and also how he articulated that identity partly through the discourse of the US prison system as I outlined it in the preceding chapter.[6]

James Carr's *Bad* also uses the prison conversion narrative to demonstrate how he changes into a revolutionary, but his autobiography pushes Jackson's logic further. Whereas Jackson changes from criminal to revolutionary, Carr celebrates, even exaggerates his own violent criminality, ultimately producing an autobiographical subject rarely seen in prison life writing – the violent, chaotic, and dangerous African American "hard man." In the second half of this chapter, I consider how Carr's *Bad* brings the hard man into prison life writing, what such a subject position reveals about prison life that is otherwise excluded from autobiography, and why engaging with such a troubling and often disturbing voice is worthwhile. I argue that Carr and the men who helped him write his autobiography bring the hard man into autobiographical discourse by hybridizing autobiography with a genre that circulates in US prisons called *lying*. *Lying* – which does not denote the misrepresentation of facts, necessarily – has very different rules than autobiography when it comes to representing violence and crime, and the hard man is one of the central figures of the genre, if not *the* central figure. *Bad* thus forms what Caren Kaplan calls an "out-law genre" because it "breaks many of the elite literature's laws" by "mixing two conventionally 'unmixable' elements."[7] Although Kaplan suggests that out-law genres blend "autobiography criticism and autobiography itself," I suggest that Carr's mixture of *lying*, an oral storytelling mode found in US prisons in the 1960s and 1970s, with autobiography, a written storytelling mode that is often associated with "high" cultural formations, likewise breaks rules of self-narration and disturbs the common sense of autobiographical discourse and prison life writing.[8]

Soledad Brother and *Bad* are invaluable resources for understanding the prison resistance movement, Black Power, and the Black Panther Party. In this chapter, I discuss how these men adapted narratives of power in their writings, but it is worth emphasizing that their work is heavily indebted to the prison resistance movement and the radical politics that were central to social justice movements outside prison, from Maoism to Black Power. As I will show, both men adapted the prison conversion narrative to better express revolutionary thought and praxis behind bars.

Their work is also representative of life writings by incarcerated African Americans who were involved in these movements, including Eldridge Cleaver's aforementioned *Soul on Ice* but also Richard X. Clark's *The Brothers of Attica*, which tells the story of the Attica uprising, and even Albert Woodfox's *Solitary: My Story of Transformation and Hope*, published only in 2019, which represents Woodfox's political struggle in Angola prison as a Black Panther during and after the Treatment Era.[9] Jackson's book is also representative of epistolary works in prison life writing, including

Abbott's *In the Belly of the Beast*. Perhaps, Jackson's missives from prison also resonate with the non-fiction work, from essays to journalism, of incarcerated people who report on the abuses of the prison system, including Mumia Abu-Jamal and Wilbert Rideau. As I will show, Carr's *Bad* also aligns with a long tradition of African American storytelling about "badmen," including prison life writing like *The Naked Soul of Iceberg Slim*.

But while these books are important for what they reveal about their historical moment and prison life writing as a genre, they are also important for what they *do* with life writing. Both men draw on the cultural work of imprisoned people – as with Jackson's use of corruption and Carr's adaptation of lying – in order to redefine the genre's conventions. Importantly, their literary innovations also emerge from their engagement with rather than resistance to the prison system, prison discourse, and the institutional mandates of the Treatment Era. Thus they exhibit the ingenuity, and the often overlooked creative work, of imprisoned people telling stories about themselves in institutions seeking to produce stories about them too.

SOLEDAD BROTHER

Before considering Jackson's *Soledad Brother*, including his use of the prison conversion narrative, I provide a brief overview of Jackson's incarceration, because his life and death behind bars changed the California prison system – indeed, prison systems across the country – in the 1970s. George Jackson was raised in Chicago, but he moved with his father, Lester, to California because his parents worried that George was becoming increasingly involved in small-time crime in the neighbourhood and attracting the attention of the police.[10] George did not change as a result of his move to Los Angeles. Instead, beginning in 1957, he started getting arrested for crimes ranging from vehicle theft to burglary. In 1960, when he was nineteen, he was convicted of robbery and given a one-year-to-life indeterminate sentence. He would never leave prison.

While incarcerated at Deuel Vocational Institute at Tracy, he met James Carr, and the two men helped form a prison gang called "the Wolf Pack," which would eventually serve a political purpose for them in prison.[11] Jackson regularly committed disciplinary infractions that landed him in solitary confinement. But time alone meant time to read. In solitary, Jackson became increasingly politicized. According to Carr, after Jackson was released from solitary he organized "political education classes" for the Wolf Pack, whose members had to read black nationalist literature such as the writings of Marcus Garvey.[12] This group would eventually form the nucleus of the Black Guerilla Family (BGF), which counted James Carr, W.L. Nolen, and William Christmas among its early members.[13]

Jackson and Nolen were transferred to Soledad Prison in 1969 at a time when the prison was saturated with racial tensions and violence. Those tensions were being stoked by the mostly white prison guards. In fact, Nolen filed civil suits against the warden, the Department of Corrections, and a few guards. He charged that "the guards were aware of 'existing social and racial conflicts'; that the guards helped foment more racial strife by helping their white inmate 'confederates' through 'direct harassment.'" Nolen "swore that Soledad officials were 'willfully creating and maintaining situations that creates and poses dangers to plaintiff [Nolen himself] and other members of his race.' Nolen said he 'feared for his life.'"[14] He had reason to.

On 13 January 1970, Nolen was released into the prison exercise yard along with several other imprisoned African Americans. They were assigned to the yard along with imprisoned white people who were known to be their mortal enemies. The guards were well aware of the tensions between the two groups, which meant the decision to bring them together in the confined space of the exercise yard was either incredibly stupid or (more likely) deliberate and malicious. When, predictably, the incarcerated men began to fight, a guard sharpshooter named Opie G. Miller fired into the group, killing Nolen and two other imprisoned African Americans, Cleveland Edwards and Alvin Miller. One imprisoned white man was injured by a stray bullet. No imprisoned white people were killed. As Sun Min Yee writes in a 1973 article for *Ramparts* (republished later that year as part of *The Melancholy History of Soledad Prison*),

> the murder of W. L. Nolen, on January 13, 1970, began an incredible chain of tragedies that led the California prison system to disaster. The initial consequence [of Nolen's murder] was the first killing of a guard in Soledad history, a revenge murder, and from there the poison spread. In the 19 months following the January 13 incident, at least 40 persons were murdered as a result of events and circumstances in the California prison system. Of the 40 murders, 19 are directly linked to the series of tragedies which began with the shooting of W. L. Nolen.[15]

After the murder of the men in the exercise yard was ruled a justifiable homicide three days later, a rookie guard named John V. Mills was attacked by imprisoned people, beaten, and thrown to his death from a third-floor tier. As Yee has already noted, this was "the first killing of a guard in Soledad history." Three men were charged with Mills's murder: Fleeta Drumgo, John Clutchette – and George Jackson. They came to be known as the Soledad Brothers.

In 1968, Huey Newton, co-founder of and Minister of Defense for the Black Panther Party, who was in prison for the murder of a police officer, heard about Jackson and asked his lawyer, Fay Stender, to review Jackson's robbery charges and indeterminate sentence.[16] When Jackson was charged with Mills's murder in 1970, Stender served as his lawyer. Stender helped organize the Soledad Brothers Defense Committee, and it was out of these efforts to solicit support for Jackson, Clutchette, and Drumgo that Stender suggested they publish Jackson's letters, which would become *Soledad Brother*.[17] Jackson's epistolary autobiography was a literary sensation. It helped garner support for the Soledad Brothers and ensured that Jackson's reputation in prison as a scholar-warrior would spread among his supporters outside of prison.

Before the publication of *Soledad Brother*, Jonathan Jackson, George's seventeen-year-old brother, had carried out a brazen attack on the Marin County Courthouse in an attempt to force the release of three imprisoned African Americans who were in court because one of the imprisoned men, James McClain (a friend of George Jackson), had been charged with stabbing a San Quentin prison guard. Jonathan Jackson, reportedly declaring, "All right, gentlemen, I'm taking over now," took out a machine gun and passed guns to three of the imprisoned people who had agreed to participate in the escape attempt (including the aforementioned BGF member, William Christmas).[18] They took five hostages, including the judge, Harold Haley. In a firefight outside the courthouse, Jackson and two of the imprisoned men – McClain and Christmas – were shot and killed. Ruchell McGee, wounded but alive, was the only San Quentin prison escapee to survive the incident. (He would be tried later alongside Angela Davis, who had been accused of providing Jonathan Jackson with the guns he used in the attack.[19]) Judge Haley was killed by a blast from the shotgun that had been strapped to his neck when Jackson and the imprisoned men initially took him as a hostage. Two of the other hostages were wounded: one of the jury members was shot in the arm, and the assistant district attorney in the trial, Gary W. Thomas, was shot in the back and paralysed.[20]

Jonathan Jackson's attack on the Marin County Courthouse framed the reception of – and was actually used to promote – *Soledad Brother*, which was published six weeks later.[21] The book ends with a letter in which George Jackson explains his brother's attack as a revolutionary act and his death as a martyrdom.[22] In this final letter, which is addressed to Joan Hammer (incidentally,

James Carr's mother-in-law), George Jackson expresses a desire that people interpret his brother's attack within a specific revolutionary framework. The letter is dated "August 9th, 1970 Real Date, 2 days A.D.," meaning, two days after the violent death of Jonathan Jackson at the Marin County courthouse. He writes that he wants people to be forced to ask themselves why a young man like Jonathan was compelled to violence and how his brother could embody the courage to boldly and aggressively confront the state. In the same letter, Jackson describes his brother as an example for others to follow, defining him as a revolutionary whose violent resistance to the criminal justice system should inspire the masses to action.[23] He explains Jonathan's attack as revolutionary vanguardism, which he theorizes at length in *Blood in My Eye*. "In order to develop revolutionary consciousness," he writes, "we must learn how revolutionary consciousness can be raised to the highest point by stimuli from the vanguard elements."[24] When, one year later, George Jackson mounted an attack from within San Quentin prison, killing three guards before being shot in the yard by a prison sharpshooter, he was likely staging an event that he hoped would be interpreted according to a similarly revolutionary hermeneutic – as a lesson for the masses, an inspiration for a much larger uprising against the state.

However, while Jackson was interpreted as a revolutionary by imprisoned African Americans (most notably, he inspired the Attica rebellion) and by many on the left and in the African American community, he was viewed as a deranged murderer by those on the right and by some in the mainstream. Indeed, as Dan Berger writes in *Captive Nation: Black Prison Organizing in the Civil Rights Era* (2014), Jackson's image was complicated by different and often competing interests: "The story of George Jackson is a story of cross-cutting narratives in which both Jackson the person and *Soledad Brother* the book were distinct figures among a large cast of characters. Jackson was caught between the story he wished to tell about himself not just in books but in actions and the stories that publishers, journalists, activists – and a long list of antagonists – wished to tell about him."[25] But even before Jackson was interpreted by "publishers, journalists, activists," he was interpreted, and closely scrutinized, by a massive ocular system in the prison that served the parole board – or, as it was called in California, the Adult Authority. Berger and others rightly suggest that in order to understand Jackson, we must look to his public persona and consider how it was shaped by multiple competing interests, from his lawyer to his editor to the Black Panther Party to Angela Davis to the Soledad Brothers Defense Committee. However, as I will show, understanding Jackson also means considering how Jackson was shaped by the prison system and how that shaping affected *Soledad Brother* – the book that made him famous in the first place.

"LOOKS BAD ON THE PAROLE BOARD REPORT": *SOLEDAD BROTHER* AND THE REHABILITATIVE GAZE

George Jackson's image as a revolutionary whose incarceration and resistance to that incarceration is representative of the black experience emerges out of a reckoning with prison discourse and the rehabilitative gaze of the prison system. By "rehabilitative gaze," I am referring to the innumerable figures who observe imprisoned people – including prison guards, censors, counsellors or therapists, doctors, teachers, even the families of other incarcerated people – and whose observations are recorded and compiled in imprisoned people's files to be read and interpreted by the Adult Authority (as well as other official bodies in the prison and criminal justice systems). Of course, this observatory network, which watches and also seeks to affect imprisoned people's behaviour, resonates with Michel Foucault's description in *Discipline and Punish* of the prison as a panoptic and disciplinary institution. As Foucault writes, the prison "has to extract unceasingly from the inmate a body of knowledge that will make it possible to transform the penal measure into a penitentiary operation; which will make of the penalty required by the offence a modification of the inmate that will be of use to society."[26]

Prisons in Treatment Era California conducted massive biographical projects about each individual incarcerated person. They tried to manage, control, and change imprisoned people by first collecting a vast "body of knowledge" about them. Although Jackson's *Soledad Brother* certainly mounts a sustained challenge to the prison system's legitimacy, especially insofar as the prison has the right to determine the lives of black, brown, and poor white people, it is also deeply influenced by this rehabilitative gaze. Examining how Jackson's revolutionary identity is a reaction to this gaze – and to the indeterminate sentence, the Adult Authority, and the prison conversion narrative – helps explain some of the aesthetic choices of *Soledad Brother* as well as the pressures that prison discourse exerted on prison life writing during this period.

The prison censor is perhaps the most immediately relevant example of how the rehabilitative gaze impacted *Soledad Brother*. The letters included in the book were invariably read by prison censors, who not only adjudicated which letters to repress and which letters to mail but also forwarded relevant information from those letters to prison officials to be compiled in Jackson's file, which would in turn be read by the Adult Authority. San Quentin warden Clinton Duffy explained the role of the censor this way:

> We keep a careful record of every letter written or received by the inmates, and our censors read every line. This is a prodigious book-keeping job, but in the long run it benefits the men themselves. Letters are clues to a man's thinking and emotions – they show progress or despair; they reveal an unreported illness, a family crisis that has affected a man's behavior, or even evidence that may be vital to his chances for parole.[27]

As Duffy suggests, prison censors read an incarcerated person's letters in order to cull "evidence that may be vital to [their] chances for parole." This was hardly as benevolent as Duffy made it sound, since the censor also searched for "clues" that justified denying their release. Invariably, whatever censors' particular motivations, their capacity to telescope the Adult Authority's rehabilitative gaze impacted how imprisoned people represented themselves in their letter writing. When Jackson's letters were gathered together into a book like *Soledad Brother*, the prison censor's proscriptive and prescriptive work was undoubtedly there too.

The prison censor, and by extension the Adult Authority, thus constitutes another implied reader in *Soledad Brother*. In other words, when Jackson addresses a letter to his lawyer, Fay Stender, and is thus writing to her most immediately, he is also writing with an awareness of the censor and the Adult Authority's interpretive work, which subtly impacts what he includes in and excludes from his letter – and thus what appears or does not appear in *Soledad Brother*. Sometimes the impact of the prison censor on Jackson's writing is not so subtle, however. For example, in a 30 March 1970 letter to Stender printed in *Soledad Brother*, Jackson shifts between addressing Stender and implying that he is also addressing a prison censor who, he explains, would "read these letters" before forwarding them out of the institution.[28] At one point in his letter to Stender, Jackson addresses this institutional gaze directly. He names one of the captains at Soledad Prison in his complaint about imprisoned white men throwing feces at him when guards escort them past his cell: "I'm putting you on notice, *Moody*, the first time I get shit thrown at me the whole country will know how it displeases me" (Jackson's emphasis).[29] Although Jackson's letter is addressed to Stender, he knows that his letter will be received and read by multiple institutional readers, who will convey Jackson's warning to Captain Moody. So, in this moment, he is openly hailing an institutional reader whose influence on him and his letters is usually harder to gauge.

Typically, the effects of the prison censor on his letters would appear as absences (letters returned rather than mailed, information excised or redacted). Or, Jackson would acknowledge the prison censor in ways that are harder to identify – for example, through self-censorship, or by using coded language or allusion to circumvent the censor's rules. In other words, by directly addressing this institutional reader in a letter to Stender, Jackson is indicating how his letter-writing is constructed with an awareness of this institutional reader and is thus, to a degree that is usually difficult to determine, influenced by this reader's interests. *Soledad Brother* – an epistolary autobiography compiled almost entirely from letters that were read by prison censors, a collection that must have been shaped with this institutional reader's criteria in mind – suggests how the prison and its discourse is productive inasmuch as it is restrictive, and how it affects prison life writing, including the life writing of someone deeply opposed to the prison, like George Jackson.

The prison censor exerts pressure on *Soledad Brother*, sometimes shaping what is and what is not included in the letters compiled in the book, but it is the Adult Authority that sets limits on, and establishes boundaries around, the kind of identity that Jackson can enter into discourse. As mentioned, Jackson was serving an indeterminate sentence for his part in a robbery, so he had to visit the Adult Authority on a yearly basis, a visit that he regularly discusses in his letters. Indeed, the Adult Authority is one of the most frequent topics of discussion in Jackson's book, indicating the degree to which his life – and, by extension, his writing about his life – was constantly responding to this organization and the observation system that informed it.

Jackson's early letters actually seem to suggest a desire on his part to conform, or rather to *seem* to conform, to the figure of the rehabilitated prisoner so that he would be released from prison. This indicates the degree to which the Adult Authority affects Jackson as an autobiographical subject. In a February 1965 letter to his mother, he writes that he expects to be released that year because he has obeyed the orders of prison officials and judiciously followed their guidelines. He asks his mother to write to the Adult Authority in support of his release, and he coaches her to clearly identify him as someone who has matured and changed as a result of his imprisonment. "You know what to say: that I was young then and you see a vast change in my character now," he tells her. Obviously, Jackson would not be out of prison that year – or any year. But what is suggestive about this letter is his avowed interest in meeting the rehabilitative gaze with a presentation of himself that he hoped would be deemed acceptable by the Adult Authority. He knows that he is being watched, and that his every action is being interpreted and analysed, and he responds to that gaze by going to counselling and school, keeping a "clean conduct record," and avoiding confrontations with prison staff. In other words, he organizes his life in such a way that it will be interpreted as the story of a rehabilitated prisoner, someone who has undergone "a vast change" – a subjectivity that (at first) seems anathema to the revolutionary figure described in most accounts of him.[30]

Similarly, in a 1966 letter to his father, he once again describes anticipating his meeting with the Adult Authority and explains how he is positioning himself so as to be read approvingly by the members of the board. He writes that he wants to "fit in with the rest of the herd and look as ordinary as possible" when they see him and assess him for potential release. "I don't want to stand out," he tells his father.[31] Once again, Jackson is cultivating a "look" in order to garner the approval of the Adult Authority; he is participating in the forced dramaturgy of an imprisoned person's life during the Treatment Era. Whether he is genuinely trying to be rehabilitated is unimportant here. Certainly, James Carr's descriptions of Jackson during this period suggest that he was far from rehabilitated in the way the Adult Authority presumably wanted him to be.[32] What is important, what I want to underscore, is how the rehabilitative gaze, the indeterminate sentence, and the Adult Authority affected

Jackson as an autobiographical subject – how, like other prison life writings, *Soledad Brother* is invested with prison discourse rather than simply resistant to it. Jackson's claim in *Blood in My Eye* that he has "always" said "just about what [he] want[s]" elides the degree to which *Soledad Brother* registers not only a hesitation to speak truth to power but a willingness to accept this institutional inter-pellation of him and respond accordingly – at least for a while.[33]

Jackson's revolutionary identity is certainly a response to the inequalities of capitalism, white supremacy in America, and the entrenched racism of the US prison system. But the way it appears in the book, the nature of its emergence, is also as a response to the prison's Treatment Era methodologies and what I have been calling the rehabilitative gaze. At a certain point, Jackson realizes that the Adult Authority had no intention of releasing him from prison. His letters record his numerous parole denials, like one from January 1967, where, according to Jackson, the board rejected him outright even though they had promised him at the previous year's review that he would receive a parole date. Although cer-tainly disappointed, he is "not surprised." He was "prepared" for the rejection, he writes.[34]

After his January 1967 denial, though, Jackson seems to have taken a more belligerent posture. He writes that he would like to be released and live a long life on the outside but that he is no longer willing to "surrend[er] the things that make [him] a man, the things that allow [him] to hold [his] head erect and unbowed." To him, this is a clear "choice": surrender or leave his "bones ... on the hill." He has chosen to live the remainder of his life – a life that he suspects may be short and lived entirely behind bars – "on [his] own terms." Here, Jackson outlines a binary: self-expression and pride ("on my terms"), resistance to the authorities, death (leaving his "bones ... on the hill"), and imprisonment on one side; acquiescing to the demands of the prison system ("surrendering"), the possibility of freedom, subservience, and a lack of dignity on the other.[35] He may have entertained the possibility that he could preserve his dignity and even revolutionary potential while also performing the role of the rehabilitated prisoner, but the Adult Authority's repeated rejections of him seem to have convinced him otherwise.

Jackson clarifies this position in a 1970 letter to his lawyer, Fay Stender, in which he reflects on the relationship between parole and revolutionary action. In that letter, he explains that the promise of parole ensures that imprisoned black men remain obedient. Because of parole, they mostly resist directly opposing the criminal justice system. But, he explains, degenerating prison conditions, along with a growing awareness among the incarcerated that they have been "slated for destruction," has changed them into "an implacable army of liberation."[36] Here, Jackson is presumably reflecting on his own liberation from the control of the parole system, for as a result of his murder charge (a capital crime for which he expects to be "slated for destruction"), he is no longer a candidate for early release. Once he is charged with murder, he can behave as he likes; before he was charged with murder, he was, to some degree, under the influence of the parole system.

Here, then, Jackson is providing a conceptual framework for understanding the relationship between his life writing and the Adult Authority. Although he is certainly articulating a position of resistance to the system, he is also acknowledging how, for a time, the rehabilitative gaze and the Adult Authority played a determinative role in his discursive identity. And this is important: by understanding how prison discourse is imminent to his work, setting limits on and shaping his identity, we can better see the conditions of his revolutionary identity's emergence.

Let me be clear: I am not in any way suggesting that Jackson was, at any time, subservient to the prison system, or that his revolutionary identity was in any way inauthentic. Almost certainly, his performance of the rehabilitated prisoner was a tactical decision since to do otherwise would have meant he would never be released and would remain behind bars, a captive of the system he sought to overthrow. Setting that aside, Jackson's performance of the rehabilitated prisoner demonstrates how difficult, at times even impossible, it was for imprisoned people writing during this period to resist the pressures of prison discourse. It also illuminates the stakes of prison life writing; the costs of openly challenging the prison during the Treatment Era; and the need to either acquiesce to the pressures of prison discourse, fight the system and live within it until death, or make aesthetic innovations in prison life writing that accept the prison's discursive modalities while evading or even challenging institutional power. In many ways, all of these different strategies appear in *Soledad Brother* at various points. But it is Jackson's acceptance of the prison system's discursive modalities, and his innovative use of the prison conversion narrative, that enables him to articulate a revolutionary identity – a technique that I argue emerges organically out of prison culture, which I call *corruption*.

CORRUPTION AND THE PRISON CONVERSION NARRATIVE

Jackson's letters in *Soledad Brother*, when read together, create the impression of a revolutionary teleology that, as I have suggested, struggles with the pressures of prison discourse before seeking to take a more confrontational posture in relation to the prison, capitalism, and white supremacist America (with the exception of the first two letters of the book, which frame the entire narrative and are written out of chronological order). However, as Dan Berger has argued in *Captive Nation*, Fay Stender, Jackson's lawyer, and Gregory Armstrong, the book's editor, helped shape *Soledad Brother* so that it would appeal to a wide audience interested in left-leaning causes. They hoped the book would elicit sympathy for Jackson and the other Soledad brothers, Fleeta Drumgo and John Clutchette. As Berger writes, "Armstrong and Stender sought to portray Jackson as the symbol for an individual and collective search for justice, even as Jackson himself seemed to prefer an image more heroic and less sentimental."[37] Moreover, as Berger suggests, Jackson was not altogether pleased with the finished work since their efforts to make it amenable to an outside audience, which surely involved making the book fit the genre expectations of a (mostly white) readership, softened the militancy of Jackson's revolutionary vision.[38] So it is important to keep in mind the degree to which the narrative I identify in the book is not solely the product of Jackson's thinking but emerges in tandem with a white editorial framework, what John Sekora might call a "white envelope," one that massages the work into a particular narrative framework (a dynamic I will revisit when I discuss James Carr's *Bad*).

A product of this sometimes fraught writerly and editorial negotiation, Jackson's story in *Soledad Brother* is one of revolutionary enlightenment, but it is less a departure from his performance of the rehabilitated prisoner than it is an amendment, a reshaping of it. In particular, he adapts the prison conversion narrative in a way that I think reflects a prison-specific technique of (mis)using found objects so that they serve alternative and even subversive purposes. In *Bad*, James Carr describes how imprisoned people use sanctioned objects in the prison system to make new, often illicit cultural artifacts. For example, Carr describes how he and George Jackson combined an inner tube, a rubber hose, matchboxes of yeast, vegetables, a five-gallon can, and a prison toilet to make a "distillery":

> George got to work: Made a furnace out of the can, then cut the air nozzle out of the inner tube, and stuck one end of the hose in the inner tube and one end in the toilet ... So he and his cellmate got it cooking and coming out with all this wine, and the fumes went right down the toilet ... With the sediment from the wine they boiled up white-lightnin' moonshine and sold it by the Jergens Lotion bottle for five dollars a taste.[39]

Here, Carr recounts how they modified and combined sanctioned materials in order to produce new, unsanctioned products, which were then funnelled into the prison system's *sub rosa* economy. This prison economy has burrowed its way into the licit systems of the prison: the imprisoned people who work as trash collectors, for instance, are the sellers and traders of these products, and they connect all the different, often segregated sections of the prison, thus enabling an underground trade in a wide variety of illegal goods.[40] This art of (mis)using is what Michel de Certeau calls an "ingenious wa[y] in which the weak make use of the strong."[41] It is a transformation of the dominant cultural economy from within in order to "adapt it to [an incarcerated person's] own interests and [their] own rules."[42] To some degree, the incarcerated person's process of modifying things is methodologically similar to the "regeneration through misuse" that Raymond Malewitz identifies in the practices of some post-industrial workers: "rugged consumers [who] find alternative ways of practicing their skills by creatively misusing, repairing, and repurposing the objects in their environments."[43] However, unlike post-industrial workers, who may choose to repurpose objects or not, incarcerated people have few options but to misuse their things: restrictions on material goods along with the hyper-constrained conditions of prison make such repurposing a virtual necessity. Imprisoned people depend on misusing the materials and systems of the prison, turning them to ends that are very different from their original purposes.

This misuse of prison materials is also a literary aesthetic in prison life writing. In his introduction to *Soledad Brother*, Jean Genet, himself a formerly incarcerated person, describes prison life writing as functioning according to a similar methodology as imprisoned people's repurposing of things. According to Genet, an incarcerated African American like Jackson is forced to articulate his opposition to the dominant culture through that culture's own language. "The prisoner must use the very language, the words, the syntax of his enemy, whereas he craves a separate language

belonging to his people," explains Genet. He notes that, for someone like Jackson, writing is invariably "hypocritical and wretched":

> He can express his sexual obsessions only in the
> polite dialect, according to a syntax which enables
> others to read him, and as for his hatred of the white
> man, he can utter it only in this language which
> belongs to black and white alike but over which the
> white man extends his grammarian's jurisdiction.
> It is perhaps a new source of anguish for the black
> man to realize that if he writes a masterpiece, it is
> his enemy's language, his enemy's treasury which is
> enriched by the additional jewel he has so furiously
> and lovingly carved.[44]

Genet describes how African American prison life writing's dependence on the literary forms of the "white man" – his "language" or
"syntax" – makes it susceptible to appropriation and domestica-
tion. This is certainly true of the prison conversion narrative: an
imprisoned person who describes changing himself through reading
and writing risks reproducing the rehabilitative logic of the system
within which he is constrained.

Genet suggests an alternative. He writes that an imprisoned
African American has only one available option: "to accept this
language but to corrupt it so skillfully that the white men are
caught in his trap. To accept it in all its richness, to increase that
richness still further, and to suffuse it with all his obsessions and all
his hatred of the white man."[45] In other words, Genet introduces
Jackson's autobiography by explaining its literary method in a way
that I read as reflecting, perhaps even emerging out of, the practice of misuse that governs imprisoned people's illicit economies.
Although many incarcerated people use the discourse of the prison
in their life writings, then, there are ways to use that discourse so
as to radically alter or "corrupt" it.

Now, I use the term "corruption" with some hesitation to describe Jackson's aesthetic strategy since the word has a pejorative quality and thus risks implying that a work like *Soledad Brother* is somehow a perversion or a debasement of a more legitimate form of writing. It is important that Jackson's work, like the writing of other imprisoned people, be recognized for its aesthetic sophistication, and perhaps the term risks occluding the importance of Jackson's writing. I use it because it emerges out of Jean Genet's introduction to Jackson's book and is thus a creation of a formerly imprisoned person to theorize the work of someone who is incarcerated and struggling against a white supremacist system, and also because it is suggestive of the kind of language – "the forbidden and accursed words, the bloody words" – that according to Genet reflects the violence of prison life.[46] In other words, the term, as used here, does not mean to suggest that Jackson perverts language or narrative. Instead, my use of the term "corrupt" is more in line with the root of the word: the Latin *corruptus*, the past participle of *corrumpere*, which means to "mar, bribe, destroy" (from "*cor*- 'altogether' + rumpere 'to break'").[47] It is this sense of the word that I want to preserve and illuminate here: it is a breaking, a smashing of the machinery of power, but also a reconstitution of that machinery so that it serves subversive ends.

Jackson's use of the prison conversion narrative in his auto-biography demonstrates how he turns "the syntax of his enemy" into expressions of subversion, defiance, and resistance. Rather than outright reject the terms of rehabilitation that, at other times in his letters, he submits to, Jackson uses but misuses, accepts but corrupts them. Notably, *Soledad Brother* turns to the trope of the incarcerated person transformed through reading and writing that was promoted by the Treatment Era prison system. Jackson writes that his imprisonment provided him with "the time and opportunity" to "research" and contemplate his condition, which ultimately "motivated" him "to remold [his] character." Had he not been incarcerated, he writes, he would have been on the street, a gambler or an addict or dead.[48] Jackson describes how prison has saved him from a life of crime or an early death and how his prison education has changed his life, a narrative arc that seems to articulate the rehabilitative mandate of the California Department of Corrections.

Most of *Soledad Brother* records Jackson's research – his prison education, including the specific books he is reading and how he tries to obtain them – in the sense that it chronicles the ideas he developed out of those readings. In his letters, Jackson is pre-occupied with his studies, often discussing his readings with his interlocutors and frequently requesting books and educational materials from them. In a letter to Angela Davis, for example, he asks Davis to coordinate with his parents in order to ensure that he has access to the reading materials he needs, from Frantz Fanon to reference books, noting in his letter that he needs cheap editions of any books that are mailed to him because the guards take them, often without justification.[49] Although Jackson is violently opposed to the prison system, he is nonetheless compelled to "accept" the "language" of the institution: the prison conversion narrative, with its promise of conversion and redemption through education, is not rejected in *Soledad Brother* – it is *employed*.

But, as Genet points out, Jackson "accept[s] this language but … corrupt[s] it … skillfully." He reconstitutes the prison conversion narrative in revolutionary terms, beginning with the *kind* of reading he does: "I met Marx, Lenin, Trotsky, Engels, and Mao when I entered prison and they redeemed me," he writes.[50] His reading might be redemptive, but his reading materials – Marxism, post-colonial and revolutionary theory, philosophy, African history, and African American history – help him recognize his criminality and imprisonment in different economic and racial terms. His reading does not induct him into American society – indeed, it teaches him to challenge its legitimacy. No longer an individual criminal, he is instead a victim of wide-scale racialized violence: an African American man trapped in a racist system that criminalizes black masculinity and makes crime a predictable response to poverty, which makes his petty crimes the consequence of wider economic and racial determinates.

This inversion of the criminal justice system – one that figures America as the criminal and the imprisoned African American as a victim – is not new, necessarily. In his autobiography, Malcolm X describes how Elijah Muhammad explained to him that "the black prisoner ... symbolized white society's crime of keeping black men oppressed and deprived and ignorant, and unable to get decent jobs, turning them into criminals."[51] Jackson goes further than this, defining the African American experience as a *colonial* experience.[52] He calls for "a true internationalism" with colonized people, who were, at the time, mounting their own revolutions against colonial powers.[53] Here, Jackson draws on theories developed within the broader Black Power movement, notably by Stokely Carmichael, whose *Black Power: The Politics of Liberation in America*, co-authored with George V. Hamilton, explains that African Americans "stand as colonial subjects in relation to the white society."[54] Moreover, reflecting the increasingly radical and confrontational turn within the movement, Jackson argues that, just as anti-colonial struggles used violence to overthrow their colonizing forces, African Americans need to use violence to incite their own revolution. Clearly, then, Jackson may be using the prison conversion narrative, but he is entirely inverting its meaning, advocating violence against the very society into which the prison was supposed to indoctrinate him.

Finally, it is worth noting how important corruption was to Jackson's role as a teacher. Some scholars (Bryant, Berger) have argued that Jackson's *Soledad Brother* is a pedagogical document. Through his letters and during his personal visits with family (which he describes in some of his letters), he tries to teach his parents, Georgia and Robert Lester Jackson, about his revolutionary ideology, and his letters register his frustration with their lukewarm response to his message (especially his father's resistance to it).

Jackson was also invested in teaching his younger brother, Jonathan, and his letters trace his evolving interest in his brother's education.

But Jackson was most immediately working to teach his fellow imprisoned people. To circumvent regulations around what could and what could not be taught in prison, he employed a form of corruption to turn prison education into a revolutionary pedagogy. In *The Road to Hell: The True Story of George Jackson, Stephen Bingham, and the San Quentin Massacre* (1996), Paul Liberatore writes that Jackson "led study groups on Marx and Fanon under the guise of ethnic awareness classes."[55] In other words, Jackson and his fellow incarcerated men corrupted sanctioned classroom spaces; the ethnic awareness classes provided them with a subterfugal pocket for agency and resistance within which they pursued a very different curriculum than the prison intended.

According to Jackson, many other incarcerated African Americans were corrupting the prison conversion narrative in precisely the same way. Thus, his personal revolution was part of a wider movement behind bars. He writes that while some imprisoned black people continue to see themselves as "criminals," they are rare. Most black people in prison have learned to use their time behind bars to "study," like him. As a result, he explains, "no class or category" of people is more angry and "desperate" and ready for "revolution."[56] Jackson's corruption of the educational branch of the prison system further illustrates how he used rather than simply resisted the prison and its resources, a methodology he extended by teaching his adaptation of the prison conversion narrative to other imprisoned African Americans – including to James Carr.

JAMES CARR: JACKAL DOG

James Carr's *Bad* reflects George Jackson's tutelage, especially insofar as the book similarly uses the prison conversion narrative to forge a revolutionary teleology. But Carr also observed Jackson's meteoric rise to fame and his violent death. He believed that

Jackson's image-making, and the construction of Jackson as an icon and then martyr for the prison resistance movement, was exploitative, so *Bad* resists representing Jackson as a political figure, instead characterizing him as a normal, albeit quite violent, incarcerated person who managed to exploit the system in order to gain some semblance of control for himself and his co-conspirators. Whatever Carr's intentions were in representing Jackson this way, *Bad*'s depiction of Jackson risked validating the popular view from the right that he was merely a dangerous criminal, not an important political leader.[57]

And *Bad* is hardly an apolitical book. For one thing, in its conclusion (which is sharply different in tone from the rest of the book – a point I will return to later), Carr accuses left-wing elements of fetishizing crime, and he rejects their moral stance against the prison system and their revolutionary rhetoric. He argues that they seek out and manipulate imprisoned people to serve as "convict martyrs."[58] Carr's claims about the left do not occur in a vacuum. Dan Berger notes that there were accusations that Carr was "sabotaging the Bay Area prison movement for his own ends" (and even stealing money from the Angela Davis Defense Committee), so Carr's critiques of the movement in his book are part of larger, messier conflicts that he was having with organizations like the Angela Davis Defense Committee, the Black Panther Party, and the Soledad Brothers Defense Committee.[59] But at the same time, Carr's eventual rejection of black radical politics opened space for alternative modes of expression within the prison life writing genre. Having rejected black militancy, Carr turned to an innovative form of genre-mixing that turned out to be useful for what it says about African American prison life writing and for what it reveals about proscriptions placed on some of the central concerns of the genre, such as violence, race, and sexuality.

Before delving into all this, I want to provide a general overview of his biography, at least as it is recounted in *Bad*. Resisting the psychoanalytic paradigm that often frames contemporary autobiography, Carr chose not to discuss his early childhood in his autobiography. He told Dan Hammer, one of the book's two editors, that it was a typical "'ghetto'" childhood indistinguishable from innumerable stories of racialized childhood poverty in America.[60] Instead, Carr's story begins with his first encounter with law enforcement. When he was nine years old, he burned down his elementary school in East Los Angeles to get even with a white boxing instructor who had banned him from the boxing ring and the playground for swearing.[61] Carr was quickly caught by the police, who tricked him into confessing to the arson. Thereafter, Carr's story of his adolescent street life in Los Angeles progresses from crime to crime – including arson, violent assault, theft, rape, and gang activity.

Almost nowhere in his narrative is he outside the purview of law enforcement, state institutions, or prisons. At the end of the narrative, he is no longer incarcerated but is still on parole, which is a conditional state that he describes as an extension of the California carceral system: police and parole officers routinely shadow him and closely monitor his activities.[62] (That said, Carr was also being closely watched – including by the FBI – because of his involvement with the Black Panther Party and his friendship with Jackson.) Resonating with Michel Foucault's concept of the "carceral continuum," then, Carr's life follows a pattern of ever-increasing degrees of punishment and containment that landed him an indeterminate sentence in the California prison system.[63] There is no temporal or spatial location outside of the carceral apparatus in Carr's book: Carr's story, and the story of his emergent sense of himself as a self, occurs in relation to the law and the prison.

The majority of *Bad* focuses on Carr's adolescence and young adulthood in California's sprawling carceral system during the late 1950s, 1960s, and early 1970s. Carr writes that the first "prison" where he was incarcerated was "Alexander's Boys' Home"; he was eleven years old.[64] When Carr was fourteen, he was incarcerated at Paso Robles, a youth detention facility in California's Central Valley.[65] When he was sixteen, he was sent to a youth detention camp near Yosemite called Mt. Bullion.[66] After participating in the gang-rape of another young incarcerated person at Mt. Bullion, Carr was transferred to the Deuel Vocational Institute in Tracy, California.[67] As mentioned, Carr met and befriended George Jackson at Tracy, and it was there that they formed "the Wolf Pack." Carr's close friendship with Jackson gained him a degree of notoriety inside and outside the prison. After this stretch of time behind bars, Carr was paroled, but he was soon charged with robbery and given a "five-to-life" indeterminate sentence and sent to San Quentin.[68] Several years later, Carr performed the role of the repentant prisoner in order to dupe the Adult Authority into thinking he was rehabilitated so that they would release him, which they ultimately did in 1971.

After his release, Carr joined the Black Panther Party and for a time served as Huey Newton's bodyguard and enforcer. In the short period when he was outside of prison, Carr, who had earned the nickname "Jackal Dog" on account of his braying laugh, was rumoured to have been involved in several high-profile murders, kidnappings, and prison escape attempts related to his involvement with the Black Panther Party and his close relationship with Jackson. Whatever the rumours, Carr was never charged with any crimes, except for the charges that were brought against him for fighting at one of Jackson's hearings – hearings that were part of the Soledad Brother trials for the murder of John V. Mills. As a result of his fight at Jackson's hearing, which constituted a violation of his parole, Carr spent nine months in county jail. After he was released from jail and reinstated on parole, he teamed up with Dan Hammer (his wife's brother, and the son of Joan Hammer, who worked on the Soledad Brothers Defense Committee and with whom Jackson wrote letters, some of which were published in *Soledad Brother*) and Isaac Cronin, who agreed to help write his life story. Several days after the first draft of *Bad* was completed, on 6 April 1972, Carr was gunned down outside his home by two Panther-affiliated assassins – Lloyd Mims and Richard Rodriguez.

"READY FOR REVOLUTIONARY WAR"? THE BADMAN AND THE PRISON CONVERSION NARRATIVE

As I have suggested, Carr's autobiography uses the prison conversion narrative in a way that is at least initially similar to that of Jackson's *Soledad Brother*. Like Jackson, who makes an early attempt to appear rehabilitated so as to be paroled, Carr presents himself as rehabilitated before the Adult Authority since he realizes that under his indeterminate sentence he must demonstrate that he has experienced a dramatic self-transformation if he hopes to be released. At his yearly parole board meeting, a member of the Adult Authority nicknamed "Mad Dog" Madden tells him he has to take part in education programming and group therapy, learn a trade, and receive no more infractions if he is ever to be released.[69] School and counselling: Madden prescribes the therapeutic and educational cornerstones of the Treatment Era. And Carr participates in this programming with relish, performing the requisite role of "guilt and repentance" required of him by the board.[70] As George Jackson's frustration over his repeated parole rejections demonstrates, interpreting the Adult Authority's criteria was notoriously difficult for imprisoned people, so Carr uses Madden's conditions as a guide: he enrols in school, learns a trade, and visits the prison counsellor. Unlike Jackson's attempts at parole, Carr's achieve results. Gordon, a member of the Adult Authority at Carr's next parole hearing, tells him they are going to release him because he has changed. Carr looks "like a different person," Gordon explains.[71]

However, like Jackson, Carr exploits the prison system's educational programs in order to further his own revolutionary activities, thus transforming the prison conversion narrative into a story about his revolutionary development. Carr finds that when he participates in the prison's vocational and educational programs, and dramatizes his rehabilitation (by pursuing long hours of solitary study in his cell, for example), the prison authorities generally leave him alone. "I was the big strong black dude" who preferred to study alone in his cell, he writes. He cultivates an image for the other imprisoned men and the guards, and his performance works.[72]

Of course, Carr had learned about revolutionary theory from George Jackson when he was in San Quentin. He recalls how he and the other members of the Wolf Pack always consulted Jackson, even relied on him, because of his considerable intelligence and because he was well-read and thoughtful. "We sort of let him do our thinking for us," he remembers.[73] At the time Carr is pretending that he is furthering his rehabilitation, he is on his own at a medium-security facility called California Men's Colony at San Luis Obispo (CMC-East), but Jackson's influence is very much in evidence. Like Jackson, Carr uses this time alone to study Marxist and postcolonial theorists like Lenin, Mao, and Fanon, and he is further radicalized as a result. His performance as the solitary, studious prisoner serves as an envelope within which he has a pocket of agency where he can engage in very different self-definitional strategies than those prescribed by the prison system.

Yet Carr later explains that the revolutionary mindset he cultivated in prison led him foster to unrealistic expectations about life on the outside. In *Bad*'s conclusion, Carr writes that after his release from CMC-East in 1970, he looked for an army of revolutionaries prepared for battle but instead found a small group of radicalized but drug-addled criminals whose thinking was hardly revolutionary and more like his own had been when he was "a poolhall hustler."[74] As mentioned, he criticizes the left, the prison resistance movement, and even (in veiled terms) the Black Panther Party. He even claims that the vanguardism central to George Jackson's philosophy was tragically misdirected – a kind of "false consciousness" based on seeing the prisoner as a martyr and a "victim," which Carr finds demeaning rather than empowering. He argues that this image of the victim was used in the civil rights movement to gain sympathy from a wide audience and that imprisoned writers were guilty of conforming to this view of them in their work.[75] While the arguments levelled against the left in the conclusion of Carr's book may need to be considered with some skepticism because they are tonally and rhetorically quite different from the rest of the book, the image of the incarcerated person as martyr or as victim – both of which clearly reference the left's treatment of George Jackson – is one that Carr seeks to reject in his autobiography. Instead, as the book's title suggests, *Bad* embraces and even exaggerates Carr's criminality, taking a position in prison life writing that radically departs from the genre's conventions.

By refusing to play the role of the rehabilitated prisoner as well as that of the revolutionary in his autobiography, Carr dramatically restricts the discursive scripts available to him within the prison life writing genre. Perhaps as a result, he draws on African American folklore, which enables him to break prison life writing's rules. In his aforementioned introduction to *Soledad Brother*, Jean Genet alludes to these rules when he talks about bad language. He explains that writing a book in prison is not like writing elsewhere. In prison, one does not write so much as hurl words on the page – words that are "spit out in a lather," ejaculated with semen, and sprayed with blood. According to Genet, words that speak about life in prison are unsafe and threatening. They are "dangerous, padlocked words." Genet writes that the "forbidden and accursed words" that really speak to prison life are "not accepted" outside the prison, in civil society. He insists that writing about prison is circumscribed by proscriptions and prescriptions, which he presents as a kind of violence done to an already violent language. For the "bloody words" of the prison to enter into the discourse of civil society, they have to be "maimed" and "mutilated," "pruned" of their brutality and their shocking immediacy.[76]

Writing about *Soledad Brother*, Genet is specifically addressing prison life writing. As Genet suggests, prison life writing has rules about what kinds of speech, and what kinds of speaking subjects, can enter into official (that is, published) autobiographical discourse However, the rules of prison life writing can be difficult to identify because they are frequently tacit or implicit, *de facto* rather than *de jure*. Since the rules of prison life writing are often hard to spot, they are most quickly recognized when broken or transgressed. In "Breaking Rules: The Consequences of Self-Narrative," Paul John Eakin identifies "three primary transgressions – there may be more – for which self-narrators have been called to account" for contravening or transgressing the implicit or explicit regulations of autobiographical discourse: "(1) misrepresentation of biographical and historical truth; (2) infringement of the right to privacy; and (3) failure to display normative models of personhood."[77] Of the three rules that Eakin identifies here, it is the third – "failure to display normative models of personhood" – that is instructive for understanding how *Bad* radically breaks the rules of prison life writing, particularly the genre's tacit rules about representations of violence and crime. Prison writers who have committed acts of violence or who have engaged in criminal activity invariably seek to justify (or at least explain) in their autobiographies the violence they have perpetrated or the crimes they have committed. James Carr, by contrast, describes murdering, raping, and brutalizing men and women inside and outside the prison without justifying his violence. In fact, he resists providing any explanation whatsoever for his crimes.

There is a scene early in *Bad* that illustrates Carr's approach to the prison life writing genre. Carr describes how, when he was a boy, he stabbed another boy with a hunting knife and refused to provide the police with an explanation for the attack after he was caught. He writes that the police kept suggesting possible motives for the attack, and seemed increasingly worried, even nervous, when Carr repeatedly told them he had no idea why he attacked the other child.[78] Carr simply refuses to provide a motive for stabbing the boy; more generally, *Bad* provides no moral, ethical, political, or ideological explanation or justification for Carr's predatory violence. In fact, Carr *boasts* about his violent crimes in his autobiography.

While Carr's boasting about violent crimes places him at odds with prison life writing's normative models of personhood, it does conform to a figure that appears in African American folklore, ballads, and blaxploitation films (and later in hip hop) called the "badman." In *Born in a Mighty Bad Land: The Violent Man in African American Folklore and Fiction* (2003), Jerry H. Bryant describes the badman as the "bad nigger" who "was the white man's worst dream," the "out-of-control black man, the surly slacker, the belligerent troublemaker, and occasionally the killer of whites."[79] Hyper-masculine, the badman has historically been available to men rather than women in the African American community. This is not to suggest that there are no violent or boisterous or anti-authoritarian women in African American storytelling. But those women do not have the same purchase on a legendary "bad" identity as their male counterparts. The badman story is traditionally about a bad *man*. Bryant isolates two manifestations of the badman: what historian Lawrence Levine calls the "moral hard man," and what folklorist Roger D. Abrahams calls simply the "hard man." George Jackson is a badman figure, but he constitutes a "moral hard man" because he fights against white oppression and aligns himself with "social action."[80] Moral hard men "revolt mainly against whites within the white system," writes Bryant.[81] Clearly, prison life writing accommodates the figure of the moral hard man. The hard man is a different story.

The hard man challenges the white system, but he also preys on weaker members of his own community. The hard man, according to Bryant, was a fierce individualist, a scourge in his own community, introducing disorder and arousing fear, disapproval, and alarm as well as a reluctant admiration. He was known for his viciousness, and his excesses were material for stories around a slave-cabin fire or, later, at the barber shop or pool hall and the springboard for exaggerated tales of boundless priapic feats, triumphs over the devil, incomparable cruelties, and a cool style that young studs sought to emulate. In the black community, this "bad nigger" was the king of the street corner, the terror of the roadside honky-tonk, the superbly self-confident and solitary operator.[82]

The hard man, as defined by Bryant, is often talked *about* in prison life writing; but rarely, if ever, do prison autobiographers speak or write *as* hard men without including telling qualifications that make the violent figure of the hard man palatable for a non-prison readership. While male prison autobiographers occasionally invoke the hard man, their hard man performances are typically bracketed as politically motivated (thus constituting themselves as moral hard men), represented as manifestations of selves from the past that no longer have much in common with the book's author, or explained or rationalized, which contrasts with the hard man's devil-may-care braggadocio.

Unlike other prison writers, James Carr predominantly takes the position of the hard man rather than the moral hard man in his autobiography. As a result, much of the usual "pruning" that goes into prison life writing – for example, pruning the autobiographer's involvement in acts of violence – is absent in *Bad*. Carr's self-narration as a hard man contravenes acceptable models of personhood and uses some of the "accursed," "padlocked," censored words, sentences, and stories that Genet suggests adequately represent the brutality of prison life – and presumably the brutality of some of the prison's inhabitants.

Claiming this subject position is certainly problematic and often deeply unethical. For example, Carr, like other hard men, not only makes light of raping men and women but indeed *celebrates* that violence, gleefully affirming violent expressions of misogyny and homophobia in the process. Moreover, like other hard men, Carr with his remorseless acts of violence risks supercharging stereotypes of African American male criminality. Carr's proximity to racist stereotypes is even more concerning given the book's editorial process and the whiteness of the book's editors. *Bad* is an as-told-to autobiography: Carr told anecdotal stories from his life to two white, middle-class amanuenses – Dan Hammer and Isaac Cronin. After taping their conversations, Hammer and Cronin transcribed the tapes, ultimately turning Carr's oral text into the written narrative. *Bad*'s editorial process is reminiscent of slave narratives that were co-authored, transcribed, or edited by whites – the aforementioned "white envelope." Not only was the editorial process conducted by white men, but the introduction is written by a white man (Hammer), and the lengthy afterword is written by a white woman (Carr's wife, Betsy Carr), further enveloping Carr's story.

In his introduction, Hammer insists that Carr read and agreed to the version of the text that was subsequently published as *Bad* (an assertion that Cronin repeated to me in an interview).[83] But the book was published after Carr was murdered, which, of course, makes it impossible to verify Carr's opinion on the final version of his story. The degree to which Hammer and Cronin produce Carr as an autobiographical subject cannot be determined. Ultimately, *Bad*, and the book's portrayal of Carr as a hard man, presents a knot of ethical quandaries about racial stereotyping, power relations, credibility, legitimacy, authenticity, and authorial identity.

That said, understanding *Bad* means addressing the ethically vexed dialogic process between Carr, Dan Hammer, and Isaac Cronin that produced it. In *Race and Masculinity in Contemporary American Prison Narratives* (2005), Auli Ek writes, "Since the experience of being incarcerated is ... marginal in that it is unknown to most readers, autobiographers tend to teach us how to read this experience by educating us about prison discourse and culture."[84] Carr provides just such a pedagogical moment when he describes *lying*. He tells Cronin and Hammer that one day he was resting on his bed in the prison Adjustment Center (a form of solitary confinement), trying to guess what people did in isolation, when he heard prisoners calling out for another prisoner, named Smitty, to tell them a "lie." Soon, explains Carr, he heard "a black dude with a silkysmooth voice" respond by telling them an elaborate and graphic story about having sex with a woman he met when he was outside prison. Carr is clearly impressed with the man's storytelling skills. He writes that the other men encouraged the speaker "by using a little negative psychology." They would shout out, "'Smitty, we know you're lying! Don't just sit there and lie like that.'" He tells Hammer and Cronin that Smitty's storytelling was always entertaining and realistic, whether he was recounting sexual exploits or exaggerated stories about drug deals or memories from the Second World War. Smitty would have the other imprisoned men spellbound for hours. "He might have made it big on the stage if he'd ever made it back to the streets," Carr tells us.[85]

In describing *lying* as a storytelling practice in prison, Carr is teaching Hammer and Cronin how to receive and help produce his story. In his introduction to *Bad*, Hammer discusses how the three men used *lying* as a way to produce the taped interviews that would later be shaped by Hammer and Cronin into Carr's autobiography: "Isaac and I would move Jimmy along the way other cons used to inspire the 'liars,' the cons who helped everyone pass the time by weaving incredible tales." The more elaborate the story, and the more incredible, the more Hammer and Cronin would encourage Carr by telling him to stop lying.[86]

This dialogic practice is discussed in Hammer's introduction but goes unmentioned in the body of Carr's story (unlike in *Soledad Brother*, for example, whose epistolary form registers the prison-enforced dialogue of letter-writing). Evidence of Hammer and Cronin's complicity in producing the narrative is thus partly obscured. *Bad* is predominantly governed by Carr's univocal, autobiographical "I," which implies that the book's "autobiographical pact" is solely between the reader and Carr, whose face graces the book's cover and whose name is listed as the sole author in some editions.

Yet *lying* demonstrates that Hammer and Cronin's influence is substantial. As Hammer suggests, the two men "move Jimmy along" and "inspire" his storytelling. Hammer and Cronin's absence as possible co-storytellers in the narrative is problematic because it is quite possible that their conscious or unconscious cultural expectations (of Carr, of imprisoned people, of black criminality, for example), along with Carr's expectations of his two middle-class white readers' desires, inform how Carr tells his life story, thus influencing the shape of his narrative – what he passes over and what he selects for inclusion. Although I will discuss Carr's emergence from an African American folk tradition in this article, it is worth remembering that he is also the product of European American desires, imaginings, and expectations because, as *lying* suggests, Carr's two white amanuenses are complicit in his narrative at its most fundamental level.

While keeping these concerns in mind, I want to emphasize how *lying* interrupts what Paul John Eakin calls autobiography's "rules." *Lying* brings Carr's story into discourse: *lying* among the three men is recorded on the tapes before the tapes are transcribed into an edited written text that eventually becomes the published memoir. As a result, the generic borders of Carr's autobiography are reshaped according to a storytelling mode that circulates in prison. As its name suggests, *lying* allows for transgressive speech acts (or what Eakin calls the "misrepresentation of biographical and historical truth"). It also provides discursive space for rule-breaking "models of personhood" that circulate widely in the prison but that are absent in prison life writing.

Lying emerges out of a rhetorical tradition beyond the prison, in wider African American "speech communities" that have historically reconfigured biographical and historical truth in storytelling to subvert a dominant and threatening white culture, to share sensitive information, or to articulate registers of truth that exceed factual records.[87] For example, Zora Neale Hurston describes in her autobiography, *Dust Tracks on a Road* (1942), how men in her rural hometown would conduct "lying sessions": competitive storytelling sessions that blended community stories with individual memory, rumour, and cultural folklore.[88] The "lying sessions" were social texts that provided meaning to a localized community in ways that factual texts could not. Lying sessions had an element of subversion to them as well: something that could be difficult, problematic, or dangerous to mention publicly was brought into discourse through its subterfugal blending with myth, cultural history, rumour, the artifice of the storyteller, and the participation of the listeners, who "strain[] against each other" in telling their stories.[89]

Lying and lying sessions are variants of an African American rhetorical tactic called "signifyin(g)." The meaning of signifyin(g) is often opaque to those outside the specific speech community in which the story is told and to which the story often refers. As such it is often presumed to be meaningless or unimportant wordplay by outsiders. H. Rap Brown's description of signifyin(g) registers the genre's feigned insignificance: "I used to hang out in the bars just to hear the old men 'talking shit.'"[90] But "talking shit," which may suggest wasteful or unimportant speech, a kind of language-detritus, can have great individual, cultural, and social importance. Brown's old men, the men in Hurston's community, and imprisoned people like Smitty employ storytelling modes that are forms of linguistic subterfuge, or covert and resistant "private transcripts" whose meaning is indiscernible to those who are not members of the group or speech community. These storytellers also use modes of untruth – "lies," "talking shit," and "lying sessions" – as ways of telling truths that may not be accessible within traditional or dominant modes of speech. Furthermore, their method often uses the vocabulary of a dominant linguistic system, destabilizing the dominant vocabulary by deploying it in radically altered fashion (such as by braiding it with other generic modes, for example, as Carr, Hammer, and Cronin do with *lying* and autobiography).

Storytelling practices that blend fact with fiction, myth with history and biography, are certainly useful in prison or on parole, where stories, particularly autobiographical stories about past criminal activity, can have legal (and other) consequences for an imprisoned or paroled storyteller. Framing *Bad* within *lying* could, perhaps, have provided Carr with the discursive space to talk about crimes he might not have shared in genres that make less ambiguous truth-claims. However, *Bad* does not blur the boundaries of truth in order to hide Carr's crimes. Instead, as I have suggested, the book adamantly *asserts* Carr's criminality, in ways that constitute a radically different relationship to discourses of truth and power than has been suggested in studies of autobiography and prison life writing.

As I have argued throughout this book, most analyses of prison life writing claim that autobiography contests how the discourses of the law and the prison have constituted prison writers as criminals. As Deena Rymhs writes in *From the Iron House: Imprisonment in First Nations Writing* (2008), autobiography allows imprisoned and formerly imprisoned people "to respond to the law's authority over their public and personal identities": "In managing their texts in such a way, these writers maneuver around some of the constraints that the law places on self-representation."[91] Carr, though, does not "maneuver around" the "constraints that the law places on self-representation" so much as use them to articulate subversive forms of self-representation. Rather than contest the subject position "criminal" ascribed to him by the law, the police, and the prison, Carr embodies that position, uses it, expands and aggrandizes its signifying power.

Bad exaggerates rather than hides, qualifies, or contests Carr's criminality because the book adheres to the generic rules of *lying*, which provide space for a different relationship to criminality than what is commonly available in prison life writing. To understand the rules of *lying*, I turn to a form of signifyin(g) called the "toast." Jerry H. Bryant describes the toast as "a narrative poem, usually cast in a sort of pre-rap rhythm, designed for oral delivery by a single performer to an informal or casual audience of other street people, usually young men."[92] Toasts, which are often called lies, were important textual formations in US prisons in the 1960s and 1970s when Carr was imprisoned. In fact, Carr's description of *lying* seems to be a prose-variant of the toast. Unlike prison life writing, the toast boasts about the speaker's involvement in criminal activity and exaggerates his capacity for violence and ruthless brutality. Unlike prison life writers, toast storytellers not only talk about hard men, they talk *as* hard men, who are central figures of the genre. Because Carr, Hammer, and Cronin reconfigure Carr's as-told-to autobiography in terms of *lying*, a prose-form of toasting, Carr too can talk as a hard man and articulate aspects of prison life otherwise excluded from the prison life writing genre.

Consider, for example, how Carr's descriptions of rape resonate with the *lying*/toasting genre and accord with stories of the classic hard man, Stagolee. Stagolee – who is also known as Stagger Lee, Stackolee, or Stackalee in some versions of the toast – is the archetypal badman, first emerging in African American post-bellum badman ballads, which were precursors to the toast. Toasts that narrate variations on the old Stagolee story follow plot lines that are similar to those of their ballad predecessors: Stagolee is thrown out of his house by his wife; he wades through mud to a local bar called "the Bucket of Blood"; in a fit of fury he murders the bartender, has rough sex – in some cases forced sex – with a prostitute, and shoots dead an adversary named Billy Lyon (who is also called Billy Lions, Billy Dilly, Ben Lee, or Benny Long in other variants of the story). Some versions of the toast end with Billy's death,[93] while other versions find Stagolee before a judge, charged with Billy Lyon's murder,[94] and one version even concludes with Stagolee in hell after he is murdered by Billy's mother, fighting the devil and having sex with the devil's minions.[95]

Violent misogyny and rape play central roles in the poetics of badman figures like Stagolee, providing a generic context for Carr's rape stories. In one version of Stagolee (here called Stackolee), for example, "Stack" has violent, forced sex with a prostitute after murdering the Bucket of Blood's bartender: "Now me and this broad we started to tussle / and I drove twelve inches a dick through her ass before she could move a muscle."[96] In another version, when Stagolee is in hell, he rapes a woman "bent over shovelin' coal."[97] Stagolee's violent sexuality and misogyny are the norm in toasts, in which badmen define their masculinity against and through the bodies of women. Jerry H. Bryant writes that sex for the toast badman "is an empty erotic pleasure." "The point is to establish dominance," writes Bryant, "to overwhelm, to display a total lack of sensitivity or affection. As in the old badman ballads, the penis is employed as a weapon." Bryant concludes that the "satisfaction found in blasting away with guns is echoed in the pleasure taken in ramming penises up the vaginas and rectums of the 'ho's' [*sic*]."[98] In the badman toasts, sex is bereft of desire and is usually an expression of power, dominance, and control.

Similarly, throughout *Bad*, sexuality is an extension of other expressions of violence and domination in Carr's phallocratic street and prison life. For example, Carr regularly boasts about his involvement in gang-rapes – described as "running a train" – which always take the most vulnerable women as objects of exchange in a masculine economy that privileges men who can arrange a rape for their friends. Early in the narrative, Carr describes gang-raping women with a street gang called The Farmers. Their strategy involves finding some "sharp-looking chick" at a party and convincing her to leave with one of the gang members, ostensibly to "go to the store." They would hurry her into a waiting car, and, before she realizes that she has been duped, they would be at their clubhouse; she would be trapped and forced into "a train" – or, gang-raped.[99]

In *Makes Me Wanna Holler: A Young Black Man in America* (1995), particularly his chapter called "Train," Nathan McCall describes the dynamic of the gang-rape by relating his involvement in and witnessing of gang-rapes in the small, predominantly African American community called Cavalier Manor in Portsmouth, Virginia, where he grew up: "Different groups of guys set up their own trains. Although everybody knew it could lead to trouble with the law, I think few guys thought of it as rape. It was viewed as a social thing among hanging partners, like passing a joint. The dude who set up the train got pats on the back. He was considered a real player whose rap game was strong."[100] According to McCall, then, "running a train" was understood by its participants as a form of homosocial bonding ("a social thing among hanging partners"), which affirmed alliances between men and staged violent performances of masculinity over and through the bodies of young black women – women who were violently effaced in the homosocial exchange. As McCall indicates, rape was one way to define oneself as "a real player whose rap game was strong," much as violent misogyny reinforced the badman's masculine toughness.

However, while McCall's autobiography psychologizes gang-rape in his community and explains how he was caught up in behaviour that he eventually rejects in the course of his narrative, Carr never defines rape as something worthy of regret; in this way, he points to the degree to which his use of *lying* stretches the rules of autobiographical discourse. Carr frames gang-rape as part of the "crazy" "routine" of street life, and illustrates his point by comparing gang-rape with a slapstick story about stealing cakes from a bakery.[101] *Bad* thus flattens otherwise horrifying experiences of sexual violence into an almost ethics-free discourse that makes little distinction between rape and petty theft.

As McCall demonstrates, prison life writing makes room for discussions of heterosexual rape; by contrast, there is no space within the genre for male autobiographers to describe their involvement in same-sex rape or prison rape (or almost no space – Carl Panzram's *Killer*, which I discuss in the next chapter, constitutes another exception to this rule). Auli Ek argues that while some imprisoned people's autobiographies are told from the position of the rape victim (see T.J. Parsell's *Fish*, for example), most describe prison rape from the position of the "disinterested observer," and none describe rape in prison from the position of the perpetrator, despite the huge number of rapes that occur in US prisons.[102] Ek's observation that prison rape is talked about in prison life writing but never from the position of the rapist suggests that the prison rapist is what Paul John Eakin describes as a proscribed "model of personhood" in autobiography.

Where the prison life writing genre keeps the male prison rapist at the margins of discourse because his violence is taboo, the genres of *lying* and toasting enable the prison rapist to be a speaking subject because they frame same-sex rape according to very different ethical boundaries, defining male rape exclusively as a sign of masculine power. For example, in another version of Stagolee, this time recited in 1967 by "Big Stick," an African American imprisoned at New York's Auburn Prison (and recorded by Dennis Wepman, Ronald B. Newman, and Murray B. Binderman in *The Life: The Lore and Folk Poetry of the Black Hustler*), Stagolee rapes his adversary, Billy Dilly. First, he threatens to "fuck Billy Dilly in his / motherfucking ass" if he encounters him. Then, when Stagolee is finally confronted by Billy, Stagolee attacks, rapes, and murders him. Stagolee tells Billy,

"… you'd better get down on
your knees and slobber my head,
'Cause if you don't, you're sure to be dead."
Billy Dilly dropped down and slobbered on his
head,
But Stag filled him full of lead.[103]

Sex is indistinguishable from murder in this stanza: Stagolee's penis and gun blur; Stagolee "fill[s] him full of lead" rather than semen. And Stagolee's sexual violence in this version of the poem is directed at another man, bearing the traces of the sexually homogeneous carceral space in which the toast was recited. The sex of the rape victim in this Stagolee toast is of little significance because sexuality in the hard man's world is bereft of desire and only serves to demonstrate and enhance the potency of the hard man rapist.

By framing his autobiography in terms of *lying*, Carr breaks prison life writing's proscriptive formula for depictions of prison rape and identifies – even celebrates – himself as a prison rapist. For example, Carr describes how he and his gang repeatedly rape a newly imprisoned young man ("a kid") named Abernathy, whose victimhood is representative of the other victims of sexual violence in the book and in prisons where Carr was incarcerated. After being gang-raped in the shower, Abernathy has a psychological breakdown. He keeps himself isolated in his cell and descends into madness. He becomes incontinent. Eventually, the prison psychologist determines that Abernathy is no longer well enough to remain in the prison and transfers him to Atascadero State Hospital.[104] In this instance, Abernathy is a figure of some pathos, but once again, Carr never expresses regret for his violence.

Carr's descriptions of rape also follow the narratological format of *lying* as a genre in their carnivalesque treatment of sexual violence, as is conveyed in the brutal but jocular terms that Carr uses to narrate his actions. Thus, Carr frames gang-raping a "cute young kid" as a sadistic, humorous anecdote, for example, where the punch-line is that Carr and the other two assailants are caught because they all contracted the same venereal disease as a result of the attack.[105] Likewise, Carr boasts about gang-raping a "cute white kid" with a group of young African American men at a prison camp near Yosemite. He describes raping the white kid as though it were a prank and follows it with a putatively comedic police chase through the woods where Carr and the other rapists run amok "like Keystone Kops."[106] *Lying's* violent, sadistic, but bawdy humour provides a framework for Carr to speak about raping men because the genre's humour resists acknowledging the pain of the victim, focusing instead on the priapic exploits of the hard man rapist.

Carr's use of the adverb "cute" to modify "young kid" and "white kid" signals how his narrative deviates from the *lie/*toast genre by defining the hard man's homosexuality in terms of desire and not simply as an expression of power and dominance. In fact, throughout the autobiography, Carr describes desiring young men that he calls "homos." When he first arrives at CMC-East, for example, Carr sees "a procession of beautiful-looking boys [that] hurried across the yard and filed by me as if I was a judge in some fantastic beauty contest." He ogles their "tight short-shorts, teased hair, make-up, perfume," and he teases them and flirts with them, enjoying the attention they give to him.[107] Although Carr's interest in men radically breaks with the hard man's sexual code and with conventional representations of African American masculinity in the 1960s and 1970s, the autobiography also reinscribes homophobic (indexed most obviously in his use of the term "homos"), patriarchal, and misogynistic mores at the same time. Finally, befitting his hard man image, Carr always represents sex with men as forced sex – sex that might involve desire but that is ultimately brutal domination.

Carr's hard man persona is undoubtedly unethical. Beyond his brutal misogyny and predatory violence, his frank descriptions of prison rape potentially reify the stereotype of the "black beast rapist," which was at one time held up in the southern states as a justification for lynching black men.[108] James Baldwin, discussing Richard Wright's Bigger Thomas, calls this figure "that fantasy Americans hold in their minds when they speak of the Negro; that fantastic and fearful image which we have lived with since the first slave fell beneath the lash."[109] This "fearful image" of the violent African American male has significant cultural currency in representations of imprisoned African Americans. As John Sloop demonstrates in *The Cultural Prison: Discourse, Prisoners, and Punishment* (1996), one of the dominant images of incarcerated African Americans during the period from 1969 to 1975 – when Carr was imprisoned and when *Bad* was published – was of a nihilistically violent man: "He is violent for the sake of violence alone. This prisoner is a rapist, a liar, a spoiler of white youth. Rather than struggling against a racist culture in order to preserve his heritage, he is represented as following his nature, behaving in ways that defy transformation and thus demand restraint."[110]

Historically, the stereotype of the violent black male has been crucial to sustaining different modes of "restraint" on black bodies. "Free blacks were often characterized as degraded, vicious, and depraved, supporting the rationale that blacks must be contained within the institution of slavery," writes Jane Rhodes.[111] Likewise, Dorothy E. Roberts, arguing that legal decisions entrench and make use of racist stereotypes of black men, writes that the "stereotype of the aggressive, 'macho' Black male legitimates the massive incarceration of young Black men."[112]

Angela Davis explains that the stereotype of the black rapist also legitimates stereotypes of black women as sexually available. Davis writes that "the fictional image of the Black man as rapist has always strengthened its inseparable companion: the image of the Black woman as chronically promiscuous. For once the notion is accepted that Black men harbor irresistible and animal-like sexual urges, the entire race is invested with bestiality." It is not surprising, then, that most "African American authors 'vigilantly' resist the traditional representation of the black male as rapist."[113] Because Carr embraces the image of the black male rapist and takes the position of the violent, chaotic, and destructive hard man, he risks reifying a stereotype that defines black male criminality as an inherent condition rather than as an effect of social, racial, or economic exploitation.

Yet in a way, it is precisely *because* Carr's autobiography is irresolvably problematic that it is an important book. *Bad* indexes how prisons produce few ethically clear lines. Victim and victimizer, oppressed and oppressor are categories that are frequently blurred in prisons. But they are often artificially solved in prison life writing as autobiographical subjects are shown to transcend the petty criminality and violence that are required of most imprisoned people as conditions of existence. Let me be clear: I am in no way suggesting that Carr's violence is acceptable. My point is that *Bad* resists occluding or resolving Carr's brutality in the course of the narrative. In *Bad*, the ethical quandaries of the US prison system are exposed rather than narratologically resolved.

CONCLUSION: REVOLUTIONARIES OR HOLLOW MEN

George Jackson's *Soledad Brother* and James Carr's *Bad* show how and why the prison conversion narrative promoted in California penology during the era of the rehabilitative ideal is reproduced in prison life writing. Serving indeterminate sentences, Jackson and Carr had to represent themselves as successfully rehabilitated or they would never be released from prison, and this institutional pressure to conform is stitched into their autobiographies. In *Soledad Brother,* Jackson is often preoccupied with parole and the Adult Authority, sometimes detailing how he hopes to be released, since he believes he has met their requirements, and sometimes resisting the system's demands on him. Ultimately, he concludes that if an imprisoned person is released on parole it is because he has "crawled" into his parole hearing with the Adult Authority. For Jackson, to be paroled is to surrender one's dignity and to acquiesce to the institution – and, finally, to accept the institution's definition of him.[114] Jackson's claim that an imprisoned person must totally acquiesce to the demands of the prison system if he is to please the parole board is exemplified in *Bad* when Carr follows a "little-good-boy routine" because, as he explains to several imprisoned people who question his newly formed interest in rehabilitation, "'I've been [in prison] almost eight years and I aim to get out in the near future ... If I fuck up one more time I'm gonna die in prison.'"[115] Even incarcerated people like Jackson and Carr, who openly fight the prison system, are forced to employ elements of the prison conversion narrative in their life writings.

However, both men also demonstrate how the prison conversion narrative can be corrupted by imprisoned people, uncoupled from its disciplinary foundations in the prison, and made to serve alternative purposes in their life writings. In the Treatment Era, just as in earlier and later phases of the US penal system, prison life writing exhibits exchanges, contestations, tensions, and convergences with prison discourse, in the process sometimes justifying and sometimes subverting the prison's discursive authority.

Jackson and Carr also gesture toward another important feature of prison that tends to be overlooked in the prison life writing genre, with its abundance of narratives that feature imprisoned people who have transcended the violent conditions of their incarceration: the incarcerated person who has been irrevocably damaged by imprisonment and is thus rendered permanently unable to live a normal life. In her Afterword to *Bad*, Betsy Carr describes James Carr's cousin, Bobby Tucker, who had spent ten years at San Quentin. Tucker was released from prison, but he had no idea how to live on the outside because he had spent much of his life in some form of incarceration. "Bobby was the opposite of Jimmy [Carr]," she explains: he was "the other side of what the joint does to people." According to Betsy Carr, Bobby was rendered *antisocial* by prison rather than rehabilitated. She describes how he was mesmerized by the minutiae of everyday life: "windows, toilets with doors, double beds, refrigerators (he opened the icebox at least a dozen times, saying, 'I'm not hungry now,' as he took food out and put it back again)."[116]

In *Becoming Ms. Burton*, Susan Burton describes similar experiences among women after their release from prison. For example, she relates the story of a formerly incarcerated woman named Annie who, after her release, would hoard toilet paper because it was strictly limited in prison.[117] Burton also describes how some formerly incarcerated women struggle with basic features of life on the outside, like working a shower or riding in a car.[118] One woman who "hadn't been in a moving vehicle in well over a decade ... got car sick several times along the long drive" home from prison.[119] Burton calls life after prison "an extreme detox."[120]

These sometimes touching portraits of recently released people marvelling at or struggling with the gadgetry of the world outside have a darker corollary in the imprisoned person who has been rendered completely antisocial in prison – a figure that haunts Jackson's *Soledad Brother*. Jackson argues that prison conditions produce two kinds of imprisoned African Americans: revolutionaries and "broken men." He writes that "the broken men are so damaged that they will never again be suitable members of any sort of social unit." Bobby Tucker might learn how to live in free society, but some imprisoned people, according to Jackson, are fundamentally abnormal as a result of their incarceration. Indeed, some of these men are rendered violently antisocial because of the violent conditions of the prison system that made them. Jackson describes these men as "monsters." I explore the figure of the "monstrous" imprisoned person in the next chapter.

FROM THE TREATMENT ERA TO THE MONSTER FACTORY

CARL PANZRAM'S AND JACK HENRY ABBOTT'S ANTICONVERSION NARRATIVES AND THE DAWN OF MASS INCARCERATION

This monster – the monster they've engendered
in me will return to torment its maker, from the
grave, the pit, the profoundest pit.
—George Jackson, *Soledad Brother*, 194

FOR A FEW DAYS IN SEPTEMBER 1971, AMERICANS' ATTENTION WAS focused on a small upstate New York town called Attica. Incarcerated people had taken over a large portion of the town's nearby prison, Attica Correctional Facility. They held it for five days until state police violently returned control of the prison to the authorities, killing forty-three people in the process and dramatizing for the world the precarity of imprisoned people's lives (and, to some degree, prison employees' lives too, since police mistakenly shot to death numerous prison guards held as hostages).[1] Although the rebellion had many causes, from overcrowding to institutionalized racism to terrible food, imprisoned people cited their collective anger over the shooting death of George Jackson at San Quentin two weeks earlier as helping inspire solidarity among imprisoned people – solidarity that was necessary to transform what could have been a riot into what became a political action of historical proportions.

The Attica rebellion marks an important moment in the history of the US prison system because it illustrates the degree to which imprisoned people were politically aware and capable of consolidating diverse groups so as to openly challenge the prison system and even the state. However, Attica is also significant because many prison officials and politicians saw the uprising as demanding a new approach to prison management, one that would focus less on rehabilitation and more on control and retribution. According to Heather Ann Thompson in *Blood in the Water: The Attica Prison Uprising of 1971 and Its Legacy* (2016), "Attica had directly, albeit unwittingly, helped to fuel an anti-civil-rights and anti-rehabilitative ethos in the United States."[2] The uprising fed into an increasingly popular view among the public, prison officials, and legislators that efforts at rehabilitating the imprisoned were misguided and that prisons should no longer "coddle" criminals.[3]

This opinion was virtually legitimated in 1975 when Douglas Lipton, Robert Martinson, and Judith Wilks published *The Effectiveness of Correctional Treatment* (1975), a report on prison rehabilitation programming, which famously concluded that, when it came to rehabilitating imprisoned people, "nothing works."[4] Lipton, Martinson, and Wilks's conclusion helped usher in what came to be called a "just desserts" approach to corrections: prison sentences would fit the crime; rehabilitation played little if any role in mitigating sentencing.[5] Also helping to justify this dramatic turn in penal policy was the view that incarcerated people were incorrigible and dangerous, as having no capacity for rehabilitation, as monstrous subjects who could never fit into normal life and who thus belonged behind bars. This chapter considers prison life writing published in the transitional period between the end of the Treatment Era and the beginning of mass incarceration that produced this ideologically unstable figure – a character that conservatives and liberals, Democrats and Republicans, used to legitimate a new age of mass incarceration, one in which rehabilitation would have little to do with official prison policy.

In April 1972, just over a year after the Attica prison uprising was violently suppressed, Michel Foucault toured the prison.
When he emerged from Attica, he explained in an interview that
the infamous prison resembled "an immense machine." And if the
prison was a machine, he said, then "the question one obviously
asks is what does the machine produce, what is that gigantic instal-
lation used for, and what comes out of it."[6] In *Soledad Brother*,
George Jackson claims that the prison could "produce" revolutionaries like himself – or, one might add, like the imprisoned people
of Attica who organized the rebellion there into a coherent political
act. But the prison could also produce someone else. Like Foucault,
who in his interview suggests that the prison machine "eliminates"
imprisoned people from normal society and ensures that they are
lifelong recidivists, Jackson writes that formerly incarcerated people
are "monsters, totally disorganized, twisted, disgusting epitomes
of the parent monster. Those who aren't so upon their arrival will
surely be so when they leave. No one escapes unscathed."[7] Here,
and elsewhere in *Soledad Brother*, Jackson explains that imprisoned people are made into "monsters"; they are acclimatized to
the depraved conditions of prison, which makes their transition
to normal life difficult, at times even impossible.

Jackson's contention that people are made monstrous in prisons
inverts the rehabilitative ideal, particularly the medical model of
corrections that was popular in prisons in the postwar era until
roughly the 1970s. According to proponents of this theory, criminality is a pathology to be cured. But people are never cured in
prisons, Jackson argues. Instead, "in every instance they are sent
out of the prison more damaged physically and mentally than when
they entered."[8] At one point, Jackson suggests that this process of
socializing imprisoned people to the violent world of the prison,
sending them out "more damaged" than when they entered, constitutes a threat to the social order: "It's socially self-destructive
to create a monster and loose him upon the world."[9] Although
representing incarcerated people as monstrous – and especially

as *threateningly* monstrous – is risky since it suggests that they are subhuman (and thus inherently unable to behave as normal people, and naturally suited for places like prisons), Jackson clearly believes that this peculiarly Gothic trope is nonetheless important since it says something about prison conditions and how those conditions affect the incarcerated – their social behaviour, psychological stability, and legal identities – that cannot be articulated as effectively in another way.

In this chapter, I extend Jackson's metaphor. The monstrous prisoner – that is, the imprisoned person who has been rendered radically unfit for normal life – is a common figure in prison life writing but one that is also ideologically unstable, in that the stereotype of the incorrigible criminal haunts popular conceptions about criminality and imprisonment and can easily be weaponized to great political effect. In particular, in the late 1970s, as the public grew increasingly anxious about rising crime rates, some critics of the Treatment Era methodology, most notably "law and order" politicians, argued that imprisoned people needed to be recognized as serious threats to social stability rather than as victims of social injustice. The figure of the monstrous prisoner – that is, the formerly incarcerated person who struggles to live on the outside – would come to signify a new kind of incurable criminal, someone beyond hope who was incapable of rehabilitation and change and who thus belonged in prison. That view helped legitimate tough-on-crime legislation, retributive prison policies, a rejection of the rehabilitative ideal, and legislation that helped produce the era of mass incarceration.[10]

Of course, in adopting Jackson's metaphor I am not suggesting that the incarcerated are somehow less than human. Nor am I suggesting that all or even most imprisoned people are warped by their experiences behind bars or that they constitute a threat to people on the outside. Instead, I use the term to denote a literary trope that reappears in prison life writing, like Jackson's *Soledad Brother* – one that is often used to represent the "category crisis" that incarcerated people experience after their release.[11] In other words, the monstrous prisoner is in fact a monstrous *ex*-prisoner: someone who is "monstrous" – that is, abnormal, out of place, a threat to normative boundaries – *because* his or her subjectivity is deeply contradictory and thus difficult to sustain outside prison.

This monstrosity comes about, in part, because a formerly incarcerated person is ostensibly free but living in what Michelle Alexander calls an "invisible cage" comprised of a "unique set of criminal sanctions that are imposed on individuals after they step outside prison gates, a form of punishment that operates largely outside of public view and takes effect outside the traditional sentencing framework."[12] Once released, formerly imprisoned people exist in "a parallel universe," an indeterminate space between incarceration and freedom, exile and belonging.[13] They are thus neither alien nor citizen but instead something in between. The metaphor of the monstrous prisoner usefully addresses the invariably Gothic qualities consistently applied to this mode of existence – metaphors such as "invisible cage" and "parallel universe" abound in descriptions of post-prison life – but the monster, as a figure of indeterminacy and incompleteness, a figure that threatens the normative order because the monster has no place to belong, encapsulates the legal, social, psychological, and affective experience of formerly incarcerated peoples whose indeterminacy is often resolved only once they are returned to prison.

I focus my discussion of the monstrous prisoner on two life writings, Carl Panzram's *Killer: A Journal of Murder* (which was largely written and edited by Thomas E. Gaddis and James O. Long, who are, albeit incorrectly, listed as the book's sole authors), and Jack Henry Abbott's *In the Belly of the Beast*. Both *Killer* and *In the Belly of the Beast* use but rework the prison conversion narrative to illustrate how Panzram and Abbott have become "monstrous" – unable to live outside the boundaries of prison in normal society. Panzram, a self-described serial killer (and serial rapist and pederast, arsonist, and burglar), who was executed in 1930, inverts the prison conversion narrative by detailing how he was "educate[d]" in carceral institutions from youth training schools to maximum security prisons. However, his "train[ing]" was in myriad expressions of institutional violence.[14] In other words, the brutality of these spaces taught him to be a brutal man, and he frequently explains his killings as putting into practice what he learned in them: he is fond of explaining that by murdering people he "reform[s]" them.[15] Whereas the prison conversion narrative traces an imprisoned person's progressive socialization through education, Panzram's *anti*conversion narrative represents how his prison "training," "reform," or "education" has made him ill-suited for normal life and also, according to Panzram, justified his violent attacks on the society that he believes locked him up and mistreated him in the first place.

As I will show, however, *Killer* both condemns and legitimates the criminal justice and prison systems: the historical and biographical text that surrounds Panzram's autobiographical writings frames his work within psychological, criminological, and juridical discourses that define Panzram's life writing as a case study rather than an autobiography. I argue that this genre switching, from autobiography to case study, has several important consequences for Panzram's work that help explain the power struggles that appear elsewhere in different measures throughout the prison life writing genre: it resituates power relations within the text, including around authorship; it privileges institutional discourse (from fields like criminology, psychology, and the law) as a determinant of meaning in the story; it limits the potential for resistance or disturbance to institutional authority and norms by translating an otherwise transgressive voice into existing discourses of crime and punishment; and, perhaps most significantly, it makes Panzram *useful* by making him into an object of analysis, a specific case, that helps create a knowledge base about a criminal subculture and thus extends the criminal justice system's disciplinary and supervisory practices. Although Panzram vigorously rejects these discourses in his own writings, establishing an irresolvable tension at the heart of the book, *Killer* demonstrates how prison life writing is part of, and is always at risk of furthering, a field of knowledge that can serve institutional power.

Likely following the narrative blueprint of Panzram's writings, Abbott's *In the Belly of the Beast* for its part uses an anticonversion narrative, but in such a way that it challenges conventional presumptions around prison education and the socializing effects of reading and writing and represents the social, political, affective, and even ontological ambiguities of post-prison life, treading territory similar to that of Gothic fiction. Like Panzram, then, Abbott details how a lifetime behind bars made him monstrous – warped his identity and rendered him unfit for normal life. However, Abbott also adopts George Jackson's revolutionary narrative in his book, thus providing himself with a political identity in prison that also, given Jackson's focus on the African American experience, forces him to confront his own racial identity and address important questions about his complicity in white supremacy that are revealing for what they say about race in prison but also about whiteness writ large. I conclude this chapter by explaining how media responses to Abbott's trial weaponized the figure of the monstrous prisoner, thus helping justify a dramatic turn toward a more punitive prison system.

Of course, Panzram and Abbott are extreme representations of the monstrous prisoner, since, unlike most imprisoned people, both men *did* constitute violent threats to the social order after being released. Panzram claims to have murdered many men and boys after his release; while on parole, Abbott infamously stabbed a man to death in a late-night fight, which returned him to prison for life. However, Panzram and Abbott are important limit cases. Their experiences, being as extreme as they are – the violence they endured in prisons and the violence they in turn meted out – render highly visible the contours of more common but much less sensational experiences of prison and post-prison life: those of imprisoned people traumatized by prison violence, rendered antisocial because of years in the solitary spaces of prison cells (or, like Albert Woodfox, tortured in solitary confinement), or simply forced out of legal employment or refused housing because of their status as felons, thereby compelling them to turn to illegal avenues to live, thus making recidivism more likely.

As I have suggested, Panzram's and Abbott's stories are exemplary texts in that they speak to key features of the prison life writing genre. Their life writings are perhaps illustrative of life writing by incarcerated people who were their contemporaries: Jack London's stories about being incarcerated because he was poor, homeless, and hoboing are in very broad terms similar to Panzram's stories of poverty (although London spent very little time incarcerated by comparison, and bore none of the psychological damage nor exhibited any of the violence of Panzram), and Edward Bunker's descriptions of juvenile hall in *Little Boy Blue* resonate with Abbott's stories of his incarceration as a teenager.

But Panzram's and Abbott's life writings, which detail how unfit both men are for life on the outside, are particularly unique since most incarcerated people want to demonstrate that, if they have changed, they have changed for the better. So their stories are similar to those of many *characters* in the work of other imprisoned writers, including those characters who appear in the work of George Jackson, James Carr, or Susan Burton that I have mentioned, or even characters that appear in American life writing more broadly, like Richard Hickock and Perry Smith in Truman Capote's non-fiction novel *In Cold Blood* or Dean Moriarty (the literary avatar for Neal Cassady) in Jack Kerouac's roman à clef, *On the Road*. While Panzram's and Abbott's books resonate with other prison life writings (or with American life writing more broadly), their stories are especially unique insofar as they aestheticize violence and degradation rather than redemption and transcendence and so never fully adhere to the generic parameters of the prison life writing genre.

A DANGEROUS MAN: CARL PANZRAM AND
KILLER: A JOURNAL OF MURDER

While imprisoned in an isolation cell at Washington District Jail in 1928, Carl Panzram began a friendship with a guard named Henry Lesser. Lesser urged Panzram to write his autobiography, which he did, passing handwritten pages of it to Lesser through the prison bars. In his writings, Panzram confesses to twenty-one murders, brags about countless rapes of men and boys, and details myriad other crimes that he committed inside and outside prison, including arsons and burglaries. His confessions were taken seriously by some officials. And a few of the murders he described seemed to match unsolved crimes in Boston, Philadelphia, and New Haven. But Panzram was ultimately never charged with the murders he claims to have committed. Instead, having been sentenced to twenty-five years in prison for housebreaking, Panzram was shipped to Kansas's notorious Leavenworth Prison to serve his time. He continued to correspond with Lesser, although the Leavenworth prison censors severely limited what Panzram could share with Lesser in his letters.[16] Ominously, Panzram warned Leavenworth officials that he wanted to be left alone and that he would kill the first man who bothered him.

In June 1929, Panzram surprised a work foreman in the prison named R.G. Warnke and crushed the man's skull with a piece of iron bar, killing him instantly. The murdered man had been Panzram's employer in the prison laundry, and Panzram was exacting revenge because he believed Warnke had punished him unfairly for a minor infraction – laundering handkerchiefs on the side in order to earn money for extra food and cigarettes.[17] For this murder, Panzram was sentenced to death – but not without some effort on Panzram's part: he actively petitioned for his own execution and sought to weaken his own defence (in part by entering a not-guilty plea, since he believed it would make a death sentence more likely). He even wrote a letter to then-president Herbert Hoover asking Hoover to reject any requests for clemency on his behalf. In this respect, Panzram foreshadows how convicted two-time murderer Gary Gilmore similarly fought for his own execution by firing squad in the 1970s – a case that inspired Norman Mailer to write *The Executioner's Song*, a book that, as I will discuss in a moment, brought Jack Henry Abbott to literary notoriety.

Panzram was executed by hanging on 5 September 1930. His alleged last words were to the executioner fiddling with a strap on the leather corset around his waist: "'Hurry it up, you Hoosier bastard! I could hang a dozen men while you're fooling around!'"[18] After the execution, Lesser tried for forty years to get the manuscript of Panzram's autobiography published in some form. It is not that people lacked interest in Panzram's work. The then-renowned writer H.L. Mencken read Panzram's autobiography, and while he was shocked by its frank descriptions of violence, he was impressed with it. Karl Menninger was also fascinated with Panzram and his confession, and Menninger eventually wrote about Panzram under the pseudonym "John Smith" in his 1938 book *Man against Himself*.

But despite interest in Panzram's work, no one would publish it because of its unrepentant brutality. It is worth pausing for a moment on this point: not only does Panzram's autobiography depict in detail the multiple murders he claims to have committed, but it also describes how he repeatedly raped men and boys before he killed them. Understandably, no publisher expressed any interest in actually publishing Panzram's writings. Decades later, however, Lesser convinced Thomas E. Gaddis, biographer of the famed "Birdman of Alcatraz," Robert Stroud (whose solitary confinement cell at Leavenworth adjoined Panzram's), to work on a book that would feature Panzram's autobiography. Gaddis enlisted the help of journalist Jim Long, and in 1970 the two men finally published *Killer: A Journal of Murder*.

In *Killer*, Gaddis and Long frame Panzram's confession with their own historical research, providing a narrative that proceeds from Panzram's upbringing in juvenile facilities to his graduation to jails and prisons and, eventually, to his execution. They provide only selections from Panzram's confession (which in its original form was more than two hundred handwritten pages in length), but they also include passages from selected letters that Panzram mailed to Lesser from his cell after he was shipped to Leavenworth.[19] Additionally, they include excerpts from letters that psychologists and criminologists sent to Lesser *about* Panzram – letters whose reactions to Panzram's confessions play a significant (but, I argue, problematic) role in the ideological work of the book.

Due to its publication history, *Killer* reflects the interests of several different historical periods. Panzram's confession was written in the late 1930s, so Panzram is most immediately describing Progressive Era prisons (and prison policies) in his confession and letters. However, some of the letters from psychologists and criminologists were written after Panzram's execution in the interim between the writing of the confession and the book's publication in 1970. And, of course, Gaddis and Long's biographical narrative reflects the preoccupations of their own historical moment.

Certainly, cultural changes made the publication of Panzram's writings possible. Americans in the late 1960s and early 1970s were fascinated with the outlaw and sometimes even celebrated him (as in Hunter S. Thompson's 1966 *Hell's Angels*), and high-profile assassinations and serial killings had increased interest in murderers' motivations. Gaddis and Long remark in their introduction that notorious acts of violence, from the Kennedy assassination to the crimes of the Boston Strangler, "fixed the eye of the country upon the man who acts out of hate."[20] Indeed, as I will show, this ocular fixity "upon the man who acts out of hate" is a defining feature of the biographical and contextual work that Gaddis and Long organize around Panzram's writings in *Killer*, which I suggest helps make him a case study. This textual superstructure, this fixed "eye," tries to plumb the depths of Panzram's story ostensibly not so much to better understand *him* but to understand how his desires and motivations might help a multivalent readership – one that includes psychologists, criminologists, and penologists – understand men *like* him.

Moreover, this mode of analysis, which pivots from the specific to the general – that is, which extracts information from an individual imprisoned person's psychobiography so that it can be used to understand similar people in the abstract (a category of criminality, or a typology, such as a serial killer, for instance) – would eventually become an essential tool for law enforcement. As Colin Wilson and Donald Seaman note in *The Serial Killers: A Study in the Psychology of Violence* (1990), in the late 1970s and early 1980s, the FBI's Behavioral Science Unit interviewed and studied numerous imprisoned people convicted of violent crimes. This provided the FBI analyst with "a rare chance to probe the psyche of the *kind* of serial murderer he may encounter time and again in the investigative years ahead."[21] In other words, Gaddis and Long value Panzram's autobiography for what it can explain about some generic "man who acts out of hate"; likewise, the FBI analyst interviews an imprisoned person so as to learn more about "the *kind* of serial murderer he may encounter." In both cases, there is a shift from the specific to the general, from the individual biography to the typology. Certainly, the application of this mode of analysis in *Killer* is not directly linked with practices of criminal profiling or criminal psychology developed in the years since the book was published. However, these techniques, which see the individual biography as instructive for some general typology, employ a similar logic and constitute overlapping hermeneutics that seek to establish a field of knowledge that is at the crossroads of criminology, prison discourse, psychological discourse, and life writing.

"THE MONSTROUS PRODUCT OF VIOLENT PUNISHMENT": PRISON "EDUCATION," THE ANTICONVERSION NARRATIVE, AND THE MEANING OF PANZRAM'S PRISON LIFE WRITINGS

Having sketched the broad outline of Panzram's story and some of *Killer*'s publication history, I turn to consider Panzram's use of the prison conversion narrative and explore how the various discourses I have just discussed, especially the overlapping psychological, criminological, and juridical discourses, are engaged in *Killer* so as to normalize, and render knowable and safe, Panzram's story – that is, how autobiography is supplanted by the case study in the book.

Panzram's use of the prison conversion narrative is surprisingly similar to that of Flannery O'Connor's mass-murdering escaped-convict character, The Misfit, in "A Good Man Is Hard to Find." If, as O'Connor suggests, The Misfit is a "prophet gone wrong," then he went wrong in the penitentiary.[22] The Misfit claims that he "never was a bad boy" before his incarceration. "Somewheres along the line I done something wrong and got sent to the penitentiary. I was buried alive," he says.[23] Being "buried alive" in prison changed him. Like an inversion of the renaming trope that appears frequently in conversion narratives, he takes a new name to commemorate the person he has become: "'I call myself The Misfit ... because I can't make what all I done wrong fit what all I gone through in punishment,'" he explains.[24] The Misfit sees the penitentiary as central to his identity. He places the penitentiary at the heart of his biography, suggesting that by mass-murdering he takes revenge on the social order that wrongly, or rather excessively, punished him.

The Misfit's argument that he has been psychologically, socially, or morally damaged as a result of his incarceration and thus seeks revenge on the society that imprisoned him is uncannily similar to the argument that Carl Panzram makes in his life writings.[25] Like The Misfit's fictional biography, Panzram's story inverts the prison conversion narrative: rather than being transformed in prison into a man capable of living a normal, crime-free life on the outside, his incarceration makes him violently antisocial. Panzram claims this process began when, as a twelve-year-old, he was sent to the Minnesota Training School for burglary. Sure, he misbehaved, explains Panzram, but his disobedience was largely innocuous. Then, he says in the deadpan, sardonic tone that often marks his writing, "the law immediately proceeded to educate me to be a good, clean, upright citizen and a credit to the human race."[26] His "education" involved repeated beatings and other instances of institutional violence. Panzram writes that "the so-called training that I received while there is mainly the cause of my being the degenerate beast that I am today."[27] In other words, the brutality of the training school and the later degradation of the prisons that he was forced to inhabit acclimatized him to a world of violence. As Henry Lesser explains, Panzram was "the monstrous product of violent punishment."[28]

Moreover, Panzram satirizes the prison conversion narrative by repeatedly using pedagogical metaphors to explain how prison violence has affected him. For example, he writes that as a boy, he "learned a hell of a lot from ... expert instructors furnished to [him] free of charge" at the Minnesota Training School. His "instructors" "reformed" him. They "taught" him theft, lying, torture – and murder. He claims that his own sexual violence, his raping of men and boys, was "learned" at the reform school, from staff who raped and brutalized *him*. For Panzram, there is a clear causal relationship between the violent man that he became and the brutality of his training in Minnesota: "From the treatment I received while there and the lessons I learned from it, I ... made up my mind that I would rob, burn, destroy, and kill everywhere I went and everybody I could as long as I lived."[29]

"Reformed," "taught," "learned": Here and elsewhere in his writings, Panzram signals his awareness of Progressive Era penology. He uses penologists' rehabilitative terms to describe the violent treatment that he receives behind bars, thereby inverting their meaning and signposting the system's hypocrisy. Panzram is consistent in his use of pedagogical metaphors throughout the book: a man being whipped is "being *reformed*" (74); in prison, he was "*taught* wrong" (166); in reform school, he "*learned* to become a first-class liar and hypocrite and the beginnings of degeneracy" (emphases added).[30] By casting the litany of abuses he received as a child and young adult in various institutions in the rhetoric of prison reform and prison education, Panzram makes his autobiography a kind of deviant Bildungsroman. Just as the narrative subject of the Bildungsroman, a novel of education, matures and learns to find his or her place in society, so too is Panzram "educated" in carceral institutions, inevitably returning to them since they are where he has learned to belong.

Outside prison, though, Panzram is "monstrous," a dangerous misfit: his "education" has rendered him incapable of belonging anywhere but behind bars – an anticonversion that Panzram explains as a form of environmental determinism that resonates with models of human behaviour that were being developed in the social sciences in the early twentieth century, upon which would be built the rehabilitative ideal of the mid-century prison system. Many prison reformers believed that individual behaviour was a reaction to environmental conditions, and one of the major arguments for Progressive Era prison reform was that prisons were so punitive that they created the very problems they were supposed to solve. Famed Progressive Era prison reformer Thomas Mott Osborne used precisely this equation when he explained that "certain natural immoral acts are bound to arise ... because of the essentially unnatural social conditions" of incarceration.[31] The similarity between Panzram's story of his antisociality and these emergent theories would explain the enthusiasm with which the first reader of his work, the guard Henry Lesser, shared Panzram's writings with the many psychologists and criminologists whose reactions to Panzram's work flit in and out of *Killer*, where they serve as a kind of meta-commentary on Panzram's writing and identity, inviting readers to understand Panzram according to theories about crime and punishment that would evolve into the rehabilitative philosophy of the Treatment Era.

Lesser, who encouraged Panzram to write his autobiography, who collected Panzram's writings, and who cultivated interest in Panzram and his work over several decades, was motivated in part by his enthusiasm for Progressive Era criminology and penology. He believed that Panzram's story might provide some insight into criminality if only the right people could interpret Panzram's work correctly. So he repeatedly sent Panzram's autobiography to renowned psychologists and criminologists, who, at Lesser's invitation, provided "symptomatic readings" – readings that took "meaning to be hidden, repressed, deep, and in need of detection and disclosure by an interpreter." Those readings are included in the book.[32]

Symptomatic readings frame the narrative, signposting for readers how to interpret Panzram's work. For example, Lesser sent the manuscript to famed criminologist Sheldon Glueck, who showed great interest in Panzram, writing in a letter to Lesser that Panzram "would make a fascinating psychoanalytic study. Merely to classify him as one type or another of offender or psychopath is not an illuminative process; he should be studied by a skilled psychiatrist over a long period of daily contacts."[33] Glueck's recommendation situates Panzram's story within the theoretical framework of Progressive Era criminologists and penologists, who rejected what they saw as a one-size-fits-all approach to understanding crime – that is, classifying criminals as "one type or another" – and instead called for a bespoke approach to interpreting and ultimately changing criminal behaviour. As David Rothman writes in *Conscience and Convenience: The Asylum and its Alternatives in Progressive America* (1980), Progressives rejected the nineteenth-century belief that "deviants were of a single type"; instead, "Progressives aimed to understand and to cure crime, delinquency, and insanity through a case-by-case approach."[34] Glueck prescribed just such a methodology: Panzram needed "daily contacts" with "a skilled psychiatrist" who could properly diagnose him as an individual. Moreover, Glueck was predictably interested in Panzram as a "psychoanalytic study," a hermeneutic that, despite the dialogic process of analysis, ultimately made Panzram an object under observation rather than a subject in communication.

This case study approach to Panzram, which I suggest is repeated throughout the book, tended to seek the "true" meaning in some hidden content of his speech or writing rather than in the manifest content of his discourse. Take, for instance, how Lesser and criminologist Benjamin Karpman tried to elicit some hidden meaning, some latent motivation, in Panzram's writing by devising a series of questions for Panzram to answer. Karpman was a proponent of Progressive Era theories about the rehabilitative ideal that would play a major role during the Treatment Era, including the notion that crime was a form of mental illness.[35] A psychoanalyst, Karpman prepared questions for Lesser to ask Panzram – questions that Karpman suspected might reveal "the sexual basis of violent murder."[36]

In a letter, Lesser asked these questions of Panzram without telling him that the questions had been devised by Karpman. To Lesser's disappointment, Panzram refused to directly answer the "8 questions" in his first written response.[37] Panzram told Lesser that, yes, he found pleasure in violence, but not for the reasons that Lesser's questions intimated. Instead, explained Panzram with frustration (calling Lesser a "chump"), the brutality of the state – twenty-two years of beatings in state institutions – had made him violent; he found pleasure in taking vengeance on a world that had brutalized him. He admonished Lesser for the "tone" of his letter, which, according to Panzram, made him out to be "a bug of some kind" (*bug* is prison slang for someone who is insane). Panzram angrily called Lesser "dumb" for thinking he could be a "fire bug or a homicidal maniac."[38] He was clearly aware that Lesser's questions indicated an agenda, one that sought to interpret him rather than listen to him.

Similarly, in his next letter to Lesser, Panzram rejected the psychoanalytic dimensions of Lesser/Karpman's questions, writing, "What ever [*sic*] possessed you to think that me or anyone else ever had a sexual-like feeling when we commit a crime like a murder or arson. That's the bunk."[39] Lesser/Karpman's questions were seeking a motivation for violence in Panzram's unconscious even though Panzram has already explained that his violence was caused by social forces. Panzram correctly saw how the questions were pathologizing him, and he ridiculed Karpman's hermeneutic presumably because the questions indicated that Lesser misunderstood him but also, perhaps, because the psychoanalytic framework identified him as mentally ill, and thus his acts as irrational, which was quite the opposite of what Panzram had been saying to Lesser for some time.

Here, and elsewhere in the book, Panzram struggled against the analytical framework that Lesser repeatedly applied to his story. Although Panzram seems to have humoured Lesser's interest in prison reform on several occasions – at one point, Lesser explained to Panzram the virtues of reformers like Glueck, Elmer Barnes, and Hyman Lippman and discovered, to his surprise, "that Panzram was well read in these theories" – Panzram ultimately and vehemently rejected these analyses of him.[40] If James Carr taught his amanuenses how to read his life writing – which, as I have shown in the preceding chapter, provided the framework for the eventual production of Carr's autobiography – then Panzram taught, or tried to teach, Lesser and (by proxy) the specialists who read his autobiographical writings how to interpret – or rather, how *not* to interpret – the meaning of his work.

Despite Panzram's repeated rejections of various psychological and criminological analyses of him, however, this interpretive approach seeped into Gaddis and Long's ostensibly benign contextual and historical framework. For example, even after the letter where Panzram scoffs at Lesser's questions about his motives, they write that "the implications of this letter, and the one to follow, would afford more insight into the mind of a murderer than any prior account."[41] By claiming that Panzram's letter can provide some "insight into the mind of a murderer," Gaddis and Long are once again suggesting that his story has value insofar as it says something about people *like* him, some abstracted criminal ("a murderer"), but they are also normalizing a way of seeing Panzram according to a depth model of reading that has already been employed elsewhere by numerous psychologists and criminologists whose letters are quoted in *Killer*.

Indeed, "insight into the mind" is a conceptual metaphor that Gaddis and Long repeatedly apply to Panzram's writing; it is a penetrative hermeneutic that, like insight in psychotherapy, suggests that true meaning is to be apprehended through interpreting Panzram's writings. In other words, this interpretive approach sees value not in what Panzram *says*, necessarily, but in what his text *reveals*. This mode of analysis shifts agency – as well as control over the meaning of Panzram's story – from author to reader, from Panzram to the analyst(s) who reveal what his text *really* means (including the various criminologists and psychologists whose interlocking approaches frame how Panzram's confession appears in the book). Perhaps this accounts for the peculiar absence of Panzram's name on the book's cover. Gaddis and Long are listed as the sole authors because, within this framework, Panzram is no longer an author but is instead a site of analysis, an object of study. (Curiously, in my old library copy of *Killer*, someone has scrawled, and then underlined, "author, Carl Panzram" under Gaddis and Long's names on the title page of the book, seeking to amend the glaring omission of Panzram's name as author of what is clearly, in no small part, his story.)

As I have suggested, I see this mode of analysis – which includes a depth model of reading and a movement from the specific to the general, from the individual to the typology – as part of a broader hermeneutic that is related to genre, to framing Panzram's confession as a case study. This genre-switching, from confession to case study, pathologizes Panzram but also domesticates the unsettling qualities of his story since it suggests that his story fits comfortably within an established discourse. It is likely that this mode of analysis was essential to the book's publication since it normalized (or tries to normalize) what would otherwise have been an impossibly deviant voice – one that had, Gaddis and Long explain, impeded publication precisely because its unrepentant admissions of violence broke the rules of the genre (much as I have shown with James Carr's *Bad*). Wrapped in the scientific rhetoric of criminology and psychology, framed as a peculiar but recognizable pathology, Panzram's unrepentant voice, which would otherwise not find its way into autobiographical discourse, was thereby rendered safe enough to appear in print. Reading his confession as a case study does more than simply normalize an otherwise disturbing voice, however. It makes his confession *useful*; it weaponizes his biography by framing it as an analytic tool that could improve law enforcement's capacity to understand criminal behaviour, control criminality, and even improve the prison system (rather than indict law enforcement, the criminal justice system, and prisons, which was Panzram's stated goal in his confession).[42]

Although I have been focusing on readings of Panzram that frame him as a case study, Panzram's deep suspicion of psychological or criminological analyses of him must also be understood in relation to a psycho-legal hermeneutic imposed on him during his murder trial. Under the scrutiny of the judicial branch because he had murdered a prison employee, Panzram was feeling the pressure of a juridico-psychological analysis from the authorities, who sought to establish whether he was insane and thus exempt from capital punishment. Since Panzram *wanted* to be executed, he was determined not to be seen (or interpreted) as insane. In a letter to Lesser, Panzram wrote,

> My trial is coming up and in the meantime I am
> trying not to do anything, say or write anything
> which could be used as evidence to convict me of
> insanity. I know that there are some people who
> would like nothing better than to send me to the
> mad house. This I don't want because I would rather
> be dead.[43]

So, Panzram had good reason to be careful in his letters: they were
being reviewed for signs of potential insanity. As with George
Jackson's letters in *Soledad Brother*, Panzram's letters reproduced in
Killer are shaped in part by an unintended and unwanted reader,
the prison censor. Since Panzram was very worried that he would
be deemed insane and thus saved from the gallows, he repeatedly
insists on his sanity in his letters, knowing full well that they will
be read by prison officials.[44] For example, in a letter to Lesser, he
claims, "I knew right from wrong," insisting that his crime fulfilled
the legal requirement of *mens rea*, the mode of culpability required
to prove that his murder of the prison official, Warnke, was intentional. He knows that people think he is "just a little bit nutty,"
he tells Lesser. But those people do not know him like he knows
himself: "I know myself far better than anyone else knows me and
I am firmly convinced that I am not crazy."[45] Here, Panzram's
implied reader blurs and expands: he is writing *to* Lesser but *for*
the prison censor who has been tasked with analyzing Panzram's
writings for signs of insanity that could help determine the course
of his trial.

Now, as I have indicated, Panzram's argument that the violence
of prison made him a violent man might seem to fit Progressive
Era arguments about a kind of environmental determinism in the
prison system. But whatever similarity those arguments might
have in their diagnosis of current prison conditions stops there.
Prison reformers sought to make prisons more effective at changing

criminals into citizens. Yet Panzram in his letters describes prison rehabilitation as magical thinking: "a secret formula, some mumbo-jumbo, or hocus-pocus."[46] In a letter to Lesser, Panzram writes,

> You have it all doped out, eh! You have it all figured out that if I was given my freedom today, financial independence, moral support and a helping hand from powerful people and everything necessary that would help me to reform and lead a good clean Christian life, that's all that would be required. You figured that I would jump at it and be all reformed up the minute I hit the front gate. What a dream.
>
> You're all wet. Wake up kid you're having a nightmare ... The real truth of the matter is that I haven't the least desire to reform. Very much the reverse of that is the truth.[47]

Here, Panzram goes beyond ridiculing Lesser's optimism. The teleology he satirizes, from prison to "a good clean Christian life" with the assistance of financial backing and "moral support" and through the intervention of "powerful people," reduces what Lesser and his contemporaries in the penological community believe is a science of rehabilitation to something like the plot line of a Horatio Alger novel.

Ultimately, Panzram refuses to agree that better treatment of him might have made him a better man. Essentially, he resists the efforts of Lesser and the criminologists who read his writings to use his story as an example they could then apply elsewhere in their efforts at reforming prisons and understanding criminals around the country. Finding himself in the crosshairs of the psychological, criminological, penological, and legal traditions, whose interpretive methods were asserting their authority over the meaning of his confession and his life, Panzram resisted pathologizing his own violent criminality. And his insistence that he was a product of the prison system, that he was the prison's monstrous prodigy and thus also its responsibility, reappears in Jack Henry Abbott's *In the Belly of the Beast*, a book that helped change the direction of prisons, and that had a defining influence on prison life writing, in the final decades of the twentieth century.

FROM THE BIG HOUSE TO RANDOM HOUSE AND BACK AGAIN: *IN THE BELLY OF THE BEAST* AND THE ANTICONVERSION NARRATIVE

Carl Panzram's writings provided Jack Henry Abbott with a vocabulary for understanding how his lifetime behind bars affected his identity. But it was George Jackson who provided Abbott with a language for articulating how he could legitimately fight back against the system that he believed had destroyed his ability to live a normal life. In fact, Abbott dedicates *In the Belly of the Beast* to Panzram and Jackson (as well as to executed murderer Gary Gilmore, prison activist and "mad bomber" Sam Melville, and several unrenowned incarcerated men), essentially outlining for his readers something of the book's literary pedigree. As I will show, Abbott employs the anticonversion narrative that also appears in Panzram's life writings as well as the revolutionary narrative that George Jackson develops in *Soledad Brother*. However, Abbott extends these narrative forms so as to complicate how we traditionally understand diverse issues like prison education, identity formation, and race.

Abbott's story is as peculiar as it is tragic. While Norman Mailer was writing *The Executioner's Song*, he received an unusual letter from an imprisoned person named Jack H. Abbott. Abbott, who had served time with Gilmore, offered to provide Mailer with insight into Gilmore's life as a long-term convict – things only another long-term convict like Abbott could know. Abbott explained that, like Gilmore, he had been raised in incarceration: from state institutions like reform schools to juvenile institutions to jails to prisons to Maximum Security and long stints in solitary confinement: Abbott knew prisons. Mailer was so struck by the intensity and skill of Abbott's letters that he responded, spawning a two-year letter-writing dialogue between the two men. With the help of a young editor at Random House named Erroll McDonald, the letters were eventually developed into *In the Belly of the Beast*.

Abbott's book was published six weeks after he was paroled from prison. Although there is some debate about how much influence Norman Mailer had in ensuring Abbott's parole,[48] Mailer did promise to provide him with work and income in New York, conditions crucial to satisfying the parole board and ensuring Abbott's early release. The night before his book was published to rave reviews – most notably by Terrence Des Pres in *The New York Times* – Abbott and two friends stopped for a late-night meal at The Binibon, a café on the Lower East Side of Manhattan.[49] Abbott got into a disagreement with Richard Adan, the night manager of the café, which quickly escalated into an argument; the argument was taken outside; and moments later Richard Adan was dead on the sidewalk: Abbott had stabbed him, once, clean through the heart. After several months on the run, Abbott was finally apprehended and tried for murder. He was found guilty of manslaughter and sentenced to fifteen years to life in prison. Abbott published another book in 2001 called *My Return* (co-authored with Naomi Zack), in which he attempted to explain his role in the murder by way of a Greek tragedy made up of dialogue from the actual trial. (*My Return* is a strange piece of work: both Abbott and Adan are characters in the play; the characters re-enact the murder; and Abbott includes appendices of his own sketches of the stabbing as stage directions and supporting evidence.) A year later, Abbott was dead in his cell. An inquest concluded that he had hanged himself with a bed sheet and a shoelace.

At first glance, Abbott's story in *In the Belly of the Beast* approximates the prison conversion narrative. Like many other prison life writers, Abbott presents himself as a self-taught intellectual; through reading, he has found enlightenment behind bars.

Taking the trope of the studious, monastic incarcerated person to a dramatic extreme, Abbott describes himself locked in Maximum Security for five years without speaking to anyone but his sister, who visits him twice a month. During that period, he reads extensively from books that his sister mails to him. He writes,

> When I entered Maximum Security, I was about five feet, nine inches tall. I did not have a beard and did not know basic arithmetic. When I emerged I could not walk without collapsing; I had a full beard and was six feet tall. I had a rudimentary understanding of mathematical theory and symbolic logic and had studied in all the theoretic sciences. I had read all but a very few of the world's classics, from prehistoric times up to this day. My vision was perfect when I was locked up; when I got out, my vision required glasses.[50]

Abbott details an intellectual rebirth: before Maximum Security, he "did not know basic arithmetic"; after five years in Maximum Security, he not only understood advanced mathematics but had also studied "all the theoretical sciences" and read most of "the world's classics." Abbott's hyperbole – "I had read *all* but a very few of the world's classics," "had studied in *all* the theoretic sciences" – suggests his desire to underscore the dramatic difference between who he was before and who he became after his five years in Maximum Security.

As *Belly* demonstrates, Abbott was incredibly intelligent, well-read, and articulate – qualities that made him immensely appealing to writers. The writer Jerzy Kosinski, who like Mailer maintained a lengthy correspondence with Abbott, later claimed that he and others were infatuated with Abbott because Abbott provided them with a classic American story of self-making that writers in particular could relate to because it validated their belief in writing's life-changing potential: "'from Leavenworth to Random House,'" as Kosinski succinctly put it.[51] However, unlike most prison writers, who claim that their education has provided them with the emotional and intellectual skills to lift themselves out of lives of crime, Abbott claims that his education has made him more articulate and self-aware but no more fit for absorption into US society. Rather than presenting a teleological movement toward a coherent identity, as is typically found in a prison memoir, Abbott in his memoir sees himself becoming increasingly alienated despite his incredible self-education. Notwithstanding the book's nod to the prison conversion narrative tradition, then, *In the Belly of the Beast* follows an anticonversion narrative similar to – indeed, if Abbott's dedications page is to be believed, heavily influenced by – that of Carl Panzram.

Like Panzram's life writings in *Killer*, *In the Belly of the Beast* traces the relationship between the violent, alienating carceral spaces of Abbott's upbringing, maturation, and early middle-age with the alienated, violent person he readily admits himself to be. He writes that he is affected by "a form of instability (mental, emotional, etc.)" that "is *caused* by a lifetime of incarceration."[52] *Belly's* degradation aesthetic – which includes elaborate representations of extreme sadism and suffering and its set pieces of blackout cells, bizarre medical and psychological experiments, torture, electroshock therapy, and madness – is decidedly, even excessively gothic. This is no surprise, really. Many critics have noted the inherently gothic qualities of the prison system and the literature associated with it.[53] Especially unique is the book's rendering of this system's effects on Abbott's identity and what that identity means *outside* prison: or, how prison has made him monstrous.

As I have suggested, Abbott's monstrosity has less to do with the gothic space of the prison than it does with the world beyond the prison – a world that presents profound social, psychological, or legal contradictions for a formerly incarcerated person like him. In the book's final chapter, Abbott reflects on his potential freedom in a way that resonates with the subjective ambiguity that I have defined as central to the figure of the monstrous prisoner. He writes that he longs to be released from prison to "see and do things other people do." He then laments that freedom seems impossible for him: "Too much has happened, for too long, to me," he writes. However, he continues, he wants "to try," and he has a "right" to try to live on the outside rather than spend his life behind bars:

> *That* is what "human right" is. *My* right, the *individual's* right. We all have that right even though we know in our hearts we may be incapable of accomplishing what we have the *absolute* right to try to accomplish ... I have the right, at least, to walk free at some time in my life even if the odds are by now overwhelming that I may not be as other men.[54]

Abbott bases his appeal for freedom on a rights claim: "It is my right. *That* is what 'human right' is. *My* right, the *individual's* right." But at the same time, he insists that he likely cannot abide by the rules of citizenship: "I don't see how that would be possible now ... Too much has happened, for too long, to me."

In the very moment when Abbott contemplates freedom, he encounters a profound contradiction: he deserves to be free, but, somewhat ominously given his eventual murder of Richard Adan soon after his release, he cannot be free because he has been conditioned to behave antisocially and, he seems to imply here, would not last on the outside. Indeed, if the "monster always represents the disruption of categories, the destruction of boundaries, and the presence of impurities," then Abbott's inability to fit in is particularly monstrous since he deserves to, but ultimately cannot, belong "in the world" because he is unable to adhere to the responsibilities of citizenship.[55] Abbott presents himself not only as a social and political contradiction – as the kind of liminal figure inhabiting what Alexander calls the New Jim Crow – but also as ontologically ambiguous: he "may not be as other men."

This ontological questioning is frequently expressed as a kind of gothic affect in the book: affect that haunts, that takes possession of the feeling subject, often disrupting normal social behaviour.[56] For example, Abbott recalls how he once discovered he was crying because "little spots of water" appeared on the book he was reading in his prison cell. He writes, "I touched them with a finger and wondered at the phenomenon – when suddenly I realized tears were falling from my eyes."[57] Not only is he unaware of what causes his emotional outburst, but he is also alienated from the emotional content of it. Although after discovering his tears he "weeps uncontrollably," he initially experiences his feelings as though they were felt and produced by another person.

This sense of an alien presence that produces emotions that he is forced to address (or more often repress) is intensified when Abbott is confronted with the social world, with other people. Even in prison, social interactions make his otherness shockingly apparent to him, resulting in an admixture of paranoia and violent rage. When he is in circumstances where there are large groups of imprisoned people, for example, he feels an almost overwhelming sense of paranoia, which he describes as "an illness [that he] contracted in institutions." This paranoia manifests itself as feelings of "hostility" and "hatred" for the people around him: "It's all I can do to refrain from attack," Abbott writes. He explains that he "can't help this anger" and that he has struggled to "control" these feelings "for years": "I have to intentionally gauge my voice in a conversation to cover up the anger I feel, the chaos and pain just beneath the surface of what we commonly recognize as reality," he writes.[58] Here, the most dominant affective registers that appear throughout the book, paranoia and rage, are placed in the "spatial metaphors of interiority" that Eve Sedgwick sees as central to gothic literature, literary criticism, and psychoanalysis.[59] These feelings are "just beneath the surface" and must be willfully "cover[ed] up,"

Abbott writes. Failure to enfold his paranoia and rage in the cara-pace of a conscience that is self-aware and strong enough to manage this frightening interiority, he suggests, could result in an "attack," in violence. Judith Halberstam writes in *Skin Shows: Gothic Horror and the Technology of Monsters* that "like Mr. Hyde, the paranoiac produces the other within himself and then projects that other out into the external world."[60] Like Dr. Jekyll, then, Abbott experiences his emotions as though he were possessed – a doubling of the self whose violence, he claims, disrupts his capacity to socialize in any meaningful way. What *Belly* offers here and throughout the book is a depiction of what the social and political monstrosity of prison and post-prison life *feels* like to someone who has been raised in carceral institutions, how the liminality of prison and parole has affective corollaries that are similarly conflicted, and how those affective registers help bring about recidivism.[61]

According to the traditional cultural scripts of prison life writing, then, Abbott is profoundly contradictory: he is educated but unstable, self-reflective but not self-governing, self-made but self-destructive. Whatever Abbott's education imparts, it cannot interrupt the psychological and social effects of his long-term imprisonment. Given that it figures education as a tool for self-engineering that is blunted by rather than resistant to the damaging social and psychological effects of incarceration, Abbott's story is at odds with, and should inspire questions about, prison education, especially claims that education can change people when it cannot simultaneously change the broader social conditions in which those people happen to live.

In *Belly*, Abbott challenges the redemptive, transcendent rhet-oric associated with prison education by resisting the basic pre-sumption of education programs – that education has an inevitably positive, socializing effect; instead, he foregrounds how imprisoned people's lives are circumscribed by systems that not only enforce stasis but also encourage physical, psychological, and social degen-eration. However much Abbott "remakes" himself, he argues, he will never "come out of prison a better man."[62] Abbott's work thus fits what Dylan Rodríguez describes as writings by imprisoned people who eschew "notions of the imprisoned author defying physical incarceration by finding (intellectual/spiritual) freedom in the creative act." According to Rodríguez, these writers emphasize "the material embeddedness of their writing in the condition of imprisonment, rupturing the insistent coherence of the prison-writing genre by amplifying the incoherence of captivity, an altogether different condition of possibility for literary production."[63]

Abbott's insistence on degradation rather than transcendence as a dominant motif for his writing also brings into focus the marginalized stories of the incarcerated who do not or cannot transcend the conditions of their imprisonment – stories that are perhaps more representative than the uplifting stories of rehabilitation that recur in the prison life writing archive. And as a book that illuminates the psychological damage caused by long-term isolation, it serves as an unheeded warning, for the prison system dramatically increased its use of solitary confinement as a method of control, discipline, and torture in the decades after the publication of *In the Belly of the Beast*.

JACK HENRY ABBOTT: THE WHITE NEGRO PROBLEM

As I have suggested, *In the Belly of the Beast* is a work defined by contradiction and ambiguity. And contradiction is central to Abbott's analyses of race, especially his own whiteness. For one thing, although Abbott's mother was Chinese-American, he identifies as white and is consistently interpellated as white throughout the book. "I was the only white man there," he writes, when describing how he "was always thrown into all-black cells" as punishment by guards, who also identified him as white and who believed he would be attacked by imprisoned African Americans for it. Certainly, there are multiple instances when Abbott distances himself from whiteness, but he is distinguishing himself from a particular *kind* of whiteness – from a white middle class that reaps the benefits of a white supremacist system, which he believes has excluded him.

Yet Abbott is forced to encounter his whiteness – that is, his presumptive whiteness, with which he associates himself throughout the book. This is for a variety of reasons, but mostly because, at the time he was imprisoned, African Americans were being incarcerated in greater and greater numbers and the prisoners' rights movement, which was deeply influenced by civil rights, Black Power, and African American groups like the Nation of Islam and the Black Panthers, emphasized race as the dominant lens through which imprisoned people's experiences were to be understood. In *Belly*, Abbott describes his admiration for the movement and its leaders, especially for George Jackson. By adopting Jackson's revolutionary narrative in his book and identifying himself as a revolutionary figure, Abbott is forced to take stock of his complicity in white supremacy.

Like James Carr in *Bad*, and like many other imprisoned people who were inspired by Jackson's work, Abbott uses the revolutionary narrative as a blueprint for agency and resistance. At times, Abbott seems to follow Jackson's instructions almost by rote. In *Soledad Brother*, for example, Jackson writes, "I met Marx, Lenin, Trotsky, Engels, and Mao when I entered prison and they redeemed me."[64] Similarly, in *Belly*, Abbott finds redemption by reading "Karl Marx and Friedrich Engels ... Lenin, Stalin, and Mao" who, he claims, "teach the highest principles of human society."[65]

Furthermore, like Jackson, Abbott identifies with anti-colonial struggles around the world. In *Blood in My Eye*, Jackson explains that imprisoned people are involved in a collective, large-scale revolution beyond the prison: "Prisoners must be reached and made to understand that they are victims of social injustice," participants in a "war [that] goes on no matter where one may find himself on bourgeois-dominated soil."[66] Taking a page from Jackson, Abbott is (on his small piece of bourgeois-dominated soil) participating in what he calls "a terrible revolutionary war in its infancy." His daily battles and struggles with the guards and the prison system are framed as revolutionary acts, "flaring up in fits and starts and dying as quickly in a splash of blood and violence on a scale so microscopic as to go unnoticed to the average, everyday perception of events in the country."[67] Abbott's "vision" of his life as a revolutionary "splash of blood" on "a small scale" has meaning because it is part of something greater, historic, a "bigger 'splash of blood'" on a "'bigger scale.'"[68]

In identifying as a revolutionary, he is linking his struggles in the prison with the international wars that were waged throughout the twentieth century against imperialist powers everywhere from Cuba to China to Vietnam. Abbott might feel alienated from the normal world because of his incarceration, but he can feel connected to an imagined community of like-minded people around the world who are overthrowing imperialist and capitalist regimes. Panzram's environmental determinist theories about prison have clearly affected Abbott's understanding of his own degeneration, and similarly, Jackson's rhetoric of revolution pervades *Belly*, presumably because it has provided Abbott with a sense of agency and community in a system in which he feels largely alienated and alone.

Since the murder of Adan, however, Abbott has come to be identified as a mere reflection of the nihilistic hipster that Mailer celebrates in his notorious essay "The White Negro."[69] Carl Rollyson writes, "The vehemence of Abbott's expressions, literally underlined in nearly every page of his prose, delineates a view of repressive society that Mailer had held in 'The White Negro.'"[70] Likewise, Mary V. Dearborn argues that while it might not be fair to "hold Mailer to the standards he promoted more than twenty years earlier, it's hard to distinguish the long-term convict from the hipster of 'The White Negro' taken to extremes."[71] There seems to be a desire, prevalent even among meticulous biographers like Rollyson and Dearborn, to define Abbott as a monstrous creation of Mailer's – as a living (killing) consequence of the writer's earlier ideas.[72]

At first glance, Abbott seems like a Mailerian hipster *in extremis*, a "philosophical psychopath" hell-bent on challenging the "square" "totalitarian tissues of American society."[73] But the nihilistic hipster has no political purpose, whereas Abbott's often violent and apocalyptic diatribes, his interest in Marxist theory, and his belief that imprisoned people are part of an international anti-colonial movement express a deep political commitment (at least in the text). *Belly* has little to do with Mailer's hipster and everything to do with the prisoners' rights movement and, as I have shown, Jackson's revolutionary philosophy. In particular, Abbott's "racechanges" – to borrow a term from Susan Gubar – are part of this political lineage.[74] Abbott's understanding of race takes a page from Sam Melville rather than Norman Mailer. Melville, whose name appears on *Belly*'s dedications page alongside those of Panzram and Jackson, writes in *Letters from Attica*, "One thing is for certain: when I emerge [from prison] ... I won't be a honky anymore."[75] Here, Melville articulates a form of post-whiteness that appeals to Abbott, who seeks a similarly effaced whiteness in his memoir, arguing that he "never had much in common with [white people]."[76] To dramatize his outsider-status, his difference from "white people," Abbott provides a short series of scenes that he claims took place during his brief stint outside prison, during which he travelled to the south and observed state-sanctioned white supremacy and black victimization.

On the whole, these scenes are familiar, almost cliché settings of civil rights struggles: a segregated movie theatre, a lunch counter, and an school dance.[77] Abbott dramatizes how he is unaccustomed to the racism of white supremacist America, often blundering into white segregatory practices by accident. In one scene, for example, he watches while white police officers shoot and kill an innocent black farmer over a parking infraction as the man's son watches, horrified.[78] Abbott freezes, appalled "because [he] could not believe what he was seeing."[79]

In this scene, Abbott reproduces a familiar triangulation in post-civil rights representations of violent white supremacy: the violent white racists (here, represented by the police and members of the southern white community), the black subject(s) in pain (with a focus on the brutalization of a black body), and the sympathetic, morally tortured white witness (Abbott). This triangulation drives a wedge between Abbott and white supremacy, a wedge that reappears in what Mark Golub calls "Hollywood redemption history" dramas about slavery or Jim Crow – like *Mississippi Burning*, *The Long Walk Home*, *Amistad*, and *Glory* – where the "point of identification character [with whom the audience is expected to identify] is a charismatic white man [or woman, as in *The Long Walk Home*,] who fights (or comes to fight) against oppression."[80] The triangulation I identify, and the genre Golub brackets, together provide whites with a location from which they can view racism from a morally safe distance and divest themselves of their potential complicity in white supremacy, despite the fact that white supremacy in the post-civil rights era is usually maintained without blatant expressions of racial discrimination, let alone overt demonstrations of racial violence.

Through these scenes, Abbott dramatizes what he means by "white people": "white people who are in a position to commit these racial injustices."[81] Abbott claims that he is unable (never mind unwilling) to participate in white oppression and wield white privilege. For Abbott, his difference from white people is not due to his multiracial identity, which is never discussed or even represented in the book; instead, it is class-based. He claims to "shar[e] a common oppression" with African Americans because he is poor, even asserting that "class oppression and racial oppression are identical."[82] Claiming that poor whites are at an equal disadvantage to blacks risks occluding how whites, regardless of their anti-racist intentions or socio-economic status, invariably receive the benefits that underpin white identity, simply by being white in America.

As Abbott himself demonstrates, even poor whites benefit from the racial caste system at work in American society, including in the criminal justice system. For example, in a scene mentioned earlier, Abbott describes how guards interpellate his whiteness, suggesting its fraternal possibilities for him, its currency even when he is celled with African Americans: "We're white men like you," a white guard tells him. "Those blacks don't like you any more than they like us."[83] Regardless of his economic status, Abbott is not in a position of innocence or unaccountability in relation to white supremacy. As the guards suggest, Abbott cannot shrug off whiteness despite his experiences of socio-economic privation and his distance from a normative "bourgeois" whiteness. If the guards invoke a white racial solidarity with him, he muses, underscoring the lines of racial complicity in the prison system, then "they must do it to the other white prisoners."[84] The guards test the limitations of a post-white subject, "disaffiliated from the deployments of white supremacy and refunctioned as cross-race and cross-class struggle."[85] *In the Belly of the Beast*, always enigmatic and often paradoxical, thus asserts and subverts a post-racial whiteness. Abbott claims a fundamental difference from white people while also representing himself as inseparable from his whiteness, despite his best intentions.

This paradoxical position reasserts itself in the same chapter when Abbott describes an instance of race-based aggression outside an all-white dance in Salt Lake City. Abbott is attacked by a group of young black men, presumably in retaliation for being barred from that dance on account of their race.[86] Abbott identifies this instance of race-based violence as social rather than individual, a distinction he tries to maintain when discussing his own relationship to whiteness; thus, their attack has nothing to do with him per se: "Today I realize I have had to pay the price many times for the social injustices committed by white people in this society," he explains.[87]

However, Abbott tries to make this observation from a position exterior to whiteness. The black youth are responding to *those* "white people," argues Abbott, and their violence is supposed to "force [him] into the ranks of white society," which he resists.[88] Again, nowhere does Abbott suggest that this forced racial affiliation has to do with his multiracial identity. Instead, it has to do with his inability to reap the benefits of whiteness; it has to do with his presumed distance from a kind of white privilege. As Robyn Wiegman observes, "the desire to combat white privilege seems unable to generate a political project against racism articulated from the site of whiteness itself." Abbott's constitution of himself as what Wiegman calls an "antiracist subject," then, only occurs after he has performed the intellectual contortions of divesting himself of his own whiteness.[89] Only by disaffiliating himself from "white people" can he mount an effective critique of white supremacy. As Wiegman argues, "disaffiliation from white supremacy founds contemporary white identity."[90] This "liberal whiteness" resuscitates the US narrative of democratic progress by representing racism and white supremacy largely through articulations of virulent, explicit racism (the George Wallaces, the David Dukes, the KKK), while (for the most part) neglecting the ongoing institutional racism (in the criminal justice system, for example) that cuts against the grain of an American story of racial and social uplift.

Yet the black youth who attacked Abbott are clearly responding to existing forms of structural racism that are harder to resist (like a segregated dancehall) but that they know privilege Abbott because of his skin colour. While the men were beating him, writes Abbott, "one kept yelling something about not being able to dance."[91] Their attack establishes his proximity to white dominance even as he tries to deny "accountability and historical connection" to white systems of oppression, as bell hooks suggests post-white liberalism often seeks to do.[92] Abbott's desire to distance himself from "white people" is always in tension with his inability to entirely do so, as other people – white guards, black teenagers – remind him that he cannot divest himself of the whiteness that he eagerly seeks to reject.

Thus *In the Belly of the Beast* dramatizes a tension between an idealized post-racial subject – a white identity without what Hamilton Carroll calls the "stigma of privilege" – and a white subject who, anti-racist sentiments aside, cannot be unyoked from white power structures through the exercise of individual agency.[93] If Abbott's rejection of his own whiteness connects with arguments among some theorists that whiteness can and should be "abolished," his inability to fully realize that project despite his best intentions reflects the shortcomings of a white-abolitionist position.[94]

Moreover, Abbott's hoped-for non-whiteness turns on an argument that is also made by white men who feel as though they have been the victims of "reverse discrimination" (an argument forwarded by the affirmative action "backlash," for example): he has not created white privilege or minority disempowerment (nor has he benefited from either), so the "stigma" of whiteness is not his responsibility. He has nothing "in common" with "white people who are in a position to commit these racial injustices." Abbott shows that the unintended consequence of a white abolitionist argument is that it articulates a variation on the commonly held belief among whites that they are race-neutral or race-less, thus venturing onto the field of colour-blindness that conservatives have occupied since the post-civil rights era as a way to claw back gains made by civil rights legislation (such as affirmative action).

CONCLUSION: MONSTERS AND "NOTHING WORKS"

Carl Panzram and Jack Henry Abbott refuse to adhere to the teleology of the prison conversion narrative that dominates the prison life writing genre. Instead of claiming that they have undergone conversions that enable them to transcend the material conditions of their lives, they emphasize how they have instead been rendered violently antisocial and thus incapable of living outside a prison. Their stories are intended as indictments of the prison system that made them monstrous.

But they also risk providing evidence for a view of imprisoned people that in fact did become prevalent in the coming years, ultimately influencing the turn toward a punitive prison system, draconian laws, and mass incarceration. This is most clearly the case with Abbott's *In the Belly of the Beast*, for Abbott was associated with literary celebrities, most especially Norman Mailer, and his murder trial became something of a media circus that framed Abbott's case as a trial about the limits of rehabilitation and the dangers of liberal overreach. Ultimately, as Philip Jenkins writes in *Decade of Nightmares: The End of the Sixties and the Making of Eighties America* (2006), "media response to the [Abbott] case stressed ... the irredeemable evil of the killer, the near-impossibility of rehabilitation, and the gullibility of Abbott's admirers," which reinforced "conservative policies" that "indicate[d] the bankruptcy of liberalism."[95] Paradoxically, *In the Belly of the Beast* came to justify the argument that imprisoned people required *more* prison, not less, and retributive prison policies, rather than rehabilitative ones.

In the years since Abbott's book dramatized the horrific psychological effects of solitary confinement, prisons around the country have relied increasingly on various forms of solitary confinement for discipline and control. This includes the increased use of administrative segregation within prisons, and well as entire institutions built around isolation – so-called supermax prisons. Abbott's autobiography participated in the development of a discursive formation that enabled the reorganization of the US carceral landscape: sentences were lengthened, parole was largely eliminated, more prisons were built, isolation was used more and more as a control mechanism, and prison education programs were largely eliminated.

This revaluation of the criminal and the incarcerated person was felt most acutely by incarcerated people of colour, especially imprisoned African Americans, whose ranks swelled in the 1970s as law enforcement targeted black communities in a series of tough-on-crime measures. Somewhat predictably, given white America's long history of criminalizing black masculinity, these policies were justified by veiled or explicit references to African American men and boys, whose socialization within the ghettoes of America supposedly made them impulsively violent and incapable of living without the restraints of law enforcement and an expanding prison system. Perhaps the best-known example of this argument is John J. DiLulio, Jr.'s claim in the early 1990s that the coming years would see a dramatic wave of "superpredators" flood the streets of the country, a claim that was infamously repeated by then First Lady Hillary Rodham Clinton.[96] Imprisoned African Americans during this period were thus generally represented as impulsively and often irrationally violent – a conception of them that justified increasingly punitive prison policies.[97]

Perhaps as a reaction to this mainstream conception of the incarcerated person as a threat to the social order, and a collapse of public support for prison resistance movements, prison life writing during this period returned to the prison conversion narrative with a renewed vigour, for it provided an avenue (however limited) for social rehabilitation. Not that the prison conversion narrative ever disappeared from the prison life writing genre. But prison life writing throughout the 1980s, 1990s, and 2000s frequently relied on largely uncomplicated versions of the prison conversion narrative to articulate how an imprisoned author became a different person: although an imprisoned or formerly imprisoned person may have been a criminal before their incarceration, they had undergone a dramatic change and were prepared to be accepted back into American life as a fully functioning citizen and a productive member of the community. In the next chapter, I consider this return to the prison conversion narrative and explore how it intersects with prison discourse, especially how it unearths troubling assumptions about criminality and citizenship that earlier uses of the prison conversion narrative, especially during the Treatment Era, sought to critique.

LIFE WRITING IN THE CONTEMPORARY CARCERAL STATE

WRITING MY WRONGS, *A PLACE TO STAND*, AND THE MAKING OF A "BETTER HUMAN BEING"

SINCE THE MID-1970S, WHEN THE TREATMENT ERA DISSOLVED, THE US prison population has expanded dramatically, from roughly 200,000 to more than 1,400,000 today. Marie Gottschalk, in *The Prison and the Gallows: The Politics of Mass Incarceration in America* (2006), describes this expansion as "the construction of the U.S. carceral state."[1] In recent years, state and local officials have started to worry about the historic numbers of people behind bars (or, rather, they have been concerned about the cost of keeping so many people in prison). As well, scholars and activists have finally started to convince a public often reluctant to consider the needs of incarcerated people that the prison system is out of control.

Yet despite a dip in federal prison populations under the Obama administration and a small reduction in the numbers of imprisoned people in some states, US prison populations continue to grow.[2] The US prison system still houses Americans, especially African Americans, in historic proportions. Moreover, during this period, prisons have largely become warehouses for human bodies. The rhetoric of rehabilitation, and the reformist reimaginings of prisons as schools or asylums or hospitals, sound today like antiquated, naive theories from the past. Yet prison life writing continues to produce narratives about imprisoned people who have been educated and transformed in prisons and sent back into society ready to uphold the responsibilities of citizenship. At a time when prisons are governed by an almost nihilistic focus on punishment, deterrence, and control, prison life writing has now more than ever returned to the story that has historically driven the rhetoric (if not the reality) of the modern prison system: the prison conversion narrative.

The role of the prison conversion narrative in the life writings of imprisoned people has changed, however. For one thing, prison life writings have come to focus less on theoretical analyses of crime, punishment, economics, and race; they are now often more individualistic, even entrepreneurial. This has been the result of multiple factors, including the waning of public interest in Marxism as an explanatory model for domestic and global oppression, the collapse of the prisoners' rights movement, the rise of the "New Right," the international dominance of neoliberalism, and the fading public perception that imprisoned people are victims.

To explore how prison life writing during the era of the carceral state uses the prison conversion narrative, and to explain what such uses might mean, I consider two books that are representative of the genre's developments in recent years: Jimmy Santiago Baca's acclaimed 2001 autobiography *A Place to Stand: The Making of a Poet* and Shakha Senghor's similarly well-received 2013 autobiography *Writing My Wrongs: Life, Death, and Redemption in an American Prison*. Both books use the conversion paradigm to articulate how Baca and Senghor changed their lives through reading and writing and emerged from prison as different people capable of participating in social spheres that are largely distinct from the criminalized communities they inhabited before their incarceration. In both books, reading and writing are represented as having had an alchemical effect on Baca's and Senghor's identities while they were imprisoned, transforming them from impulsive and violent to introspective and sympathetic, qualities that made them more amenable to social inclusion outside prison but that also have complicated ideological underpinnings that trouble their books' humanist projects. In *A Place to Stand* and *Writing My Wrongs*, reading and writing produce the emotional and psychological qualities associated with good citizenship, but the acquisition of these qualities risks reproducing narratives of personality development and belonging that are also marked by problematic histories of race and class.

The act of writing and publishing an autobiography also inoculates Baca and Senghor from their past criminality – a beneficial effect of prison life writing. Both *A Place to Stand* and *Writing My Wrongs* are written by formerly incarcerated men (although an initial draft of *Writing My Wrongs* was composed in prison), and their use of the conversion narrative paradigm, with its clear division between a pre-conversion identity of the past and a post-conversion identity of the present – a distinction that is repeatedly defined in conversion narratives as near-absolute (although, as I will show with Senghor, that distinction can simultaneously be permeable) – enables them to acknowledge and discuss their criminality even while distancing themselves from it.

That said, the *ways* these books inoculate their authors have quite different ideological effects. In *A Place to Stand*, Baca represents his conversion as a metaphorical transformation from animal to human. However, as he changes from animality to humanity, he concurrently represents other imprisoned people as increasingly animalistic and primitive. This has strong parallels with Cesare Lombroso's thinking about the "atavistic criminal." Lombroso, a nineteenth-century proto-criminologist, associated animality with criminality. In this way, Baca simultaneously breaks and reinforces the raced and classed boundaries between imprisonment and US citizenship, unintentionally justifying the prison as rehabilitative (for him) but also as a necessary method of control (for the other incarcerated people).[3]

By contrast, *Writing My Wrongs* funnels Shaka Senghor's story into the techno-capitalist figure of the African American "community builder," an entrepreneurial role that bridges diverse and often incongruous fields such as community organizing, activism, and finance capitalism. Senghor places his prison experience at the centre of his role as a community builder, using the prison conversion narrative's peculiar dichotomy between old and new identities both to immunize himself from his past criminal self and to legitimate his work as a public figure, mentor, and motivational speaker who consults on topics such as "Prison Complex and Reform," "Atonement and Literature," understanding PTSD, and non-violent conflict resolution.[4]

With the help of his autobiography, which provides the blueprint for personality development that made his post-prison career possible, he commodifies his criminality, converting what I call *carceral capital* into economic capital, a process that challenges historically racist assumptions about black masculinity even while legitimating the prevailing economic system that has long directed economic opportunities down racialized paths.[5] For good reason, African American prison life writing has long been deeply suspicious and even openly hostile to capitalism (as exemplified most notably by Black Power era writers like George Jackson). As *Writing My Wrongs* demonstrates, contemporary prison life writing often has a less confrontational relationship with capitalism even as it continues to draw from the revolutionary rhetoric and practices of earlier anti-capitalist traditions.

Like all the life writings discussed in this book, *A Place to Stand* and *Writing My Wrongs* are unique but also exemplary. In particular, Baca's and Senghor's works illustrate two trends in prison life writing. Of course, Baca's work epitomizes the story of the incarcerated person turned creative writer. This tradition includes Chester Himes, Edward Bunker, and Malcolm Braly. But Baca's story about becoming a poet in prison also resonates with the many stories of people who find poetry behind bars, including Etheridge Knight (who wrote that he "died in 1960 from a prison sentence and poetry brought [him] back to life"), Norma Stafford, and Reginald Dwayne Betts.[6]

Senghor's memoir self-consciously aligns itself with the African American prison life writing tradition, particularly with the work of activists and political prisoners, including Malcolm X and George Jackson, but while his work does address the socio-economic and racialized features of mass incarceration, his memoir follows an entrepreneurial narrative that is increasingly being used by formerly imprisoned people. It has been used by, or has been applied to, formerly incarcerated people like Divine, the founder and CEO of BLAK Fintech, a tech-finance company that provides financial and banking services to the "financially excluded"; Frederick Hutson, the founder of Pigeonly, a tech company focused on easing communication between incarcerated and non-incarcerated people; and Trevor Brooks, the founder of GunBail, an app that allows people to exchange illegal weapons for a reduction in bail money.[7] Along with Senghor, these men participated in a speaking tour called "From Incarceration to Innovation," a title that encapsulates how the conversion narrative has, in recent years, been grafted onto narratives of black entrepreneurship.[8]

Ultimately, while *A Place to Stand* and *Writing My Wrongs* set out how white supremacy and socio-economic status are causal factors of crime and imprisonment, their narratives emphasize personal responsibility, individual choice, and hard work as the qualities that ensured their authors' successful transition from prison to citizenship – features that fold their stories into traditional American bootstraps narratives and thus make them more amenable to a reading public that is often more interested in stories of individual uplift than in addressing the structural features of systematic inequality that make mass incarceration possible. There are limited avenues available to imprisoned and formerly imprisoned people to demonstrate to a public highly suspicious of them that they belong in the outside world and can develop the requisite qualities of citizenship. This is most especially significant for formerly incarcerated people of colour like Baca and Senghor, who may have been released from prison but who still must navigate the *de facto* and *de jure* restrictions of the New Jim Crow. The complexities of post-prison life in the Progressive and Treatment Eras, which profoundly affected white men like Panzram and Abbott, have dramatically increased since the 1980s, particularly for imprisoned people of colour, and this has left formerly incarcerated people with very few options for legitimating themselves in the outside world.

Finally, I would be remiss if I did not note that both Baca and Senghor are actively involved in supporting and advocating for incarcerated and formerly incarcerated people. Baca's not-for-profit, Cedar Tree, Inc., promotes literacy among underserved communities, including people in prisons. Senghor is involved in different kinds of advocacy work, including the Atonement Project, a class at the University of Michigan that was co-taught by Senghor and Dr. Ashley Lucas from 2013 to 2015.[9] Baca and Senghor are representative of the many formerly incarcerated men and women actively involved in bettering the lives of imprisoned people.

"MY DEEPEST MOMENT OF REFLECTION": BACA, SENGHOR, AND THE PRISON CONVERSION NARRATIVE

Before exploring how *A Place to Stand* and *Writing My Wrongs* diverge aesthetically and ideologically, I want to consider their similarities, particularly how both books follow the rehabilitation-through-education paradigm of the prison conversion narrative and how Baca and Senghor's reading and writing has changed them emotionally and psychologically – a transformation that is a common feature of prison life writing that engages conceptions of personality development associated with the acquisition of full citizenship.

In his International Prize–winning memoir, *A Place to Stand*, Baca recounts his traumatic childhood, his involvement in the drug trade, and his incarceration. Family is central to Baca's memoir. He tells his story for his sons, he explains in the book's prologue, employing a common framing device in the American autobiographical tradition that can be traced to Benjamin Franklin's *Autobiography* (which begins with the salutation "Dear Son").[10]

In the book, Baca's parents play a formative but tragic role in his life. His father, Damacio, is an alcoholic who leaves his family for long stretches of time; when he returns, he is often drunk and abusive.[11] Baca's mother, Cecilia, abandons the Baca family when Jimmy is only seven years old. She leaves to live with a white man named Richard and tries to pass as a white woman named "Sheila" (though she is Latina). Cecilia and Richard eventually have children of their own, and Cecilia refuses to acknowledge the Baca children as part of her family.

Jimmy Baca lives with his grandparents for a time, but when his grandfather dies, he is taken to St. Anthony's Boys' Home in Albuquerque with his older brother, Mieyo. (We later learn that his brother and mother die tragically. Mieyo is found murdered in an alley. Cecilia is shot and killed by her husband, Richard.) After repeatedly running away from St. Anthony's, Baca is transferred to a detention centre for boys, the first in a long line of increasingly punitive forms of incarceration that govern his adolescence and young adulthood. Holding cells, drunk tanks, and jails ultimately circumscribe his young life after he absconds from the detention centre for boys with his brother. In 1973, Baca is charged with drug-trafficking, sentenced to five years in prison, and incarcerated at Arizona's maximum security Florence State Prison (FSP). In prison – actually, initially in solitary confinement – against all odds, he teaches himself to read and write. He begins to write poetry, which becomes an outlet for him in prison and eventually a calling. That is, writing poetry becomes both a form of employment and an identity for him after he is released (hence the subtitle of his memoir, *The Making of a Poet*).

Although Senghor's *New York Times*–bestselling autobiography, *Writing My Wrongs*, shares narrative (and other) features with Baca's *A Place to Stand*, his story is in many ways quite different. Most obviously, *A Place to Stand* is a southwestern story that engages with a Chicano cultural experience and literary (and penal) tradition (which B.V. Olguín in *La Pinta: Chicana/o Prison Literature, Culture, and Politics* [2010] calls "the pinto picaresque," a subgenre that features "a Mexican American underclass antihero who animates the unique subcategory of modern picaresque literature"),[12] whereas *Writing My Wrongs* speaks to African American urban life, particularly to life on the margins in a post-industrial Detroit that has been profoundly impacted by the loss of manufacturing jobs, white flight, and the crack epidemic.[13] Senghor describes how, after his parents' divorce, he increasingly involved himself with drug-dealing on Detroit's East Side. Selling crack cocaine was dangerous work. In 1990, Senghor was shot during an argument. He survived, but experienced symptoms of psychological trauma after recovering from his wounds, which he says motivated him to carry a gun for self-defence. In 1991, he would use that weapon to murder a man in a late-night argument after a party.

For shooting and killing this man, Senghor was convicted of second-degree murder and given a forty-year prison sentence. Like Baca, though, he changed in prison, a transformation he attributes to family – particularly to his desire to be a better father to his children – and to inspirational mentors who helped him in prison, but mostly to the transformative power of literature, both reading and writing. And, like Baca, Senghor took to writing behind bars. He also studied the business end of publishing with the intention of establishing his own publishing house upon his release.

After serving nineteen years of his sentence, Senghor was released from prison. He then worked to establish himself as a publisher, writer, and, for a time, part-time journalist with *The Michigan Citizen*. Senghor also pursued work as a public speaker, counsellor, mentor, and community leader. He earned a community fellowship through BMe (Black Male Engagement), a pilot program established by the Knight Foundation, a not-for-profit organization focused on cultivating community development, the arts, and journalism. Through this work, Senghor became involved with a group of entrepreneurs, post-secondary institutions, and not-for-profit organizations – particularly the MIT Media Lab, IDEO (a design firm), and the University of Michigan – who were interested in providing community support and development in Detroit. As I will show, although much of his autobiography was written in prison before he was released, the story of conversion and transcendence reproduced in his autobiography has played an important role in establishing his legitimacy on the outside, including in relation to these various institutions.

Baca and Senghor map their stories of crime, imprisonment, and redemption according to the prison conversion narrative paradigm in similar ways. Notably, they foreground the conversion narrative in their respective prologues – similar writerly decisions that are common in prison life writing and that are likely bound up with concerns about legitimacy. For example, in his prologue, Baca writes, "If prison was the place of my downfall, a place where my humanity was cloaked by the rough fabric of the most primitive manhood, it was also the place of my ascent. I became a different man, not because prison was good for me, but in spite of its destructive forces. In prison I learned to believe in myself and dream for a better life."[14]

Fall, conversion, renewal: Baca's "downfall" in prison, like the "rock bottom" of the Alcoholics Anonymous conversion paradigm, is both his lowest point and the circumstance that produces his conversion, his "ascent" toward a hoped-for "better life." Baca becomes "a different man," employing the defining metaphor of the conversion narrative, the new self. Baca writes that the prison is "destructive" rather than rehabilitative and contends that he converted into a different man "in spite of" his incarceration. However, as I have shown, the prison has, at least in discourse, a productive function as well. It demands that imprisoned people change. Baca's account of his conversion is similar to the one laid down by prison reformers and penologists, particularly in the postwar period – a rhetorical convergence that, as I will show, troubles Baca's self-representation in the book as a "witness" who records the experiences of his fellow incarcerated people and speaks on their behalf.[15]

Shaka Senghor's prologue to *Writing My Wrongs* features a similar scene that draws on the rhetorical features of conversion: "I stared at the mirror, watching the tears roll slowly down my face, each drop carrying the pain of my childhood. I was on my second year of a four-and-a-half-year stint in solitary confinement. It was my deepest moment of reflection, a sacred moment of clarity when I came face-to-face with true forgiveness."[16]

Here, Senghor is using the vocabulary of conversion: solitary confinement produces the conditions for his "deepest moment of reflection," a "sacred moment of clarity" that results in self-recognition – a metaphor for self-awareness made literal here since he is "face-to-face" in the mirror, an experience that results in the cathartic experience of "true forgiveness." The prologue foreshadows a more detailed description of this moment, which happens later in the narrative, and which he calls his "true awakening," his "transformation," when, like Malcolm Little becoming Malcolm X, he takes a new name, thus memorializing his conversion: "the man Shaka was born and the boy Jay was laid to rest."[17] Like Baca, Senghor foregrounds his conversion in the prologue, establishing in advance of the narrative proper a way to perceive the direction of his story.

By foregrounding their conversion experiences in their prologues (and even in their subtitles: *The Making of a Poet* and *Life, Death, and Redemption* underscore the personal transformations featured in their life writings), Baca and Senghor provide framing devices that help sanction their books as worthy of readers' attention. As I have suggested in this book's introduction, readers are often suspicious of imprisoned (or formerly imprisoned) writers, so prison life writings sometimes seek to address and mollify readers' ethical concerns, particularly in the crucial opening pages of a book.

This technique can take a number of forms. Earlier imprisoned writers sometimes bookended their narratives with brief explanations about the pedagogical value of their stories: by reading a particular story of crime, a reader was supposed to be dissuaded from the temptations of criminality (even though this moral component competed with the cultivation of a reader's interest in the narrator's life of crime, which usually took precedence in the story itself). This moral framework may be a holdover from criminal narratives that appeared in the eighteenth century, before the American Revolution, which similarly bookended a criminal's exploits with moral instruction.[18] Providing a conversion narrative in the prologue performs a similar function. It seeks to appease a wary reader by situating a story of crime within a moral structure; it ensures the reader that however far the story might drift into seemingly unethical territory, it will inevitably return to its morally acceptable mooring. In other words, by previewing their conversions in their prologues, Baca and Senghor provide narrative templates for the events that follow in their books, thus guaranteeing that, whatever happens, their stories will eventually cohere around the narrative subjects' self-transformation into recognizably moral people. Foregrounding their conversions thus invites readers to trust the formerly incarcerated authors; it also assures those readers that they are different from the men who committed the crimes related in their stories.

Like most authors of prison life narratives, Baca and Senghor figure their conversions as largely the result of reading and writing. For both men, this happens in solitary confinement, the most restrictive form of incarceration, the deepest level in the prison's disciplinary hierarchy. In *A Place to Stand*, Baca presents his transformation in solitary, or what he and the other imprisoned people at Florence call "the dungeon," in this way: "poetry helped make me the person I am today, awakening creative elements that had long lain dormant in me, opening my mind to ideas, and enabling my intellect to nourish itself on alternative ways of being."[19] In the dungeon, Baca begins to exchange letters with a man named Harry, who picked Baca's name from a church list of imprisoned people who had no one on the outside with whom they could correspond. Harry supplies Baca with a dictionary, and, like Malcolm X in Norfolk Prison Colony, Baca spends time looking up words, copying their meaning, and writing short letters. Baca also copies the religious pamphlets that Harry sends to him, not for their religious content but to "practice writing sentences." At first, he struggles with the language, "plodding word by word to write a clear sentence," but soon his efforts at writing develop into more critical engagements with his past and with the prison environment.[20]

Around this time, Baca also begins to write poetry – a literary form that, for him, becomes constitutive of his identity. If, as *A Place to Stand*'s subtitle suggests, Baca's memoir is *The Making of a Poet*, then that "making" is both autogenetic, since he is entirely self-taught, and under conditions that precede him: as I have shown, prison discourse and the prison life writing genre have already redefined the prison cell (and especially the solitary confinement cell) as an educational space, as what Zebulon Brockway calls "a college."

Similarly, Shaka Senghor's biography on his website summarizes the transformative role that studying played for him: "I spent my time [in prison] reading and writing, using books to free my mind and expand my thinking. I clung to words – my own and others – as I pulled myself out of the anger that led me to prison and kept me from reaching my full potential." In *A Place to Stand*, Baca reimagines his prison cell as a kind of monastic space; in *Writing My Wrongs*, Senghor literally reconstructs his prison cell as a "school." While in solitary confinement, he tries to create a classroom environment by designing his own curriculum, which covers "political science and African history" and "religion and psychology." These homemade courses involve developing his own quizzes and tests, which help ensure that he is "retaining the information," as well as borrowing heavily from the prison library. In what feels like a self-conscious nod to the imagery of Malcolm X's self-transformation, Senghor describes himself reading "late into the night." "But," he writes, "real changes came when I started keeping a journal. Anytime I got angry at one of the other inmates, I would immediately grab a lined notepad and begin writing down what I wanted to do to him and why."[21]

In Senghor's "school," writing serves multiple purposes: it is educational, recreational, and therapeutic. This therapeutic component is especially interesting in that Senghor's journaling introduces autobiography into the educational and rehabilitative space of his cell. These personal autobiographical acts are reflective, like the reflective surface of the mirror in his prologue where he has a "face-to-face" interaction that catalyses his "deepest moment of reflection" and results in his finding "true forgiveness." He describes his journals as similarly reflective surfaces: they allow him to record his experiences, and his emotional reactions to those experiences, so that he can return to contemplate them later. When rereading his journals, he encounters a reflection of himself in his notebooks, and that reflection slowly changes his behaviour and eventually his identity.

I deliberately underscore the language of reflection here because it is a metaphor that prison reformers have often used to explain the work of the solitary confinement cell. Senghor's aforementioned "deepest moment of reflection" in solitary confinement, which happens before a mirror and thus pairs a literal reflection with a figurative reflection, also enacts how early prison reformers believed solitude would affect an imprisoned person's consciousness. As Beaumont and Tocqueville wrote in their report, solitude was supposed to "conduct [the prisoner] to reformation by reflection."[22] Similarly, according to a commissioned report about Eastern State Penitentiary, Robert Vaux, one of the early prison reformers who developed the penitentiary, hoped that total seclusion would force the incarcerated person "to have an opportunity to reflect on his transgressions so that he might repent."[23] In *The Prison and the American Imagination*, Caleb Smith explains that this was the point of the early penitentiary's solitary confinement cell: "the stone walls of the cell were not supposed only to confine the offender's body"; "Instead, the reformers imagined that the walls would become the mirrored surfaces of *reflection*, leading convicts to reckon with themselves and their crimes" (Smith's emphasis). What distinguishes Senghor's experience from the plans of the early reformers, of course, is the centrality of reading and writing to this reflective process. Solitude may give him time for introspection, but writing produces a specific kind of reflection that has an effect on his behaviour and, notably, on his emotions.

Baca and Senghor are both changed through reading and writing, and part of that change is figured as a reconstitution of their emotions – an affective transformation that repeats characteristics that figure widely in Western discourse around education, emotion, personhood, and citizenship. In *A Place to Stand*, Baca's education does more than provide him with reading and writing skills. He finds that writing improves his "self-esteem"; he learns self-discipline; he increases his capacity for introspection and self-reflection, which are the buds of his blossoming sense of empathy and civic responsibility; and, as his pen-pal Harry suggests, writing begins to provide him with a vocabulary for "mak[ing] a better human being of [him]self."[24] Harry's peculiar rhetorical turn here links the book's subtitle (*The* Making *of a Poet*) with a humanist teleology that will become an important but problematic metaphor in the book as Baca tries to articulate the depth of his self-transformation and how that change distinguishes him from the other imprisoned men around him.

Similarly, Senghor repeatedly explains how his labours change him emotionally: from unthinking to thinking, from unfeeling to feeling, from violent to compassionate. Before his conversion, his feelings were dominated by fear, impulsive anger ("the toxic hatred from my past"), and an inability to feel empathy: "I didn't realize it then, but I was growing desensitized to the suffering of others."[25] Beginning with the drug trade and extending into the prison, he transforms "into a callous, apathetic, coldhearted predator," he explains.[26] But through reading and writing, he changes. He feels himself "becoming a leader, a deep thinker, and a man of self-control – the kind of man that [his] readings of African history had inspired [him] to become."[27] As a result of his readings, he learns to be compassionate; he feels empathy for the other men imprisoned with him.[28]

The discovery of these emotions is consistently represented through metaphors of depth: "Deep down, I was ashamed of my own fear"; "I needed to get my thoughts and feelings out"; "I had changed the deepest parts of me."[29] Now, depth metaphors are obviously the most common way to conceptualize interiority and introspection, or one's unspoken thoughts and feelings. But in *Writing My Wrongs*, the very capacity for depth is figured as an *effect* of reading and writing: through reading and writing – especially journaling – Senghor creates the conditions for self-reflection and contemplation that he claims were lacking when he was on the streets dealing drugs or in prison, before he began his educational regimen. So for Baca and Senghor, reading and writing are civilizing technologies since they change both men from being impulsive, violent, angry, and unfeeling to self-controlled, introspective, and compassionate: qualities that dovetail with narratives of education and personal growth that figure reading and writing as demarcating the boundaries of citizenship.

Baca and Senghor illustrate how the linkages between literacy, literature, affect, and citizenship that critics have argued cohere around the teleology of the Bildungsroman are also at work in the conversion narratives of American incarcerated people. In *Human Rights, Inc.: The World Novel, Narrative Form, and International Law* (2007), Joseph Slaughter shows how the Bildungsroman shares with human rights law a narrative of "human personality development" where reading and writing produce the emotional, intellectual, and social qualities necessary for civic participation in modern society.[30] These qualities are precisely what Baca and Senghor achieve through reading and writing in prison; they include rationality, interiority (a "highly interiorized stage ... of consciousness"), self-regulation, and compassion: as Slaughter explains, citing Lynn Festa, these qualities ostensibly enable "an act of imaginative, affective 'extension of humanity to hitherto disenfranchised subjects'" – like other imprisoned people.[31] According to Slaughter, the capacity to read and write is, in the rhetoric of human rights discourse, a prerequisite for someone to participate in the Habermasian liberal public sphere: "With its discursive, idealized alignment with modernity, democracy, and liberty, literacy becomes the primary qualification and capacity for participation in ... 'a free society' – a society that writes about itself as a 'lettered city.'"[32]

For incarcerated people seeking inclusion in American society after their incarceration, or formerly imprisoned people claiming that they belong in American life despite the myriad legal and extra-legal ways that they are reminded they are outsiders (from limited voting rights to "checking the box" when seeking employment), reading and writing are the figurative keys that unlock the gate to full participation in the "lettered city" of American liberal democracy. Moreover, the stories of affective and intellectual growth presented by Baca and Senghor are not simply seeking to illustrate how they acquired the requisite characteristics of citizenship; their published books, which attest to their status as authors, legitimate their social inclusion in this literate society.

Baca and Senghor use the prison conversion narrative to articulate how reading and writing changed them from abject outsiders, who seemingly could not bear the burden of citizenship, to notable insiders, who met and exceeded the characteristics for civic participation and belonging (including belonging within the rarified space of the literate public sphere). However, as I will show, this seemingly benign celebration of the transformative power of literature can have problematic consequences. Now that I have identified some of the features of the prison conversion narrative in *A Place to Stand* and *Writing My Wrongs*, and explained how both books present reading and writing as having had psychological and emotional effects on their authors that made them fit for citizenship, I want to consider how they have taken this belonging in different directions – directions that indicate how using the prison conversion narrative, which is already freighted with meaning in prison discourse, can funnel claims of belonging into forms that can undercut the progressive projects that both books pursue.

FROM "PRIMITIVE MANHOOD" TO "HUMANITY": *A PLACE TO STAND*, PRISON IDEOLOGY, AND THE ATAVISTIC CRIMINAL

In *A Place to Stand*, Baca's conversion from illiterate imprisoned person to poet turns on a metaphor of becoming human – what he explains in his prologue as changing from "primitive manhood" to "humanity" – that is also a foundational metaphor for the US prison system. Caleb Smith, in *The Prison and the American Imagination*, argues that the early prison, the penitentiary, was conceived as a system for re-creating the teleology of the social contract, a narrative of social development that pivots on a transformation from animality to humanity. Deriving his claims from an analysis of Jean-Jacques Rousseau's classic text of Enlightenment political philosophy, *The Social Contract*, and the writings of early prison reformers, Smith writes that

> the social contract, as it was conceived in the enlight-
> ened and sentimental discourses of the late eight-
> eenth and early nineteenth centuries, required the

> figurative sacrifice of natural (or animal) life as a pre-
> condition for the acquisition of the citizen's spiritual
> (or human) subjectivity. The civil state was founded
> through a process of mortification and reanima-
> tion. This was the new political myth that was to
> be played out in the rituals of the new institution
> of punishment ... In the modern age, the peniten-
> tiary would enact the abjection of the body and the
> birth of the citizen's refined, self-governing soul – it
> would sacrifice [what Jean-Jacques Rousseau called]
> the "stupid, limited animal" and conjure, from its
> remains, an "intelligent being and a man."[33]

For Rousseau, writes Smith, the process of conversion from the "natural (or animal) ... to the spiritual (or human)" state by way of an imagined contractual agreement had "transpired in a mythic past." In the figurative death of the (animal) criminal and in the resurrection of the (human) citizen, this originary drama of human self-making and political formation was "reanimat[ed]" in the US penitentiary.[34]

Smith celebrates Baca as a prison writer "whose project is one of resistance, even revolution." However, Baca stages his self-transformation through the citizen-making technology of literature as the movement from animality to humanity, one that Smith argues is a central metaphor for the rehabilitative project of the US prison system. This reveals how Baca's memoir and prison discourse are linked, and possibly even mutually reinforcing, though they may also be antagonistic.[35] As noted, in *A Place to Stand*, reading and writing produce the requisite qualities for citizenship, such as interiority, industriousness, self-discipline, and sympathy. Baca's acquisition of these qualities is dramatized in several key scenes that, importantly, distinguish him from the other incarcerated people. For example, Baca's newly acquired self-restraint and empathy are both revealed when he fights an imprisoned person named Boxer, a struggle that puts in motion the animal/human dichotomy that Baca uses to distinguish his pre-literate criminal past from his literate poet-self – the self who authored the memoir (and the "poet" whom the book's subtitle suggests is being "made" in the book). After overpowering Boxer, Baca kneels over the bloodied man, shank in hand, ready to strike a death blow. For an instant, he defines himself as Rousseau's pre-social contract animal, as violent and impulsive: "I towered over him like an animal with a survival instinct to kill."[36]

But the humanizing, citizen-making influences of literature intervene in the form of the imagined voices of Pablo Neruda and García Lorca, two poets who have proven influential to Baca and who function here as what Rousseau might call "voice[s] of duty": "While the desire to murder him was strong, so were the voices of Neruda and Lorca that passed through my mind, praising life as sacred and challenging me: How can you kill and still be a poet? Do you know you will forever be changed by this act?"[37]

What Smith describes as the social contract's "figurative sacrifice" of the animal as a "precondition for the acquisition of the citizen's spiritual (or human) subjectivity" is expressed here as an Abrahamic non-sacrifice where Baca seals his covenant with civil society: Baca, moved by a sense of human feeling for the other man, drops the shank and lets Boxer live. By refusing to murder Boxer, Baca is not just empathizing with Boxer as a fellow person with emotions and desires; he is also responding to Boxer in accordance with the Rousseauian "general will" that identifies and promotes the value of social interdependence.[38] In other words, to kill Boxer would not just harm one man and, perhaps, his family and friends; it would also inflict damage on the social body. Consequently, Baca is "forced to act upon other principles and to consult his reason before heeding his inclinations," a turn to reason and deferred desire that Baca continues to dramatize when he is faced with the violent demands of prison culture and the abjectivity of his fellow incarcerated people.[39]

And here is where the ideological implications of *A Place to Stand*'s use of the prison conversion narrative are acutely problematic: Baca's acquisition of the Enlightenment ideals of humanity and civility is facilitated by the imagined degeneration of his fellow imprisoned people. Like a bucket passing its counterweight in a well, his ascent is made possible by their fall. The more he reads and writes, the more he develops the paradigmatic attributes of the ideal Enlightenment subject: he is endowed with reason, self-determination, self-discipline (including deferred desire and sublimated anger), empathy, and civic responsibility. These characteristics are defined *against* those of the other imprisoned people, whom Baca sees by comparison as impulsive, violent, vulgar, bestial, and grotesque. The more human he becomes, the less human they appear as a result.

The animality of Baca's fellow incarcerated people is first made apparent after he tries unsuccessfully to persuade the prison reclassification committee to allow him to participate in the prison's educational programs. He registers his frustration with the prison's decision by refusing to work or engage in any form of socialization. As a result of his boycott, he is seen by the administration to pose a threat to its authority; so, after three weeks, prison guards remove him from his cell and march him to "the dungeon" (the aforementioned segregated section of the prison where he eventually learns to read and write). Baca's forced removal effects a permanent division between him and the other imprisoned people, one that he conveys through the imagery of wild animals waiting to ravage their prey: "[A guard] jabbed me with his stick and marched me down into the landing in the middle of the block. Cons stood at the bars as one voice then another and another cursed in a deafening roar. They shook the bars, yelping like hyenas snarling over a fresh kill. Their eyes were hard and glassy. I tried to tell myself they were cursing the guards, but it was me they were condemning."[40]

The image of imprisoned people shaking the bars of their cells like caged animals recalls Robert Lowell's poem "In the Cage," where incarcerated people, like "canaries," "beat their bars and scream."[41] But while Lowell's ornithological metaphor might destabilize the order of the prison through the use of "colour and sound," Baca's depiction of his fellow imprisoned people as blood-thirsty hyenas affirms the prison's retributive, control-oriented philosophy.[42] If incarcerated people are animals – particularly if they are hyenas, which in figurative terms would suggest they are "cruel, treacherous, and rapacious" – their incarceration can be justified, for it means containing their instinctive, innate, and involuntary violence.[43] Baca learns to develop a new capacity for self-reflection and interiority; conversely, the other imprisoned people seem to have no interiority whatsoever, just "hard and glassy" eyes. And as Baca learns to be more articulate through reading and writing, the other incarcerated men's speech is effectively reduced to a zoo-like cacophony of snarling and growling.

Baca experiences his expulsion from the community of imprisoned people as a revelatory moment. Through their bestial demeanour, the incarcerated men "revealed their secrets" to him.[44] In turn, this revelation initiates a process of self-revelation for *him*. He writes, "Their rage and censure were forcing me to find something out about myself which didn't exist yet but which I felt struggling to come out."[45] These reciprocal revelations are mirror-images of each other: when the other imprisoned people uncloak their *in*humanity, to invert the terms used by Baca in his prologue, Baca begins to see "something about [him]self" – assumedly the "humanity" that his prologue has allowed us to anticipate will be uncloaked over the course of the narrative. From this moment on, Baca increasingly defines himself as human and the other imprisoned people as animalistic or grotesque. Unlike Baca, they are unable to overcome their abjectivity. Ultimately, the human/animal binary establishes a *cordon sanitaire* between those who belong in American society and those who are, by nature of their seemingly inherent difference, destined to be excluded.

Certainly quite by accident, then, *A Place to Stand* reproduces the terms of savagery, animality, and primitivity that have haunted the figure of the criminal since at least the nineteenth century, when Cesare Lombroso studied people in prison and noticed that "there [was] nearly always something strange about their appearances."[46] For Lombroso, that something was frequently animalistic – for example, a criminal's "ape-like" physiognomy.[47] In the first edition of *Criminal Man* (1876), Lombroso developed these observations into an early criminological "science," famously concluding that criminals were "atavistic," prehistoric throwbacks to an earlier period of human evolution. He notes, for instance, that "the most horrendous and inhuman crimes have a biological, atavistic origin in those animalistic instincts that, although smoothed over by education, the family, and fear of punishment, resurface instantly under given circumstances."[48]

Lombroso's zoological study of criminals, which he refers to as "criminal anthropology" in the book's third edition (1884), pathologizes criminal behaviour and links it to an evolutionary theory of human development that places criminals in a hierarchy alongside animals and "savages."[49] Moreover, his study's insistence that crime was biological rather than environmental meant that criminals were largely unable to change, for crime was in their nature. This reduced any possible causal explanations for crime to the nature of the individual; it followed that structural problems such as poverty were largely incidental, perhaps influencing the outburst of primitive behaviour but not really constituting a legitimate determinate for crime, since crime was secondary to the primitive nature of the criminal.[50]

This biological understanding of crime was shared by eugenicists, who, like Lombroso, developed theories of white superiority and non-white savagery, and who ushered their racist theories of crime into legislation and criminal law, determining who was and who was not fit for social inclusion. The infamous Lothrop

Stoddard, whose work is satirized in F. Scott Fitzgerald's *The Great Gatsby*, writes in *The Revolt Against Civilization: The Menace of the Under Man* (1922) that "Asia, the American Indians, and the African Negroes" are "barbarian stocks," "congenital barbarians [who] have always been dangerous foes of progress."[51] These "congenital cavem[e]n, placed in civilization, [are] always in trouble and usually in jail."[52] They reappear in the criminal justice system, ultimately "eliminate[d] ... by prison and the scaffold."[53] Stoddard was an extreme example, but his virulent racism was nonetheless part of a much broader discourse that saw race and crime as linked within animalistic or primitivistic imagery.

This discourse changed over time, but it continued to play a role in representations of race and crime, including during the present era of mass incarceration, a period that often figures the incarcerated as animalistic or savage, immune to rehabilitation and change, and thus requiring a severely punitive and controlling prison system. For example, John Sloop, in *The Cultural Prison: Discourse, Prisoners, and Punishment* (1996), his exhaustive study of "mass-mediated representations of prisoners" (particularly in magazines), shows that the "violence of inmates is characteristically represented [during the period of mass incarceration] as animalistic and senseless, arising from warped personalities."[54] Although the conception of criminals as animalistic and violent that Sloop claims is endemic in popular representations of imprisoned people during the era of mass incarceration might be distinguishable from earlier theories developed by Lombroso or Stoddard, they are certainly share a similar pedigree. Baca's representation of the incarcerated as animalistic also participates in this tradition. Ultimately, *A Place to Stand*'s mapping of savagery and humanism, of radical otherness and assimilation, onto emotional and psychological qualities impedes rather than enables a view of imprisoned people as worthy of readers' sympathy.

The argument that incarcerated people are ontologically different from the non-imprisoned and therefore unable to uphold the requirements of citizenship is not part of the manifest content of *A*

Place to Stand. Instead, the book shows through Baca's story how his poverty and his experiences of racism and social exclusion set the stage for his criminal behaviour, and how prison makes its own violent subjects. Baca's memoir seems to function as a counter-narrative. As Baca himself laments in an interview, mainstream society predominantly regards imprisoned and formerly imprisoned people "as less than human, and therefore irredeemable." His work seeks to challenge this by "chronicl[ing] their hopes, doubts, regrets, loves, despairs, and dreams."[55] But what John Bender argues of *Oliver Twist* is also true of *A Place to Stand*: "Though [it] is plainly written as a humane attack on the institutions that help produce the delinquent milieu, the very terms of the attack strengthen the perception of delinquency that upholds the phenomenon."[56] Whatever its likely goals, *A Place to Stand* conflates criminality with animality, citizenship with humanity. As a result, the categories of criminality and citizenship that constitute the historical sediment of the US prison system's concept of rehabilitation achieve a degree of autobiographical truth because these terms are reiterated in the form of a memoir, which suggests that criminal/animal and citizen/human are not simply theoretical concepts, but represent, in fact, the "real life" of someone who has been imprisoned.

THE "WORLD HE REPRESENTS": *WRITING MY WRONGS*, THE COMMUNITY BUILDER, AND CARCERAL CAPITAL

Sometimes, like Baca, Senghor uses humanist rhetoric to represent his prison conversion experience. For example, when explaining that his desire to be a good father motivated his conversion, he writes, "I had to reclaim my humanity and soften my heart so that I could be a voice of reason and wisdom for my boy." Reading and writing helps him "reclaim [his] humanity," but this reclamation does not turn on a human/animal binary the way it does in *A Place to Stand*. However, Senghor's use of the prison conversion narrative commodifies and perhaps even fetishizes imprisonment.

The commodification of prison and crime is a common feature of prison life writing: prison writers are aware of their readers' prurient interest, so the genre often oscillates between sympathetic depictions of imprisoned people and sensational depictions of their crimes and misfortunes. Senghor, though, commodifies his imprisonment in a different way. His role as a public figure – a role in which he earns a living as a teacher, mentor, writer, and public speaker –depends on his making valuable and sellable his image as a reformed criminal and formerly incarcerated person, and this image is fraught with contradictions that the prison conversion narrative resolves but also exacerbates.

Senghor's autobiography plots the seemingly organic evolution of – and thus works to cohere and legitimate – his public identity as a reformed incarcerated person. In a way, the cultural work his autobiography performs is similar to that of a presidential candidate's autobiography, which is used to "project a whole, self-contained story" that is mobilized to "animate, iconize, and stabilize" a political identity.[57] Just as a presidential candidate's autobiography organizes the narrative subject's past so that its events lead, seemingly inevitably, to the candidate's public image, Senghor's story relates how the key features of his public image as a writer, mentor, and public speaker (the person who appears on his website, on Oprah, or on a TED Talk) emerged seamlessly out of his efforts at rehabilitating himself in prison.

In *Writing My Wrongs*, this process accelerates after Senghor is released from solitary confinement. After his release into the prison's general population, he immediately acquires a word processor and begins to type out the books he had written earlier on prison stationery in his solitary confinement cell. He seeks out a fellow imprisoned person who had started a publishing company when he was on the outside, and he starts to learn about the publishing business in the hopes of starting his own company. He also takes a business computer technology class, for he realizes that computers have come to dominate communication since he was incarcerated.

With the help of his then-fiancée, he works to shape his writing into a marketable commodity. Baca's story about becoming a poet adheres to a romantic notion of authorship as an ontological quality, where the poet is a kind of visionary, whereas Senghor's writing is in the service of his public identity, an identity that is itself a marketable commodity.

Senghor's evolution as a writer and publisher is also braided with his evolution as a public speaker and mentor – key components of his post-prison identity in the public sphere, represented most prominently in his lectures and most recognizably in his TED talk. After his stint in solitary, he and another incarcerated person, named BX, mentor younger imprisoned African Americans. They create "a males' rites of passage program" that teaches young black men skills like reading, studying, and responding "to life from a position of personal responsibility, reciprocity, and respect."[58] Here, and increasingly after his stint in solitary, he begins to apply the terms of his own rehabilitation to mentoring others – a practice that will become central to his entrepreneurial work after he is released from prison.

Senghor translates mentoring inside the prison into public speaking and self-help programs outside the prison. For instance, his website employs his prison conversion to advertise his mentoring and lectures: his "powerful talks [are] designed to change," and his work promises to help you "escap[e] the prison of your mind." In this way, he turns his redemption story into something commodifiable and transferrable.[59] According to his online promotional materials, his workshops reproduce the techniques he developed in prison. For example, in his workshop on "Atonement and Literature," he writes:

> Unpacking baggage from my past and getting to the
> core of my anger allowed me to take responsibility
> for my crimes and redirect my energy and talents.
> After years of self reflection [*sic*], I've been able to

transform and begin atonement for my mistakes ... In this talk, I address the themes of acknowledgement, apology and atonement. And discuss 'The Atonement Project,' an initiative that helps the healing and understanding between victims of violence and violent offenders through art, literature and tech. Also, the role that literature played in my transformation and the possibilities for others to do the same.[60]

Here, Senghor is linking his own "transformation" – a conversion that is fleshed out in his autobiography, which is prominently displayed on his website – with his public speaking, demonstrating how he enlists his prison experience, and even the rehabilitative discourse of the prison system itself, for his own entrepreneurial ventures. Where George Jackson corrupted the prison conversion narrative in order to critique the prison and the white supremacist, capitalist society that he believed the prison supported, Senghor has monetized that narrative, turning disciplinarity into self-help and self-promotion.

As I pointed out in this chapter's introduction, Senghor's multiple and interlocking post-prison roles as writer, mentor, activist, teacher, and public speaker can be consolidated under the rubric of "community-builder." The community-builder is an African American entrepreneurial figure who often balances not-for-profit work like community organizing, advocacy, and public speaking with work in investment banking, the technology industry, the university, and the entertainment industry. I take the term from the BMe Community website, which uses it to define the community work and social and civic responsibilities of some of the men whom they celebrate and to promote their workshops, which seek to cultivate the values BMe commends. This term also appears in Trabian Shorters's introduction to *Reach: 40 Black Men Speak on Living, Leading, and Succeeding*, a collection of brief biographical sketches of African American men who fit the community-builder role, from designers and entrepreneurs like D'Wayne Edwards to authors and celebrities like Van Jones.[61] Among other things, that book aims to provide positive examples of black masculinity for young black men while counteracting negative representations of black masculinity in American culture.

A recurrent theme of *Reach*, and one that is especially resonant in *Writing My Wrongs*, is the significance of black fatherhood. As noted earlier, Senghor in his autobiography represents fatherhood, or the desire to be a good father, as an important force behind his conversion. He reiterates his role as a father throughout his book; indeed, his own father's steadfast support of him while he was incarcerated and his father's role as a pillar of his family illustrate the moral values around parenting that are similarly promoted in *Reach*. The valuation of fatherhood is obviously inward-looking in the sense that it seeks to cultivate a positive identity for black men within black families and communities. But it is also outward-looking in that it resists popular misconceptions about black fatherhood in American culture that have often found expression in policy documents like *The Moynihan Report*, which blamed black poverty on single-mother homes and the absence of strong father figures.[62] By demonstrating his commitment to fatherhood, even while he was imprisoned, and figuring a desire to be a good father to his children as a motivating factor for his reform, Senghor counteracts myths about black masculinity and black criminality.

Yet Senghor's role as a community-builder is based on a monetization of his criminality. This monetization takes the form of repeated confessions: his website, his public speaking, his role as a mentor, and, of course, his autobiography all underscore that he has had to foreground his criminality and imprisonment in order to be accepted in the public sphere. This is a shrewd rewriting of the formerly incarcerated person's script, whose consequences I will address in a moment. But instead of feeling ashamed of his incarceration and allowing his prison record to limit his involvement in American life (including around employment, housing, and voting), he uses his story of redemption as a mark of his suitability for public life as a mentor, teacher, writer, and speaker in a move that I call using the prison as *carceral capital*.

In *Forms of Capital*, Pierre Bourdieu explains that cultural capital is the non-economic, often class-based cultural material that can be converted into money.[63] Bourdieu's concept has proven quite useful for explaining the more ambiguous but nonetheless valuable cultural elements of capital. For example, in *Club Cultures: Music, Media, and Subcultural Capital* (1995), Sarah Thornton reconfigures Bourdieu's term in order to address how dance cultures from the late 1980s and early 1990s established group identities and maintained hierarchies through non-tangible forms of cultural capital such as "hipness."[64] However, Thornton's groups are typically subcultural by choice, so their value in the public sphere is quite different from that of stigmatized groups like criminals and imprisoned people. *Carceral* capital alludes to how incarcerated and formerly incarcerated people can monetize their prison experiences by selling them to the reading public (as with prison life writing) or to a television or film audience (as in Danny Trejo's "authenticity"). Those same experiences can also serve as cautionary tales (as in the *Scared Straight!* television program), as a means to acquire a kind of street credibility that is valued by the entertainment industry (as with rappers who serve time), or even as a new fitness regimen (in the peculiar but seemingly successful "prison style bootcamp," ConBody).[65] Certainly, Senghor's monetization of his story of redemption and transcendence is using prison in a similar way, converting what might otherwise be a mark of exclusion in this New Jim Crow Era into money and even prestige.

However, Senghor uses his carceral capital in a way that depends heavily on the duality of the prison conversion narrative. He can speak to his experiences of crime and prison, which are alien to many readers and audiences, but he can do so without being perceived as a threat to his reading and listening public, for he has demonstrated (and he must continuously demonstrate) that he no longer belongs to a perceived criminal class. The liminality of his position – between an imagined criminal class and a non-criminal public – is what makes him appeal to readers, and perhaps also to not-for-profit organizations, post-secondary institutions, and entrepreneurs; all of these are helping him legitimate his role in the public sphere through the affiliations they offer him on the outside (from his fellowships with the MIT Media Lab and the Kellogg Foundation to his role as the Director of Strategy and Innovation with #cut50, a not-for-profit organization whose focus is on reducing US prison populations) and who have effectively sponsored his autobiography in the form of a foreword by Joi Ito, the director of the MIT Media Lab. This is not to suggest that Senghor does not deserve these affiliations or that they are in any way inauthentic – quite the contrary. But Senghor's liminal position, his balancing act between a criminal identity (of the past) and a public identity (of the present), has been partly stabilized by these institutional affiliates, which help validate his role in the public sphere and help ensure his employment as a public speaker, mentor, and teacher.

But these organizations demand something from him, too. In particular, they require him to serve a representative function, one that illuminates some of the complexities of Senghor's position as someone who speaks about an abject, often racialized and criminalized, subset of the population to people from very different social and economic spheres. For example, in his foreword to *Writing My Wrongs*, Joi Ito explains why he made "Shaka an MIT Media Lab Fellow": "He'd be our man in Detroit – our connection to the incredibly important world he represents."[66] In this formulation, Senghor "represents" a "world" that is foreign to the MIT Media Lab and its university, not-for-profit, and entrepreneurial affiliates. Ito and his organization are not necessarily claiming Senghor as a kind of native informant who speaks on behalf of "Detroit" – or rather, on behalf of an African American abject, poor, or working-class segment of the Detroit population that they want to help by launching various urban projects. But something of this relationship is at work here. Senghor plays an advisory role for organizations whose make-up is racially and economically distinct from the community they want Senghor to represent, and the rhetoric of "our man," with its discomfiting valences of ownership ("*our* man"), clandestine work (as in *Our Man in Havana*), or police supervision (as in the expression "that's our man"), certainly underscores the ideological slipperiness of Senghor's role in this relationship between groups with very different levels of power.

And Senghor often *participates* in this image-making. For example, when he is first introduced to Ito and Colin Rainey, a representative of IDEO (the aforementioned design firm), at a meeting organized by the Knight Foundation where Ito and Rainey introduce their vision for the City of Detroit, their approach to helping revitalize the city sounds interesting and courageous to Senghor, but he explains that their plans "were based not on actual, firsthand experience, but on the romanticized version of Detroit that often gets sold in media and the public imagination." Senghor explains to them during and after the meeting that they need to access and understand "the real Detroit":

> I felt like they hadn't understood the real Detroit or recognized the people who were already work-ing feverishly to make a difference in the city. So I decided to speak up. I raised my hand and told them that their ideas sounded great, but if they really wanted their work to make a difference, they needed to include the real Detroit in the conversation.[67]

Here, Senghor establishes a binary between romantic and "real," inauthentic and authentic, and moves to establish himself as a representative of the authenticity that is lacking in their approach to the city. After Ito and Rainey concluded their presentation,

Senghor approached the two men, introduced himself, and offered to "take them around Detroit and introduce them to some people who were doing amazing work. Colin and Joi looked at each other and agreed on the spot."[68] Authenticity, in this framework, denotes the activists in the city whose work Senghor wants to highlight and connect with these wealthy enterprises. But this authenticity is racialized and class-based, associated with the parts of the city that people like Ito and Rainey cannot readily access because, presumably, their manifest privileges would mark them as outsiders. Here, authenticity also risks collapsing innumerable connotations associated with this inaccessible geography, such as criminality, street life, poverty, incarceration, and, of course, blackness. Senghor is certainly doing good by seeking to intervene in a philanthropic project so as to best serve the community where he lives. But he occupies a difficult position when he mediates between very different positions of power, especially when activating social expectations about inner-city life.

Although Senghor promotes himself as a representative figure for this ostensibly inaccessible but authentic Detroit, he also registers his discomfort with this role, especially after these organizations enlist his help as a cultural intermediary so that they can make investments and interventions. In particular, the complexities of his position are illuminated when Colin Rainey asks him to act as a "tour guide" for a group from his organization that wants to visit Detroit. Senghor finds himself shepherding a group of MIT Media Lab affiliates around the city, and he takes note of the way they perceive the city and the people in it:

> As we drove down block after burned-out block in the capital of the Rust Belt, I watched the varied expressions of my passengers through the rearview mirror. Their faces registered emotions ranging from disbelief and sadness to intrigue and hopefulness. In my own heart, I felt a twinge of embarrassment

for our city, for the people who call Detroit home
– including myself. It felt like I was seeing Detroit
objectively for the first time, and it was painful to
witness what had happened to my beloved city.[69]

Senghor's "twinge of embarrassment" arises from a complex of
affective responses that he sees – or, rather, that he believes he sees
– register on the faces of the people who are looking at his city:
"disbelief and sadness to intrigue and hopefulness." Of course,
Senghor is not "seeing Detroit objectively" here but is instead
watching people from very different class (and likely racial) positions surveil his hometown, and their looking is invested with
myriad predetermined notions of what they expect to see on their
tour. Especially given how "surveillance in and of black life [is] a
fact of blackness," and how that watching is so heavily invested with
cultural presumptions about black identity (what Fanon in *Black
Skin, White Masks* calls the "thousand details, anecdotes, [and]
stories" woven around blackness by white people), this collective
observation of an impoverished black community from within the
confines of a moving car is ideologically unstable and unreliable,
as likely to drift into concerning stereotypes as it is to align with
the pedagogical goals of his tour.[70]

Senghor's tour participates, quite unintentionally, in a much
larger practice of ruin tourism that centres on Detroit, which is
often voyeuristic and fetishizes racialized poverty.[71] And the problems with this kind of touring are similar to the complications
that arise with Senghor's commodification of his past criminality
and imprisonment. His transformation of carceral capital into
economic capital on various media platforms fetishizes the prison
as a transformative space and his own experience behind bars as a
kind of self-help, besides promoting an idea of prison that is out of
step with most imprisoned people's experiences. Furthermore, as I
have suggested, he monetizes precisely what makes life so difficult
for most people who have been convicted of a felony: the inability

of formerly incarcerated people to be free of their ex-convict status, the requirement that they must always live in the blare of a criminal identity, and the fact that they must perpetually relitigate the terms of their release. What makes Senghor money is what makes most formerly incarcerated people's lives precarious. Although he keeps his redemption story in plain view so as to monetize it, and although he makes his story of prison rehabilitation shareable and marketable, most other imprisoned people are blocked from participating in American society because they have been forced to carry with them a stigma that is reflected back to them in myriad ways in American life, often until they find their place back in some form of incarceration.

CONCLUSION: PRISON LIFE WRITINGS AS *LOCUS STANDI*

Both Jimmy Santiago Baca in *A Place to Stand* and Shaka Senghor in *Writing My Wrongs* use the prison conversion narrative. *How* they use it takes their work in very different directions. For both men, the duality of conversion acts as a kind of social inoculation. For Baca, it enables him to transgress the boundary between outlaw and citizen, but at the same time, it rewrites those boundaries, even dredging up old paradigms of criminal animality in order to articulate how he achieves his citizenship. For Senghor, the duality of conversion enables him to foreground his criminality even while distancing himself from it, a dialectic that makes his public persona possible but also monetizes, even fetishizes, his criminality and imprisonment. Both books are about an identity-making that involves the constant reiteration of their status as formerly incarcerated people and a rejection of that status at the same time – a circle squared in the conversion narrative. And both books use the prison conversion narrative in order to find "a place to stand" in the American public sphere, a *locus standi* as either a poet or a community-builder that provides them with a measure of firm ground despite the precarity of post-prison life.

"LOVE IS CONTRABAND IN HELL"

WOMEN'S PRISONS, LIFE WRITING, AND DISCOURSES OF SEXUALITY IN *ASSATA* AND *AN AMERICAN RADICAL*

"The problem of the woman offender in Illinois
is not a criminal problem. It is a sex problem."
—Women's reformatory advocate, quoted in
Nicole Hahn Rafter, *Partial Justice*, 58

Love is contraband in Hell,
cause love is an acid
that eats away bars.
—Assata Shakur, *Assata: An Autobiography*, 130

SO FAR, I HAVE FOCUSED ON THE CONVERSION NARRATIVE TO explain how prison discourse has become woven into prison life writing, affecting what is sayable in the genre. But I have discussed exclusively the work of incarcerated and formerly incarcerated *men*, since conversion rarely features in the life writings of incarcerated and formerly incarcerated women. Of course, women's prison life writings also work with, and struggle against, prison discourse, but the dominant discourses that have been available to women, and that are enforced by women's institutions, are different. While women's prisons have historically been governed by similar philosophies as men's prisons, and while women's institutions have also sought to transform their incarcerated charges, they have generally focused with surprising consistency on changing women's sexual behaviour. As I will show, prisons have used sexuality to define, control, and discipline incarcerated women since the inception of women's separate institutions after the American Civil War.

Perhaps unsurprisingly, then, imprisoned women often describe, contest, and use the prison system's sexual discourses in their life writing. Their work demonstrates that sexual discourses are hardly static; they can align with power or resist it. As Foucault writes, discourse can be "an instrument and effect of power, but also a hindrance, a stumbling block, a point of resistance and a starting point for an opposing strategy." Understanding sexuality as constituting a "multiplicity of discursive elements that can come into play in various strategies" clarifies how, in women's prisons and women's prison life writings, sex can bolster or undermine power; it can legitimate patriarchal systems of control or enact alternatives to them.[1] Whereas the conversion narrative is a form of discipline that can be retooled to serve alternative and even subversive purposes in the life writing of imprisoned men, sexual discourses, which have coercive and disciplinary functions in women's institutions, can be adapted in the life writing of imprisoned women in a similar way.

In this chapter I explore the links between sexuality, power, and resistance in Assata Shakur's *Assata* and Susan Rosenberg's *An American Radical.* Shakur and Rosenberg both describe how their lives were transformed through their imprisonment; but *how* they represent those transformations (or not) illustrates how women's prison life writings work with some discursive materials that are notably different from those taken up by men. Shakur describes significant changes in her life while she was incarcerated, including giving birth to her daughter and, eventually, escaping prison. Rosenberg describes educating herself in prison and undergoing ideological changes, including revising her views on violence in the service of her political goals. But neither woman uses the plot or rhetoric of conversion to represent those experiences, and in this respect, their work reflects a general feature of women's prison life

writing as a genre. Women's prison life writing emphasizes different forms of transformation – ones that do not accord with the
conversion narrative structure that is virtually ubiquitous in the
life writing of incarcerated and formerly incarcerated men.

Instead of the conversion narrative, discourses of sexuality
feature prominently in their work. Through readings of Shakur and
Rosenberg's life writings, then, I consider how sexuality can be an
expression of, but also a mode of resistance to, violent institutional
power. I first provide a historical overview of how women's carceral
institutions were often developed as systems for policing seemingly aberrant sexualities. Then, through Shakur and Rosenberg's
autobiographies, I explore different ways that the prison system
seeks to define women's sexuality, thus functioning as a normative
institution in American society, while also using sexual violence as
a form of discipline. Both women relate how the prison uses the
discourse of sexual violence – particularly sexual abuse as a strategy
for shaming, humiliating, alienating, and dehumanizing its victims
– in order to assert its institutional authority. Their work demonstrates how women's prisons use violent sexuality to do gendered
ideological work that is particular to women's rather than men's
carceral institutions, even when similar forms of institutionalized
sexual violence happen in men's prisons too.

However, Shakur and Rosenberg's life writings also detail how
incarcerated women resist the prison system's use of sexual discourse
and sexual violence to isolate and control them by creating alliances, kinship groups, friendships, and even communities through
different performances of sexuality. As I will discuss in this book's
conclusion, reading for alliances, and identifying how incarcerated
people represent themselves as belonging and how diverse communities make belonging real for incarcerated people, is especially
important.

Of course, sexuality is by no means the only site of resistance
available to incarcerated women, perhaps especially for political
prisoners like Assata Shakur and Susan Rosenberg, who can draw

on a wide variety of supporters and alliances in order to resist the criminal justice system much like other incarcerated women political prisoners, from Emma Goldman (see her autobiography, *Living My Life*) to Marilyn Buck to Angela Davis.[2] And political prisoners like Shakur and Rosenberg detail the many ways that, with the help of outsiders who take an active interest in their well-being and their causes, they resist the prison and criminal justice systems as well as a "matrix of domination" that includes patriarchy, white supremacy, and capitalism, which they have committed their lives to combating.[3] For example, both books detail how Shakur and Rosenberg use the court system to assert their political positions, often at quite serious costs.[4] But I focus my analysis on sexuality because, as I have suggested, sexual discourse is a central focus of the US women's prison system; it is one of its guiding discourses, and, as with the conversion narrative, stories about women's sexuality produced in and about the prison system find their way into women's prison life writings in ways that reveal the complexities of writing about an institution with so much cultural power in American life.

"A SEX PROBLEM": WOMEN'S PRISONS AND DANGEROUS SEXUALITIES

Notwithstanding that women's prisons have seen significant changes since their inception in the nineteenth century, there have always been two fairly consistent guiding narratives at work in women's institutions: first, as I discussed in Chapter 1, the two different kinds of women's prisons – custodial institutions and reformatories – have long sought to return women to the domestic sphere as dependent subjects; and second, women's institutions were created to control women's sexuality. Nicole Hahn Rafter cites one nineteenth-century proponent of women's reformatories who underscored the centrality of women's sexuality to women's institutions and the wider criminal justice system: "'The problem of the woman offender in Illinois is not a criminal problem. It is a sex problem.'" Her solution, and the solution for many reformers of the period, was incarceration, which would isolate and contain dangerous women who might otherwise "scatter disease through every community."[5]

Women's reformatories initially focused much of their attention on retrieving fallen women, curing them of their promiscuousness, and returning them to the domestic sphere as chaste "angels in the house." Later, during the Progressive Era, the eradication of prostitution became a national project, and the anti-prostitution movement sought to establish women's reformatories throughout the country to curb out-of-wedlock sex (which was often grouped with other forms of non-marital sex and defined as prostitution) and to slow the spread of venereal disease.[6] Moreover, eugenicists believed that reformatories might limit the regeneration of natural-born criminals by locking up "promiscuous, feebleminded women," who, they argued, were the source of "generations of criminals, moral imbeciles, and the insane."[7] After the reformatory movement came to an end in the 1930s, a new generation of women who did not subscribe to the separate spheres ideology changed the focus of women's prisons. Even so, the concern with women's sexuality, most especially with prostitution and the spread of venereal diseases, remained a prominent focus of later women's institutions.

Throughout the history of women's prisons, black women's sexuality has been seen as especially dangerous. While reformers did not believe that black women were capable of what Barbara Welter calls "True Womanhood" (and so were presumed unfit for reformatories), they did believe that black women's purported licentiousness should be curtailed through women's custodial institutions. The defining of black women as especially promiscuous has a long history in America, and this characterization has consistently been used to legitimate white supremacist, patriarchal violence. Black women were repeated victims of sexual violence at the hands of white men under the slave system and during the violent backlash against Reconstruction; indeed, the myth of the overly sexual black woman transformed rape into consensual sex in the minds of many white Americans.[8] In *Colored Amazons: Crime, Violence, and Black Women in the City of Brotherly Love, 1880-1910*, Kali N. Gross describes how the myth of the sexually available black woman evolved in the twentieth century into that of the dangerous (but still sexually licentious) "colored Amazon," particularly after the Great Migration:

> White men's prior ownership, control, and uninhibited sexual access to black women had been, at least in theory, subverted in the modern era. As a result, somehow the ultimate submissive was transformed into what whites perceived as a dangerous urban aggressor. Moreover, depicted as large, dark, dangerous, and hypersexual, the Colored Amazon starkly contrasted with mainstream symbols of domesticity. Resting upon stereotypes that supported negative criminal inscription, the caricature chiseled out ideological boundaries of middle-class social and cultural values through its opposition.[9]

In other words, white, middle-class womanhood did not exist in isolation but was instead defined in opposition to a caricature of black womanhood. And predictably, stereotypes of black women as hypersexual *and* dangerous played a significant role in the increased policing and incarceration of black women in the twentieth century.[10]

But prisons did more than try to control women's sexuality; they also used – and continue to use – sexual violence against women to assert institutional dominance over them, which I see as a corollary to Foucault's theory of the carceral continuum. Foucault suggests that prisons are part of a wider network of punishment, discipline, and control that has saturated American culture.[11] I suggest that the institutional application of sexual violence in women's prisons is similarly linked with disparate forms of sexual violence outside the prison; this linkage functions as a kind of feedback loop, or Möbius strip, in the sense that sexuality is used to assert dominance and control over women and their bodies *within* prisons in ways that accord with men's use of sexual violence to dominate and control women *outside* prisons. Like musicians playing from a score composed elsewhere, and providing their own variations and improvisations on a theme they did not themselves compose, prison officials use sexual discourses that circulate throughout the wider culture, performing something that is unique to the institution (as in legal cavity searches) but also horrifyingly familiar to those who witness or experience it.

Sexual violence is part of many men's prison experiences (as I have discussed), and it is certainly a concern in men's prisons, but it does not interlock with sexual violence outside prison in the same way for men as it does for women. Men rarely experience sexual assaults outside prison. So sexual assault in men's prisons is generally understood as an exceptional rather than a normative form of violence. By comparison, as the authors of *Inner Lives: Voices of African American Women in Prison* write, "In 1997 ... the GAO [Government Accounting Office] reported that approximately 40 percent of female inmates in federal prisons and approximately 57 percent of female inmates in state institutions had histories of physical or sexual abuse prior to their incarceration. Sixty-nine percent of women under correctional-system authority reported that physical or sexual abuse occurred before they reached eighteen years of age."[12] Thus, as Angela Davis writes in *Are Prisons Obsolete?*, "sexual abuse – which, like domestic violence, is yet another dimension of the privatized punishment of women – has become an institutionalized component of punishment behind prison walls." For women, Davis explains, "prison is a space in which the threat of sexualized violence that looms in the larger society is effectively sanctioned as a routine aspect of the landscape of punishment behind prison walls."[13]

Although Davis writes that this kind of abuse has become part of the institution's violence, it has a long history in women's carceral spaces. For example, in the "southern carceral regime" of the early twentieth century, writes Sarah Haley in *No Mercy Here: Gender, Punishment, and the Making of Jim Crow Modernity*, "the state institutionalized gendered racial terror as a technology of white supremacist control, and often this state violence compounded intraracial intimate abuse that [black women] faced in their homes."[14] As I will show in my discussion of Assata Shakur's autobiography, what Davis describes as the "threat of sexualized violence" that women experience outside prison – which interlocks with white supremacy in especially insidious ways – has been, and continues to be, employed by the state as a disciplinary technique inside prison that normalizes sexuality as an expression of patriarchal dominance and control.

REVOLUTIONARY SEXUALITY: WOMEN'S PRISON LIFE WRITINGS, STATE AND NON-STATE SEXUAL VIOLENCE, AND *ASSATA: AN AUTOBIOGRAPHY*

In 1973, Assata Shakur and two other members of the Black Liberation Army (BLA), Sundiata Acoli and Zayd Malik Shakur, were driving on the New Jersey Turnpike when they were pulled over by a New Jersey state trooper named James Harper, who was supported by another state trooper, Werner Foerster. A shootout ensued, Foerster and Zayd Malik Shakur were killed, and Assata Shakur was seriously wounded. After she surrendered, Assata Shakur was incarcerated and charged with first-degree murder, along with numerous other charges stemming from the New Jersey Turnpike shootout and the murder of trooper Foerster. However, over a span of four years, she was tried in seven criminal trials on a variety of different charges, including bank robbery, murder, and attempted murder, stemming from multiple incidents. Although she was repeatedly acquitted in most of the cases, she was eventually convicted in 1977 of the charges associated with the New Jersey Turnpike shootout and sentenced to life in prison. In 1979, members of the BLA freed Shakur from New Jersey's Clinton Correctional Facility for Women by taking guards hostage with guns and a stick of dynamite. In 1984, Shakur turned up in Cuba, where she was granted political asylum and where she continues to live today. The US government, in conjunction with the State of New Jersey, has made repeated efforts to have her extradited, so far without success. Her autobiography was published in 1987.

Assata: An Autobiography dramatizes what I have described as a feedback loop, where sexual violence outside the prison interlocks with sexual violence inside the prison. In her book, Shakur explains how, well before she was incarcerated, she had to repeatedly fend off multiple incidents of sexual assault and attempted rape. For example, she describes how, when she was younger, the manager of a cafeteria where she was employed as a server would repeatedly grope her while she was working and use his position of authority to continue assaulting her until, later the same day that she started the job, she quit.[15] In the same chapter, she relates how several boys tried to gang-rape her; she managed to escape by fighting back and alerting a neighbour.[16]

The boys who tried to rape her were black, but she remembers thinking that they were behaving "as if [she] wasn't even human, as if [she] was some kind of thing," a dehumanization of her that she traces back to the plantation era, when slaves internalized white men's view of black women as sexually available and less than human, as "breeders."[17] Here, Shakur's autobiography provides a critical counterpoint to the stories of sexual violence in the life writings of black men like James Carr and Nathan McCall (and, one might add, Eldridge Cleaver, who famously claims in *Soul on Ice* that at one time he thought of rape as "an insurrectionary act").[18] Shakur explains how the violent dehumanization of women is misogynistic and also reinforces white supremacy, clarifying how the anti-racism of men like Carr, McCall, and Cleaver is compromised by their participation in sexual violence against black women.

Shakur's experiences of sexual violence intersect with white supremacy in more direct ways as well. She writes that black women are routinely "approached, propositioned, and harassed by white men" because many "white men consider all Black women potential prostitutes."[19] For a while, she learns to manipulate the desires of white men by conning them out of their money without having sex with them, but she stops once she learns from an older woman that it is a dangerous ploy, that "they got some crazy mens [*sic*] around here that is killing up young girls like you and one of 'em cuts their titties off" – an explanation that underscores the latent brutality at the intersection of patriarchy and white supremacy, particularly for poor women of colour.[20]

By demonstrating how racism, sexism, and sexual violence overlapped in her life before she encountered the criminal justice system, Shakur shows how the prison system's sexual violation of her body, and the bodies of other women (particularly women of colour), does not occur in a vacuum but instead participates in a wider system of sexual violence that works as a form of gendered social control. For example, like many other incarcerated women, Assata Shakur experiences the prison cavity search, a commonplace behind bars, as sexual violence. She describes the cavity search as a proto-medical procedure involving a nurse and a doctor (an inclusion of the medical establishment that I will return to), but she explains that the "internal search," where some nurses "try to put one finger in your vagina and another up your rectum at the same time," is "humiliating and disgusting."[21] Barbara Deming, who was imprisoned on several occasions for her part in various civil rights protests, similarly describes how a cavity-search functions as a technique of debasement and humiliation rather than (or as well as) a search for disease or hidden contraband:

[The guards] have neglected to look in my ears, or up my nose, or between my toes. They wouldn't be able to admit it to themselves, but their search, of course, is for something else, and is efficient: their search is for our pride. And I think with a sinking heart: again and again, it must be, they find it and take it.[22]

Erving Goffman, in his famous study of carceral institutions, *Asylums*, calls this kind of search "mortification": "a series of abasements, degradations, humiliations, and profanations of self" that are central to the control and indoctrination of imprisoned people.[23]

But Goffman's interpretation here is not entirely accurate. Without saying so (or, probably, realizing it), he is describing an exceptional experience for imprisoned *men* rather than a violent but normative experience for imprisoned *women* – an extension of existing forms of violence that occur outside as well as inside prison. Shakur describes how the other incarcerated women she encounters before her initial strip search emphasize how the mortification of the cavity search is sexualized: "the women call it 'getting the finger' or, more vulgarly, 'getting finger-fucked.'"[24] In other words, those women who undergo the cavity search understand it as a sexual violation that links with pre-existing experiences of unwanted sexual touching outside prison that are all too familiar to them.

So for incarcerated women, and especially for those who have experienced sexual abuse outside prison (as most women who enter prison have), the cavity search is a mortification of a different order. It is not, as Goffman suggests, a brutal indoctrination into a new social world; instead, it is a legitimation of rape culture by a government institution – an institution that is part of a wider system of justice that is supposed to *combat* sexual violence. Of course, the criminal justice system notoriously tends to exhibit a pattern of neglect or complicity in incidents of sexual violence – a pattern that includes victim blaming, failing to properly investigate sexual assaults, and compounding victim trauma through police interrogations and hostile court proceedings. And other forms of sexual abuse occur regularly in prisons – most notably the sexual exploitation of imprisoned women by male guards. So for imprisoned women, the cavity search does not exist in isolation; it is part of a network of sexual violence, institutional neglect, isolation, and silencing that seeks to define women as gendered (and often as racially gendered) subjects in a (white) man's world.

Sexuality is not represented simply as an oppressive force in women's prison life writing, however – as something the prison wields against women as a violent form of control and domination. With some consistency, women's prison life writings tend to identify how acts of resistance are articulated *through* sexuality. This is especially notable in Assata Shakur's autobiography when she represents her experience of sex behind bars as revolutionary, as displacing what Patricia Hill Collins calls "controlling images" about black women's sexuality and motherhood – images that helped criminalize black women and enabled the intervention of the state into black families. While in jail awaiting trial for bank robbery, Shakur is left alone for long periods of time with her friend and co-defendant, Kamau Sadiki. She describes how the two of them become increasingly close to each other and how their friendship intensifies into sexual intimacy:

> We spent whole days laughing and talking and listening to the Kourtroom madness in between. Each day we grew closer until, one day, it was clear to both of us that our relationship was changing. It was growing physical. We began to touch and to hold each other and each of us was like an oasis to the other. For a few days the question of sex was there. Then, one day, we talked about it. Surely, it was possible. But, i thought, the consequences! Pregnancy was certainly a possibility. I was facing

life in prison. Kamau would also be in prison for
a long time. The child would have no mother and
no father.[25]

Here, Shakur represents how sex with Sadiki is part of a slowly
evolving and thoughtful relationship, one that involves an in-depth
discussion about the consequences of sex before it happens, including a lengthy conversation about and meditation on the possibility
of pregnancy. In this way, she subtly counteracts stereotypes about
black women's sexuality that had become pervasive during the
period of the black power movement and that likely constituted
the subtext of the "sordid" articles that she says circulated after her
pregnancy became public.[26]

As an incarcerated black woman, she found that her sexuality
was particularly suspect to a white public attuned to viewing black
women as unthinkingly promiscuous, hypersexual, and overly
fertile – elements of a controlling image that Patricia Hill Collins
identifies as "the Jezebel": "Because efforts to control Black women's
sexuality lie at the heart of Black women's oppression, historical
jezebels and contemporary 'hoochies' represent a deviant Black
female sexuality" that functions as the binary opposite of a "white
heterosexual normality," which, she explains, had historically been
expressed through the cult of true womanhood.[27] By representing
sex as planned, thoughtful, and pragmatic rather than impulsive
and desiring, Shakur displaces the controlling image of the jezebel,
but at the cost of largely evading the question of pleasure, effectively placing heteronormative, reproductive sex as a solution to
the problem of how best to represent black women's sexual desire.
Shakur jokingly refers to her unborn child in a way that reproduces this logic: "I'll tell 'em [the FBI] that this baby is the new
Black messiah, conceived in a holy way, come to lead our people
to freedom and justice and to create a new black nation."[28] If
jokes sometimes reveal suppressed content, Shakur's joke about her

child's immaculate conception indicates how the book subsumes her sexual desire under the sign of the maternal.

Just as Assata Shakur's representation of sex is a rejection of the stereotype of the jezebel at a moment when that controlling image might bubble up from white supremacist America to explain her pregnancy, her pregnancy displaces controlling images about black motherhood by redefining the traditional meaning of family. In particular, her redefinition of family displaces the image of the black "matriarch" that was the focal point of the 1965 *Moynihan Report*.[29] Infamously, that report – officially titled *The Negro Family: The Case for National Action* – reduced massive dynamics of inequality in America to what the report called instability in the structure of black families, blaming the economic and social disadvantages of the black community on homes headed by black "matriarchs": "In essence, the Negro community has been forced into a matriarchal structure which, because it is so out of line with the rest of American society, seriously retards the progress of the group as a whole, and imposes a crushing burden on the Negro male and, in consequence, on a great many Negro women as well."[30] Along with claiming that black women held too much power and authority in the household relative to men, the report blamed mothers for working outside the home and leaving their children unsupervised, which – so the report alleged – undercut black civil society.

Because Shakur was about to be given a life sentence and was unlikely to ever be released from prison, many Americans probably interpreted her pregnancy according to this controlling image about black motherhood, for she would be unable to supervise, let alone care for, her daughter after she was born. But Shakur provides an expansive definition of the family structure – her daughter would be raised by a family-as-community – thus rejecting the presumption that the (white and middle-class) nuclear family, on which the stereotypes about black motherhood like those in the *Moynihan Report* were made, is an essential norm for healthy childrearing.

This definition of family first appears when Shakur and Kamau Sadiki discuss the possibility of having a baby while the two of them are incarcerated. Sadiki says, "'If you become pregnant and you have a child, the child will be taken care of. Our people will not let the child grow up like a weed."[31] As Margo V. Perkins writes in *Autobiography As Activism: Three Black Women of the Sixties*, Shakur "was able to rely upon a supportive community of other women to care for [her child] in [her] absence."[32] Perkins explains that this communal support follows an "African tradition" where "the child belongs less to individuals than to an entire community."[33] As Patricia Hill Collins writes, "Within Black civil society, notions of interpersonal relations forged during slavery endured – such as equating family with extended family, of treating community as family, and of dealings with Whites as elements of public discourse and dealings with Blacks as part of family business."[34] This expansive view of family, which is notably different from the normative family promoted and defended by white society (and, historically, reinforced through women's prisons), is realized as both a personal and a political unit in Shakur's autobiography: family and friends help her raise her daughter while she is incarcerated, and members of an underground revolutionary organization free Assata from prison, allowing her to reunite with her daughter in relative safety. In this way, her redefinition of motherhood and family as expansive and inclusive, involving a community of people, undercuts controlling images that frame black motherhood since these narratives identify parenthood as a shared, communal responsibility.

Finally, Assata Shakur's definition of family as expansive, involving a community of parents who help raise her child, complements how Angela Davis sees the political prisoner as someone who sees her political identity as relational – as interconnected with and supported by a community (rather than heroically individual). In her autobiography, Davis repeatedly defines her role as a political prisoner as inextricably linked to a wider network of people, figured variously as an "organized mass" or "mass movement," a "collective," a "community," or "the people."[35] Importantly, this diverse network includes activists but also regular imprisoned people: rather than see herself as somehow different from the other women incarcerated with her, Davis sees regular imprisoned people as allies, and particularly black, brown, and poor women as part of an oppressed network, a "people," of which she is a member.

This collective is inherently resistant to the prison system, given that the goal of the prison is to isolate individual imprisoned people in order to better control them. That isolation is especially acute for political prisoners. In discussing how a newspaper sought to create a rift between her and a fellow defendant in her trial, Davis explains why separation matters to the institution: "They wanted disunity and division; for divided, we would both be most vulnerable."[36] As I will show, Susan Rosenberg, too, sees her interconnections with other incarcerated women as providing the necessary materials for resisting the prison's efforts to isolate and control her, to "unmake" her world, to use Elaine Scarry's term from *The Body in Pain*. Rosenberg shows how "remaking" her world involves establishing connections with other women – connections that frequently occur along sexual lines.

UNMAKING AND REMAKING THE WORLD: SUSAN ROSENBERG, PRISON SEXUAL VIOLENCE, AND LOVE

Susan Rosenberg had been a political activist throughout the 1960s and 1970s, working with several revolutionary organizations, including the Weathermen, the Black Panther Party, and the BLA. In the early 1980s, she was placed on the FBI's most wanted list for two reasons: first, she was suspected of participating in a 1982 Brinks armoured car robbery during which two police officers and a security officer were shot and killed; and, second, she was suspected of being involved in Assata Shakur's prison escape. In 1984, Rosenberg, while in hiding, was caught by police in a truck filled with weapons and explosives. The following year she was convicted of weapons and explosives charges and given a fifty-nine-year sentence. In prison, she became a committed AIDS activist, while earning a master's degree from Antioch University. In 2001, her sentence was commuted by President Bill Clinton, and she was subsequently released. Her autobiography, *An American Radical: Political Prisoner in My Own Country*, which focuses mainly on her more than a decade and a half behind bars, was published in 2011.

In *An American Radical*, Susan Rosenberg explains how her middle-class whiteness (and her status as a political prisoner with broad support and connections on the outside) protected her from some of the worst forms of violence in the institution: "My associates and I were not similarly ground down and thrown out, in part because we were a political group and because we were of the white middle class – and even in those most profoundly appalling and anguished conditions, that made a difference."[37] Still, like Assata, Rosenberg was subjected to the sexual violence of the institution. And, like Assata, in her book she highlights the cavity search as a sexual assault – specifically, as rape.

Rosenberg describes how, during a prison transfer, she and another political prisoner, Alejandrina Torres, were "hustled into the medical building" to be subjected to a cavity search, which the prison officials used as a means to isolate, control, and dominate them. She explains that a cavity search is an act of vengeance: the prison officials "were going to pay us back for being who we were" – political prisoners who fought against the state. Rosenberg and Torres are first asked to sign a form with the heading, "Permission/ Notification for High Security Contraband Search," which has the boxes checked for "'cavity search'" and "'rectal' [search]"; they refuse. Twice, they explain to the officials and guards that they could conduct an X-ray instead, but the "captain laughed. 'No, we don't have to and we won't. You are going to a control unit and it's our call on this. We have the right to do it.'"[38]

In invoking "the right," the captain is summoning the law to conceal what the women experience as an attack. As Robert Cover famously writes in "Violence and the Word," "Interpretations in law also constitute justifications for violence which has already occurred or which is about to occur."[39] Cover is discussing judicial interpretations, but his explanation of the law's capacity to legitimate violence can be extended to show how "the right" to conduct a legal search camouflages the prison officials' use of sexual violence as a form of vengeance and as a technique for ensuring obedience and subservience. Here, then, "the right" inverts a basic function of the law: instead of protecting against unjust violations of the body (as, say, it is ostensibly supposed to function in criminal law regarding sexual abuse), it *sanctions* sexual violence.

The prison officials show their awareness that the cavity search is a form of sexual violence through acts and expressions of concealment. For example, Rosenberg and Torres are moved to separate rooms so that the "searches" can be conducted privately. Although this is likely an effort to provide some measure of privacy during an extremely invasive and intimate procedure, their removal from view is also related to a series of ocular signals that indicate that this search for privacy has to do with an institutional act that is shameful, *un*sightly. Rosenberg notes that one "woman CO with whom [she had] some conversations throughout the year ... wouldn't meet [her] look" before Rosenberg was forcibly removed to the separate room. During the search, the "woman officer who had talked to [her] had to leave the room" because watching the experience "was too much for her."[40] The woman CO is unable to look at Rosenberg presumably because she feels a complex of guilt or shame as a result of her participation in the violent search of Rosenberg's body. Of course, shame is often communicated by averting the gaze, looking away.[41] As Elspeth Probyn writes, "Etymologically shame comes from the Goth word *Scham*, which refers to covering the face."[42] The woman CO's decision to leave the room, to stop looking (a physical act akin to averting her gaze, covering her face), presumably also reflects feelings of disgust at the *kind* of violence of the act ("it was too much for her"). Ultimately, we do not know with certainty why she leaves. However, based on Rosenberg's interpretation of the woman's behaviour, we can surmise that she leaves because of her desire to no longer be a direct participant in, or even a witness bearing some responsibility for, violence that is so often experienced by women in a patriarchal society as a technique for expressing, enacting, and enforcing men's domination and control of women.

Rosenberg relates her and Torres's experience of the cavity search in graphic terms, underscoring the physical and psychological trauma of the event and clarifying how the state's intervention into their bodies is experienced and should be interpreted as rape. First, both women say "no." Rosenberg initially says "no" in response to the request for a search. And she describes hearing "a long, loud scream – 'Nooooo!'" – after Torres is forcibly removed to a private room (an allusion to the anti-rape movement's slogan, "No means no"). Rosenberg then names the violence when she shouts at the COs, "'This is rape. You're fucking raping me!" She describes the physician's assistant "ramm[ing]" his "fist" into her anus and vagina, underscoring the brutality of the act, and clarifying that the violence was itself the point: "He didn't 'look' for anything." She describes her psychological and physical trauma: she feels "shoc[k]" and "pain" and anger after the attack, and when "the marshals came to transport [them] and [she] stood up, there was blood on the floor."[43] As Karlene Faith explains in *Unruly Women: The Politics of Confinement and Resistance* (2011), prisons consistently use the cavity search as a form of violence to assert institutional authority: "a forced vaginal exam is tantamount to state-authorized rape, and torturing and shaming women in this way seems clearly intended to reinforce their dehumanized prisoner status."[44] Moreover, Rosenberg shows that the cavity search, which links punishment and sexual violence with the law and the medical establishment, is a palimpsest of intentions and effects: it is, at least in theory, a search for contraband; it is a legally sanctioned way to inflict pain, to brutalize, or to enact vengeance; it is a disciplinary technique that seeks to forcibly isolate and, through isolation, dominate and control incarcerated women; and it is a way to remind women that their bodies are not their own but are instead the property of the institution.

The multipurpose quality of the cavity search – prison officials can claim that it is a necessary form of security while also using it as a particularly sinister form of punishment and control – is part of a wider logic in prisons. The same logic is at work when, for example, administrative segregation is used to "protect" imprisoned people but also to justify lengthy periods of solitary confinement. Both Angela Davis and Assata Shakur describe being placed in isolation for their own protection, yet neither woman finds that her life is under any threat once she is finally returned to the general population. They both suspect that their isolation had more to do with the institution's anxieties about their political beliefs and desire to use isolation to punish them.[45] This dual purpose of administrative segregation points to how prison staff often exploit how the institution is based on a fundamental paradox: it is tasked with the most important forms of care (from housing to food to safety and security) but is also tasked with meting out punishment. In the cavity search, these two functions of the prison overlap, blur, so that the institutional mandate to provide care and safety (by forcibly searching imprisoned people's bodies) can legitimate forms of punishment that would otherwise be illegal.

The cavity search, like torture, relies on what Elaine Scarry in *The Body in Pain* calls "inversion." In her discussion of torture, Scarry explains that two institutions that are ubiquitous in scenes of torture are the law and medicine. Both institutions are designed to provide care for people and society, but through torture they are "unmade by being made weapons."[46] For example, by involving a doctor or a nurse or some other medical practitioner in torture, "the institution of medicine like that of justice is deconstructed, unmade by being made at once an actual agent of the pain and a demonstration of the effects of pain on human consciousness."[47]

I have already described how the captain's invocation of the law constitutes an inversion of the law's capacity to protect people against illegitimate forms of violence, including sexual assault. The same can be said of the presence of the "physician's assistant" during Rosenberg's cavity search (or rather, her rape) and of the presence of the nurse and doctor in Assata Shakur's cavity search: the protective, caring role of medicine is inverted, made to produce pain, to threaten a woman's bodily security and even undermine her identity. For Scarry, the inversion of the law and medicine, two "primary institutional forms" of civilization, is a deconstruction of "larger units of civilization."[48] But the application of sexual violence in the cavity search also constitutes a deconstruction of a smaller unit of civilization: it is a ritualistic "spectacle of power" that seeks to contract the self of the person whose body is penetrated; it alienates them from other people, and it removes their capacity to control their own body – the basic parameter of their "world," to use Scarry's terminology.

However, just as *Assata* does, Rosenberg's *An American Radical* also explains how sexuality – notably, a multivalent sexuality often comprised of desire, intimacy, love, and friendship – is a form of resistance to the institution's efforts to isolate and control women and women's bodies. Rosenberg does not explicitly define sex as a form of resistance. But because of the institution's restrictions on all expressions of sexual desire (or even intimacy), otherwise benign forms of sexuality become subversive; they are interpreted by the institution as threats to its core ideology.

The way that sexuality is rendered subversive through the institution's laws and regulations is made explicit after prison officials enact what Rosenberg describes as "a witch hunt against lesbians": "We woke up one day to find the hunt had begun without warning. Anyone suspected of being in a lesbian relationship with another prisoner was sent to segregation and placed under investigation for thirty days." Many women were interrogated and locked into segregation as suspects: "The administration subjected everyone who was known to have ever loved a woman or who had created a prison family. The little shreds of hope that we had found in reaching out to one another were under attack."[49] Here, then, the capacity of lesbian relationships to expand the boundaries of self-hood so that intimacy can be shared with another person – notably explained in expansive terms as "reaching out to one another" – is criminalized, deemed subversive.

The prison officials' criminalization of lesbianism (indeed, according to Rosenberg, any form of intimacy between women) could be because lesbian relationships disrupt the system of heter-onormative binary difference that the wider criminal justice system enforces through sexual segregation and upon which the system of sexual punishment through heterosexual abstinence is based. But lesbian relationships are sometimes tolerated in women's prisons, and they were tolerated for a period in the prison where Rosenberg was incarcerated. Rosenberg suspects that the "witch hunt" is instead a response to the prison system's sexual abuse of imprisoned women:

> I could only assume that behind this witch hunt was the real issue of sexual abuse on the part of prison guards. Pat searching and voyeurism (mani-fested in constant intrusions into our lives) were two of the symptoms of systematic abuse of power. More telling was that over the past two years, more than twenty-five male officers had been removed from Danbury [Prison] for having sex with women prisoners. Hunting for sex between women was a way of deflecting the misogyny of the system.[50]

Here, Rosenberg differentiates between the prison's sexual violence and the lesbian relationships in the prison: the prison wields sexual-ity as a means to individualize – in order to control and dominate – an imprisoned person through her body; lesbian relationships in prison, by comparison, are represented as romantic and sexual, certainly, but also as mutually supportive, reciprocal, and radically egalitarian. The former isolates; the latter affiliates – a basic, elementary unit of community and belonging.

Lesbian relationships in Rosenberg's book qualify popular conceptions of incarcerated women's sexuality, which are typically represented in American popular culture as purely sexual and sensational, often as aggressive and violent, and almost always in service of a male gaze. For example, Rosenberg describes a couple, Rider and Theresa, who are inseparable; the "intensity and intimacy they shared was as clear as a day after rain," she writes. Rider is tough and wears an impenetrable expression learned through many hard years on the street and behind bars, but "this feeling she had, this love for her partner, she could never hide."[51] When Theresa is removed to a hospital because she is dying of AIDS, Rider is unable to go with her, even though the two women have been together for nine years, and this dramatizes the violence of an enforced heteronormative system and clarifies the short-sightedness of popular discourses about women's prisons that presume lesbian relationships in prison are merely situational, "gay for the stay," or based solely on desire.

Rosenberg's own relationship with a fellow incarcerated person named Frin Mullin is similarly supportive and enriching; it is also a collaborative partnership (since they work on scriptwriting together), as well as a deeply loving companionship that transcends their incarceration since they keep in touch after Mullin is released. Rosenberg writes that she has "never been so happy loving someone": "The incongruity of this happening under the worst circumstances had only intensified my joy all the more."[52] For Rosenberg, lesbian relationships involve love, friendship, intimacy, and desire, but they also provide the necessary structure for reconstructing social arrangements that the prison seeks to dismantle.

This reconstruction of social arrangements also constitutes a remaking of the home. Consistently, women's prison life writings discuss the prison "family," which queers the domestic space that prisons have historically sought to force incarcerated women to inhabit. For example, in her autobiography, Angela Davis describes how "the vast majority of the jail population had neatly organized itself into generations of families":

> Mothers/wives, fathers/husbands, sons and daughters, even aunts, uncles, grandmothers and grandfathers. The family system served as a defense against the fact of being no more than a number. It humanized the environment and allowed an identification with others within a familiar framework.[53]

Davis writes that what strikes her "most about this family system was the homosexuality at its core." Yet she also notes that "it was not closed to 'straight' women."[54] Perhaps the prison family reproduces some of the dynamics of the heteronormative home on the outside, but it also deconstructs the notion of family as normative by showing how its cultural codes – its performative roles of, say, mother or father – are mutable and can be unmoored from sex or gender. Prison families, which remake the social world of the prison in such a way that they support the interests of incarcerated women, carve out alternative domestic arrangements within a system that has historically sought to impose heteronormative sexual and gender roles on women, especially roles actualized within the middle-class domestic sphere.

Similarly, in *An American Radical*, women's cells constitute alternative homes that disrupt the patriarchal home imposed by the prison. For imprisoned people, the prison cell is a private, domestic space. Consistently, imprisoned men and women call their cells their "houses." Rosenberg's most sustained depictions of caring, supportive lesbian relationships in prison happen in these carceral domestic spaces.

If the wider prison is itself a kind of home – and this has consistently been the case since the cottage-style structure of prisons that emerged in the late nineteenth century that sought to reproduce the domestic sphere – then it is a home that has historically tried to enforce the rules and norms of the patriarchal household, often through force, including through violence. The prison-as-home, a home that is not safe but is a site of punishment, that threatens rather than cares for the body, is a decidedly *un*homely space.

By comparison, for Rosenberg, the cell is a refuge, a private, interior space where she and her lover, Frin, live together; it is an alternative home space to the one enforced by the prison. After Frin is released from prison, Rosenberg mourns the loss of the woman she loves by emphasizing their shared space: "I simply sat for a long time in what had been *our* cell, where we had lived *our* lives." She writes, "I sat in our cell for a day, smelling her, dreaming about her, and examining all her knickknacks and her prison junk that she had left me."[55] "*Our* cell": at least to some degree, and perhaps only temporarily, Rosenberg's spatial experience of incarceration is unexpectedly subversive. Stripped to one of its most basic functions, the prison uses space as punishment. Whereas rooms in a prison are supposed to punish, to inflict harm, by forcibly isolating an imprisoned person (through ceilings and floors, but, most symbolically, through bars and concrete walls), Rosenberg's prison cell is a site of refuge and comfort, a protective cover that sustains her even after Frin is long gone. It enables communion rather than isolation.

Rosenberg explains that imprisoned women repeatedly find communion, but also community, through sexuality. For example, in her autobiography, she describes hearing a whistle, which signals a serious emergency, and watching a raid on a building involving a "team of about fifteen men ... marching and chanting in step," wearing "helmets and black jumpsuits, carrying plastic shields and clubs." Following the officers are numerous prison officials, including "the captain, the warden, [and] the two associate wardens." She immediately recognizes that the raid is not a typical "shakedown" of individual cells but something of a different magnitude: "This was a bust of some kind because of the sheer number and power that was displayed." Women are hustled out of the building and individually searched by the officers, often roughly, and for four hours the institution ceases the majority of its operations while the women's housing unit is searched by the armoured men.[56]

Rosenberg then describes seeing an officer exit the building, "gingerly" clutching a plastic bag; the other imprisoned women watching the raid "moa[n]" disappointedly, and knowingly. He removes "a cylindrical object" from the bag and waves it around. "'They got it,'" explains one woman, sadly: "'It's the dildo factory. They busted it.'"[57] Rosenberg learns that the women working in the prison factory had been swiping leftover plastic, pouring the plastic into dildo molds, painting the dildos in the prison paint shop, and selling them throughout the institution. Unsurprisingly, as with incarcerated men, imprisoned women construct objects out of found materials in a kind of bricolage of necessity. However, here, they circumvent the prison's restrictions on sexuality – restrictions that extend even to the most onanistic and innocuous sexual behaviour – in ways that illuminate the importance of sex but that also show how the need for sexual gratification is achieved through a series of collaborations that illuminate a collectivity, a community.

CONCLUSION: PRISON LIFE WRITING, GENDER, AND THE LITERARY RULES OF DESIRE

Of course, the institution's use of overwhelming force as a response to dildos makes the above scene especially funny. But it also illustrates how women's sexuality constitutes a threat to the prison system for several reasons. Certainly, defining and managing women's sexuality was central to the construction of the early reformatories and has remained at the core of women's prisons since their creation, so women taking their sexual desire into their own hands (as it were) removes some measure of control from the institution. Indeed, the prison system's use of abstinence as punishment means that imprisoned people having sex, even if it is onanistic, undermines the prison's capacity to punish. Sex, love, and intimacy are essential human needs that people will almost inevitably seek to fulfil; the prison criminalizes those needs by punishing imprisoned people for gratifying them and restricting access to their fulfilment. Thus sex becomes an indispensable tool of the administration, serving variously as a form of leverage, a tool for domination, a method of control, and a technique of intimidation.

I am tempted to claim that the prison's use of sexuality as part of the punishment apparatus constitutes what Joni Hersch and Erin E. Meyers' call a "collateral consequence": "a legal penalty, disability or disadvantage ... imposed on a person automatically upon that person's conviction for a felony, misdemeanor or other offense, even if it is not included in the sentence."[58] Yet restrictions on basic sexual needs (and needs for intimacy and physical contact) are so deeply connected to the punitive function of the prison that it hardly seems right to describe the prison's restrictions around sex as in any way "collateral." Instead, and as I have shown, the prison system relies on sexuality, even sexual violence, as a central pillar of control and domination.

But also, as the dildo scene illustrates, sexuality in women's prisons articulates expressions of solidarity that the institution sees as threats to its capacity to isolate, dominate, and control women through their bodies. In this way, women's prison life writings are at odds with representations of sex or intimacy in men's prison life writings. In men's prison life writings, sex is almost always a form of domination and control that is rarely experienced as intimacy or even desire. Sex-as-domination reproduces the abjection of incarcerated men; it intensifies their isolation and even accelerates their dependence on the prison for safety. As I have shown, in women's prison life writings, sex has the capacity to build community.

Now, without a doubt, this is not always the case. How sex is represented in the life writings of imprisoned men does not necessarily conform to the real experiences of men's sexualities in prison, which are likely much more varied than they appear in literature, since, as I have shown, prison life writing has explicit and implicit rules around the representation of sex in the genre, and one of those rules seems to be that men can rarely speak of same-sex desire or intimacy or love behind bars. (T.J. Parsell's *Fish: A Memoir of a Boy in a Man's Prison* (2006) is one exception, for example, but its scenes of love and intimacy are far rarer than its scenes of horrifying sexual violence.) Similarly, although I have discussed how Shakur and Rosenberg define incarcerated women's expressions of sexuality as forms of resistance or as expressions of solidarity, imprisoned women's sexuality is varied and complex, and incarcerated women engage in sexual violence too (although at very different rates than men). For example, in *Laughing in the Dark: From Colored Girl to Woman of Color – A Journey from Prison to Power* (1994), Patricia Gaines describes how a woman tries but fails to sexually assault her after she is incarcerated.[59] My point is that these gender differences around sexuality, whatever their reality, are features of prison life writing as a genre, and they illuminate the often narrow portals through which the prison experience can enter into discourse.

Earlier, I suggested that the absence of the conversion narrative in women's prison life writings is likely due to the absence of institutional pressures on incarcerated women to see their lives according to the conversion teleology. In the next chapter, this book's conclusion, I focus on one of the rare examples of a woman's prison conversion narrative, Susan Burton and Cari Lynn's *Becoming Ms. Burton: From Prison Recovery to Leading the Fight for Incarcerated Women* (2017). I end with a discussion of Burton's book because its use of the conversion narrative is both conventional and unique, a paradox that is instructive for thinking about how we read prison life writing today: it is an individual success story, a story of dramatic self-transformation, but it simultaneously resists the all too common reading of imprisoned people's success stories as blueprints for solving the mass incarceration crisis. Instead, just as Shakur's and Rosenberg's life writings (as well as Angela Davis's autobiography) emphasize community in their work, Burton's memoir foregrounds her connections with other incarcerated and formerly incarcerated women as well as a diverse community of people outside prisons. *Becoming Ms. Burton* shows how reading for community, including in conversion narratives that are seemingly about only the person whose face graces the book's cover, is especially important right now.

"THESE WOMEN, LIKE MYSELF"

BECOMING MS. BURTON AND REREADING PRISON LIFE
WRITING IN A TIME OF CRISIS

Baca taught himself to read and write, awoke to
the voice of the soul, and converted doing time
into a profoundly spiritual pursuit.
—*Booklist* review of *A Place to Stand*

A harrowing [portrait] of life behind bars ....
Senghor writes about the process of atonement
and the possibility of redemption and talks of his
efforts to work for prison reforms that might turn
a system designed to warehouse into one aimed
at rehabilitation.
—Michiko Kakutani, *New York Times* review of
Writing My Wrongs

IN THIS BOOK, I HAVE ARGUED THAT THE PRISON CONVERSION
narrative has always been a master narrative of the US prison
system. It helped prison reformers and prison officials articulate
how their institutions might rehabilitate people and transform
them from criminals into citizens. When the first US prisons, the
Jacksonian penitentiaries, supplanted capital punishment as the
appropriate sentence for many crimes, they were described in terms
redolent of the conversion narrative, essentially transubstantiating
an earlier conversion rhetoric performed at the scaffold into the
logic of the modern prison system. The conversion narrative has
appeared in prison discourse throughout the history of the US

prison system. As well, prison reformers have always linked conversion to education in a way that I argue is reflected in the prison life writing genre that emerged after the Second World War.

Although prison life writings consistently use the prison conversion narrative, they do so with surprising aesthetic and ideological range. During the Treatment Era, when imprisoned people often had no choice but to represent themselves as rehabilitated so that they could be released, prison life writings often used but redefined the prison conversion narrative so that it expressed meanings that were quite different from the ones that prison officials intended. This was especially true for black prison writers radicalized during this period, like George Jackson and James Carr. But it was also true for imprisoned white people like Carl Panzram, writing before the Treatment Era, and Jack Henry Abbott, writing at the close of the Treatment Era, whose anticonversion narratives inverted the genre's teleology.

Additionally, although imprisoned and formerly imprisoned women rarely ever feature the conversion narrative in their life writings, they still struggle with prison discourse in their work: Assata Shakur and Susan Rosenberg, writing during the rise of mass incarceration, use but redefine the discourse of sexuality and domesticity that has historically been, and continues to be, central to women's prisons. So, as I have suggested throughout this book, and as the prison life writings I have discussed demonstrate, the hermeneutics of resistance (the "counter-text" readings) that tend to dominate analyses of prison life writing are sometimes short-sighted and often preclude important considerations of the ideological and aesthetic intricacies of the genre.

Predictably, readers of prison memoirs and autobiographies tend to focus on imprisoned authors' accounts of personal transformation because the conversions of imprisoned people are noteworthy and dramatic but also because they provide uplifting stories about the transformative potential of literature, precisely the kind of story that readers and writers would appreciate. Readers' discussions of prison life writings are instructive for what they say about how the prison conversion narrative, with its legal/penal pedigree, is circulated in American culture. For example, one *Booklist* reviewer isolates elements of the prison conversion narrative as central to *A Place to Stand* when writing that Baca's reading and writing awaken Baca's "soul," and that as a result Baca "convert[s] doing time into a profoundly spiritual pursuit." Similarly, a reviewer for *Library Journal* employs the conversion narrative's rhetoric of redemption and transcendence when writing that Baca's work "reveals the paradox of prison life. Ironically, his time in solitary confinement redeemed him, prompting lifesaving memories of his rural New Mexico childhood, which ignited his ability to use language to elevate himself above his immediate surroundings."[1] Comparable explanations about reading and writing's transformative and soul-converting power are constantly repeated in reviews of prison literature, which attests to the highly limited ways that we typically read prison life writing, as well as suggesting how those readings reinforce presumptions about the genre. Those beliefs, in turn, often inform our expectations about prison education, rehabilitation, and imprisoned people – essentially, the role of prisons in American life.

These readings, and the ways they underpin our ideas about incarceration, are especially problematic today, for prisons are in a state of crisis, with legislators and prison reformers searching for solutions to mass incarceration.[2] Michiko Kakutani's review of Senghor's *Writing My Wrongs* (in the above epigraph) illustrates my concerns about the unintended ideological consequences of prison life writing and why those consequences are especially acute at the moment. Kakutani writes that Senghor's "atonement" and "redemption" have made him a kind of "prison reform[er]." His work, she explains, might help "turn a system designed to warehouse *into one aimed at rehabilitation*." Of course, as I have shown throughout this book, prisons have always been "designed" to produce rehabilitation, at least in theory. More importantly, however,

Kakutani enlists prison life writing as part of a legislative and policy agenda that sees rehabilitation as the solution to mass incarceration. In this way, Kakutani's reading reproduces a fundamental mis-understanding of the prison system – a misunderstanding that has fuelled prison growth and made the prison central to US criminal justice: the presumption that prisons could be fixed if only they were better at changing people.

The history of the US prison system is to some degree cyclical, oscillating between periods of bust and boom: whenever prisons have become too dangerous, overcrowded, or costly, prison reform movements have intervened and championed the rehabilitative ideal as the solution to prison crises. The problem, they have suggested over the centuries, is not the prison but how the prison works. Prisons, they have argued, should be overhauled so as to better change the people incarcerated within them. The first penitentiary experiments at the close of the eighteenth century were a response to a violent and, reformers believed, decidedly anti-republican criminal justice system that allowed no room for repentance and instead housed imprisoned people in overcrowded cells, often to await their fate at the gallows. Penitentiaries like Eastern State and Auburn were ostensibly rational and humane institutions that corrected the brutality of earlier methods of punishment. Their major innovation was that they were meant to reform rehabilitated people rather than simply punish (or execute) them. By the close of the nineteenth century, Jacksonian prisons were being deemed overly violent, crowded, and expensive, and prison reformers drew on emergent scientific, medical, and pedagogical methods in order to redefine prisons as reformatories – institutions that, once again, were supposed to be better at rehabilitating people. And prison reformers of the Treatment Era, who built on the efforts of New Penologists and Progressive Era reformers, tried to fix problems with the prison system by mounting one of the most expansive applications of the rehabilitative ideal yet. In other words, every time the prison has been in crisis, prison reformers have introduced rehabilitation as a novel solution, often simply retrofitting earlier rehabilitative methods.

These efforts have accomplished little in terms of fixing the prison system. If anything, they have papered over deep problems inherent to prisons, normalized the prison as a necessary and seemingly natural way to solve criminality (even when prisons have repeatedly failed to do so), and helped expand prisons precisely when they should have been contracted or eliminated. So, while some forms of reform may be specific to historical periods, reform *movements* are cyclical or perennial: they recur throughout the history of the US prison system whenever prisons have been identified as in crisis, and these movements have tended to further legitimate the prison rather than genuinely change it into a system that, as rehabilitation efforts repeatedly promise, transforms lives.

So, Kakutani's vision of better prisons as prisons better at rehabilitating people imagines a solution to the current prison crisis that risks reproducing a historical pattern that preserves rather than dismantles a system that has caused significant intergenerational damage to vulnerable communities, particularly African American communities. Certainly, conversions can happen for some individual imprisoned people. And there are encouraging signs that educational programs can help imprisoned people change their lives.[3] But rehabilitation programs are largely incompatible with prisons, which are always ultimately focused on punishment and control – on keeping "the bad guys away," writes John Edgar Wideman, parodying popular rhetoric about crime control.[4] Moreover, rehabilitation, however effective it might be, is in stark contrast with the wider criminal justice system, which systematically blocks reintegration and encourages recidivism. Now, let me be clear: this is not to suggest that education or rehabilitation programs have no value. Notably, imprisoned people are some of the most ardent supporters of educational programs, and some programs are undoubtedly worthwhile. Yet individual change, however dramatic, is often not enough to overcome the structural barriers imposed by the very system that ostensibly seeks that change in the first place.

A fundamental problem with Kakutani's interpretation of Senghor's book (and with the many similar readings of stories of individual rehabilitation that are assumed to be exemplary of wider prison experiences) is that it focuses narrowly on the dramatic self-transformation of an individual imprisoned person. Even when a book like Jimmy Santiago Baca's *A Place to Stand* addresses how crime is partly an effect of wider social determinates such as structural racism and poverty (which it does), and even when a book like Shaka Senghor's *Writing My Wrongs* represents the difficulties faced by formerly imprisoned people trying to reintegrate into normal life (which it does), there is something about the triumphant story of overcoming these conditions that partly masks how incredibly inadequate individual change ultimately is when someone is released from prison to live in the surreal world of the New Jim Crow.

Susan Burton and Cari Lynn's *Becoming Ms. Burton: From Prison to Recovery to Leading the Fight for Incarcerated Women* (2017) seems to affirm, but ultimately disrupts, this reading, which I find helpful for understanding how we might approach prison life writing during the current mass incarceration crisis. (I will describe the book as Burton's memoir since, while Lynn is listed as a co-author, it is ultimately Burton's story.) Burton's memoir seems open to conventional readings of the prison memoir as a marker of a formerly imprisoned person's successful rehabilitation, yet it simultaneously resists such a reading. The book is a paradox: on the one hand, it relates an imprisoned woman's conversion behind bars; on the other, it foregrounds the near impossibility of change within the current criminal justice system, with its arbitrary rules and Kafkaesque bureaucracy. *Becoming Ms. Burton* adheres to the conventions of the prison life writing genre that I have discussed throughout this book. But it also complicates those conventions. And *how* it complicates those conventions is important, in that it uses established traditions in the genre to suggest a novel way to read prison life writing.

At a glance, Burton's conversion seems conventional when set alongside the prison conversion narratives predominant in the prison life writing genre. For example, the division of selfhood that is so central to the conversion paradigm – as when, say, Malcolm Little becomes Malcolm X in *The Autobiography of Malcolm X*, or when "the boy Jay was laid to rest" after "the man Shaka was born" in *Writing My Wrongs* – is an organizing feature of *Becoming Ms. Burton*, which is divided into two sections, titled "Sue" (pre-conversion period) and "Ms. Burton" (post-conversion period). Burton describes how she began to use drugs, particularly crack cocaine, in the 1980s after her son, K.K., was hit and killed by a speeding police car. For more than a decade and a half, she was repeatedly incarcerated (what she calls the "revolving door"), often for drug possession, until she began successful drug treatment and underwent the 12-step program of Alcoholics Anonymous.[5] Like other prison conversion narratives, her story moves from a long, dark period of criminalized behaviour (particularly drug use) and recidivism to a post-prison life where she becomes an important figure in the public sphere. *Becoming Ms. Burton* is also an entrepreneurial narrative, an almost Alger-like bootstraps story in which hard work, determination, luck, and the occasional benevolence of others enable her to succeed as an advocate and small business owner. In other words, her work is similar, in a sense, to many life writings by imprisoned men whose stories of personal transcendence slot comfortably into grand narratives of American culture, from the conversion narrative to stories of self-making, from *The Autobiography of Malcolm X* to *Writing My Wrongs*.

But while Burton does suggest that hard work and determination are important qualities for someone's successful transition to post-prison life, her book also repeatedly demonstrates that these qualities alone are not enough, because of wider structural determinates that make recidivism likely even for formerly imprisoned people who exhibit all the necessary personal qualities for changing their lives. In particular, Burton keeps her book's focus on the many ways that structural racism and poverty make crime and recidivism possible for black, brown, and poor people. This is, in part, because she uses the A.A. conversion narrative rather than the prison conversion narrative, a seemingly inconsequential difference between kinds of conversion that actually has important consequences in her book – and for understanding the relationship between prison life writing, ideology, and mass incarceration.

Burton's use of the A.A. conversion narrative provides her story with a structure that enables her to describe how she escaped a cycle of recidivism and changed her life, but it also resists readings (like Kakutani's reading of *Writing My Wrongs*) that narrow the scope of an imprisoned author's life writing to the all too familiar story of individual redemption and transcendence. This is achieved, in part, because, unlike the prison conversion narrative, the A.A. conversion narrative is premised on relationality rather than difference. In the prison conversion narrative, converts typically represent themselves as different from who they were before the conversion experience, and sometimes, by extension, they also tacitly or explicitly distinguish themselves from other imprisoned or formerly imprisoned people (as I have demonstrated with regard to the work of Jimmy Santiago Baca, for example).

By comparison, the A.A. narrative is based on identification and complicity: converts are *always* alcoholics, and their sobriety is sustained through repeated performances of identification with other alcoholics – for example, by supporting other alcoholics through serving as sponsors or performing "service" by visiting recovery centres, hospitals, or clinics. In the A.A. tradition, then, people maintain their conversion through identification rather than disidentification. Somewhat paradoxically, converts change, but they also see themselves as similar to, rather than fundamentally different from, the people they used to be; and they identify with people who share(d) their pre-conversion condition.

Because Burton uses the A.A. narrative, she repeatedly emphasizes how, despite her conversion, she remains like, rather than unlike, other incarcerated or formerly incarcerated women – a crucial feature that makes it hard to see her story primarily as one of individual redemption and transcendence. When a formerly incarcerated woman struggling with the constraints of the New Jim Crow tells Burton that she is successful because she is somehow different from them – "'that's for people like you, Ms. Burton,'" they would tell her – Burton corrects them: "'I'm just like you.'"[6]

This emphasis on identification happens consistently throughout the book. She repeatedly describes how she is similar to the women who remain trapped in the criminal justice system ("these women, like myself").[7] She argues that chance, rather than anything else, is what distinguishes her success from their inability to escape the criminal justice system and take control of their lives: "I knew how easily [being a lifer, someone incarcerated for life] could have been me," she claims soberly, after speaking with a woman serving a life sentence. This kinship with other incarcerated and formerly incarcerated women is at the root of her not-for-profit work: "Never again would it feel like it was just me. It was *us*," a "family" of formerly incarcerated women, she writes of her recovery home and not-for-profit, *A New Way of Life*.[8] Whereas prison conversion narratives are often premised on converts seeing themselves as fundamentally different from who they once were (criminal or unenlightened or illiterate, for example) and sometimes, by extension, often disidentifying from other imprisoned people, Burton's use of the A.A. conversion narrative helps her articulate what might otherwise be a paradox: how she changes, unquestionably, but also how she remains unchanged and "like" other incarcerated and formerly incarcerated women. Again, because she emphatically identifies with other women trapped in the criminal justice system, it is difficult to read her story as one of transcendence: rather than overcoming structural inequalities and escaping the New Jim Crow, she is perpetually struggling against these systems of injustice in her social justice work and in her business ventures, and she continually highlights her alliances with other incarcerated and formerly incarcerated women whose lives mirror her own.

Burton's memoir repeatedly emphasizes a kinship with other women by telling their stories alongside her story and by stressing how their experiences are like her experience, which is another way that she keeps in focus the structural determinates of the criminal justice system even as she relates how she has changed her own life and remained free from prison. There is often an important synchronicity between Burton's story, the stories of other incarcerated or formerly incarcerated women, and the representation of facts and statistics that explain the wider, structural forces that impact crime, imprisonment, and recidivism. For example, when Burton tells the story of a woman named Mary, who stole two sweatsuits and received a twenty-year sentence as a result of California's "three strikes" sentencing law, she explains that the law also impacts "'two-strikers'" by "automatically doubling the sentence on a second offense, regardless of the crime." She explains that "curbing repeated offenders had been the goal, [but] the result was that prisons were filled with people" – people like Mary – "serving inordinate sentences for low-level offenses."

Burton then links her explanation of the legislation, a structural force impacting the life of an incarcerated woman, with her own experience: "Rather than striking out, I had lucked out because the law wasn't enacted in California until 1994. It was only timing – not lack of offenses – that had me on this side" of the prison wall.[9] Here, and throughout the book, Burton brings together a description of a structural force that impacts the lives of incarcerated people (the Three Strikes law), with the specific story of someone living with the consequences of that structural force (Mary), and with the way that force impacts Burton's own experience with the criminal justice system (in this case, how only a question of timing ensured that she too was not impacted by that structural force). By repeatedly foregrounding the structural forces that impact the lives of incarcerated and formerly incarcerated women, and by weighing these women's experiences against her own, Burton maintains her focus on the unlikelihood of her own conversion experience at the very moment that she is describing it.

Although Burton's use of the conversion narrative to map her experiences of incarceration affiliates her work with the prison life writing tradition that I have discussed in this book, a tradition that is dominated by men's writings, her focus on telling the stories of other incarcerated and formerly incarcerated women alongside her own story also aligns her work with American women's prison life writings, such as Jean Harris's *They Always Call Us Ladies: Stories from Prison* (1988) and Piper Kerman's *Orange Is the New Black: My Year In a Woman's Prison* (2010), which similarly tend to mix biography with autobiography in greater degrees than men's prison life writings.[10] However, there are important differences within women's prison life writings around how an autobiographer identifies or disidentifies with the other women whose stories she relates. Consider Kerman's memoir, for example, which is undoubtedly the best-known book about women's prison experiences and certainly has cultivated significant public interest in women's prisons, especially since the book became a popular TV series in 2013. Like *Becoming Ms. Burton, Orange Is the New Black* focuses much of its attention on the stories of other incarcerated women, which are often told in episodic form. But *how* Kerman positions herself in relation to other imprisoned women in the book is revealing since it exhibits how life writing can distantiate the autobiographical subject, and by extension the reading public, from incarcerated women.

If Burton makes innovative use of the conversion narrative to represent her proximity to, and her complicity with, other incarcerated and formerly incarcerated women, Kerman's story, where an upper-middle-class white woman is imprisoned for drug crimes that occurred many years prior to her incarceration, represents Kerman's incarceration in terms redolent of a travel narrative, which exaggerates the differences between her and other incarcerated women.[11] By being imprisoned, Kerman has crossed what she represents as largely impermeable class and racial boundaries, entering an alien world where she ostensibly does not belong because of her privilege. This provides her with a subject position outside the framework of the prison and its discourse even though she inhabits the prison during her sentence.

Kerman's positioning is reminiscent of Late Victorian prison writing by "gentlemen prisoners" who "invoke the discourse of the travelogue" when they represent themselves in their life writings as "reliable and authoritative witness[es] who [have] made the journey to the secret country behind prison walls and [have] now returned to tell of [their] adventures."[12] Like these Victorian gentlemen, who provide an outsider's perspective on the seemingly distinct world of the prison, Kerman in her memoir repeatedly underscores her dissimilarities from regular imprisoned people. She manages to position herself as a witness, someone whose class and race mark her as outside the cultural sphere of the prison and the people who populate it. So, although she devotes much of her book to telling the stories of other incarcerated women, her memoir reproduces a distinction between self and other, insider and outsider, that reinforces how incarcerated and formerly incarcerated people are defined as exceptional legal subjects, marked out in multiple discourses, but perhaps most damagingly in criminal justice and legal discourses, as inherently different because of their felony convictions.

In contrast, Burton's memoir, which repeatedly underscores her affinities with other women who have served time, is similar to the work of writers like Angela Davis and Assata Shakur, who, as I have shown, emphasize how, as black women, they experience an intersection of sexism and racism within the criminal justice system that aligns them with other incarcerated black women, even though they may come from different backgrounds in terms of class, education, or political affiliation. Even when Burton suggests that formerly incarcerated people need to be "responsible for ... themselves" – a position that seems to approximate a conservative approach that views individual choice as the determining factor in rehabilitation or recidivism – her emphasis on responsibility is non-individualistic since it is actualized through community. For example, Burton explains that asking the formerly incarcerated women in her group home to accept personal responsibility for their reintegration into social life also means that "each woman was encouraged to participate in whatever was going on in the homes and with the organization."[13] As with A.A., where individual success is almost indefinitely reliant on an involvement in the success of others, with a collective well-being, Burton articulates individual success through community.

And this is perhaps how we could read prison life writing as a genre in an age of mass incarceration: rather than focus on the story of individual transcendence, we could read for the myriad ways that the individual story of success is premised on the love and acceptance of other people, on the ways that the self is reconstructed through community. Malcolm X changes, in no small part, because of the intervention of his family members and the support of the Nation of Islam. George Jackson, like many other incarcerated black men and women of his time, finds his sense of identity through meeting fellow incarcerated revolutionaries and identifying with "the People."[14] Jimmy Santiago Baca learns to read and write with the help of materials sent to him from benefactors on the outside, and he learns to define himself as a Chicano poet from imprisoned Chicanos who teach him about his culture. From his lengthy conversations with an incarcerated Chicano named Chelo, he begins "to see who [he] was in a new context, with a deeper sense of responsibility and love for [his] people."[15] Like Malcolm X and Jimmy Santiago Baca, Shaka Senghor learns to rebuild himself through his involvement with someone who loves him and through re-establishing himself as part of a family. From Malcolm X to Susan Rosenberg, from Jack Henry Abbott (who was released with the help and support of people like Norman Mailer and Jerzy Kosinski) to Susan Burton, resistance to the violence of the New Jim Crow, or the successful integration or reintegration into a life free from the purview of the criminal justice system, seems to be premised on the love and acceptance of other people.

Usually, we read prison life writings as stories of individual success because those stories are *there*, particularly in the narratives of imprisoned and formerly imprisoned people who managed to escape the criminal justice system's cycle of recidivism. We also read for stories of individual success because that way of reading has, over time, become the dominant hermeneutic for the genre. It is what readers expect; it is what we look for when we read prison life writing. And it is, to some degree, an effect of the individual-centred nature of the wider autobiographical tradition.

But this hermeneutic also dovetails with the disciplinary program of the prison system. The prison individualizes punishment and demands that formerly incarcerated people be as highly individualized as possible and see their faults and their successes as only their own. Viewing crime and rehabilitation as an issue of individuals flattens the complex background against which crimes occur, which is a tempting fantasy since it would mean that crime control or the problem of mass incarceration could be solved if only individual criminals would just get their act together. But – and really, this should be obvious – crime, punishment, rehabilitation, and recidivism are not exclusively individual issues. Yes, they involve individuals and their choices, but these choices happen structurally and socially. A formerly incarcerated person's successful reintegration into social life after prison rarely happens without support from some kind of community.

And community is key to most conversion narratives. Identifying how communities inside and outside prisons sustain the newly formed identities of incarcerated and formerly incarcerated people – how those communities advocate for, comfort, nurture, and love people living in the New Jim Crow – helps explain why some people never return to prison. Prison activists – from the Soledad Brothers Defense Committee to All of Us or None – know this and have been acting from this position for decades. Prison life writings, including those works that are very much within the prison conversion tradition and that seem to emphasize individual success, are telling us that successful resistance to the New Jim Crow is almost always communal and collective. They involve the power of the people.

NOTES

INTRODUCTION

1   Haslam, *Fitting Sentences*; Rodríguez, *Forced Passages*; Caster, *Prisons, Race, and Masculinity*; Smith, *The Prison*; James, *States of Confinement*; idem, *Imprisoned Intellectuals*; idem, *The New Abolitionists*; idem, *Warfare in the American Homeland*.

2   Franklin, *Prison Writing*; Chevigny, *Doing Time*; Blunk and Levasseur, *Hauling Up the Morning*.

3   For a more thorough consideration of "life writing" as a concept, see Kadar, *Essays on Life Writing*.

4   Smith and Watson, *Reading Autobiography*, 198.

5   In this sense, my position in relation to prison life writing is similar to B.V. Olguín's claim "that Chicana/o criminal and prisoner agency is complex: it is hegemonic and counterhegemonic – and sometimes both simultaneously" (23). Olguín, *La Pinta*.

6   Kaplan, "Resisting Autobiography," 121; Green, "Introduction," 1.

7   Ek, *Race and Masculinity*, 6; Young, "The Dynamic of Interrogation," 16.

8   Davies, *Writers in Prison*, 85.

9   Gready, "Autobiography and the 'Power of Writing,'" 492.

10 Gilmore, *The Limits of Autobiography*, 145.

11 Coletu, "Biographic Mediation," 384.

12 Quoted in Rothman, *Conscience and Convenience*, 57.

13 Goffman, *Asylums*.

14 My use of autobiography's etymology comes from Smith and Watson's *Reading Autobiography*: "In Greek, *autos* signifies 'self,' *bios* 'life,' and *graphe* 'writing.' Taken together in this order, the words denote 'self life writing,' a brief definition of 'autobiography'" (1).

15 Scholars sometimes allude to the conversion narrative in their work but have yet to acknowledge its centrality to US prison discourse.

For example, although Caleb Smith notes the "narrative of death and resurrection" that underpinned the early Jacksonian penitentiary, he shifts the focus of his argument away from the rhetoric of conversion to focus instead on the "political ritual" that was also part of the prison's dramaturgy (which I discuss in greater detail in Chapter 4). Smith, *The Prison and the American Imagination*, 13.

16   Smith and Watson, *Reading Autobiography*, 70.

17   Christianity is not, of course, the only religion that emphasizes the conversion experience or produces a conversion narrative. Malcolm X's conversion experiences, while clearly in line with their Christian and Puritan predecessors, are framed within Islamic traditions. See also Viswanathan, *Outside the Fold*.

18   Dorsey, *Sacred Estrangement*, 48.

19   Dorsey 46, 48–49. For more on the relationship between conversion and autobiography, see Galt Harpham, "Conversion and the Language of Autobiography," 42–50. For more about the secularization of religious conversion narratives, specifically in the twentieth century, see Lieson Brereton, *From Sin to Salvation*, 102–21.

20   For more on the distinctions between conversion and other genres of autobiography, see Walker, *The Trouble with Sauling Around*, 15.

21   James, *The Varieties of Religious Experience*.

22   Early on, critics were quick to identify Malcolm X's *Autobiography* as a conversion narrative, although no one linked his conversion to US prison discourse: Ohmann, "The Autobiography of Malcolm X," 131; Berthoff, "Witness and Testament"; Mandel, "The Didactic Achievement."

23   For more on the relationship between power and collaborative narratives, see James Olney, "'I was born': Slave Narratives, Their Status as Autobiography and as Literature," in *The Slave's Narrative*, ed. Charles T. Davis and Henry Louis Gates, Jr. (Oxford: Oxford University Press, 1985), 148–75. Or see Kathleen McHugh and Catherine Komisaruk, eds., "Something Other Than Autobiography: Collaborative Life-Narratives in the Americas," Special Issue, *Biography* 31(3).

24 Malcolm X and Alex Haley, *The Autobiography of Malcolm X* (New York: Ballantine Books, 1992), 390; Marable, *Malcolm X*.

25 Malcolm X and Haley, *Autobiography*, 181.

26 Malcolm X and Haley, *Autobiography*, 189.

27 Malcolm X and Haley, *Autobiography*, 196.

28 Similarly, Warner Berthoff writes of the "names, the folk-identities, that attach to [Malcolm X] at each new stage" of his conversion. Berthoff 318. Carol Ohmann likewise notes that the chapter titles of *The Autobiography* conform to features of Malcolm's conversion experiences. Ohmann, "The Autobiography," 144–45.

29 Malcolm X and Alex Haley, *Autobiography*, 196.

30 Malcolm X and Alex Haley, *Autobiography*, 200.

31 Malcolm X and Alex Haley, *Autobiography*, 218.

32 Malcolm X and Alex Haley, *Autobiography*, 207.

33 Cleaver, *Soul on Ice*, 56.

34 Chessman, *Cell 2455*, 359.

35 Williams, *Blue Rage, Black Redemption*, xix.

36 For more on the role of education in the early penitentiary system, see Schorb, *Reading Prisoners*.

37 Brockway, *Fifty Years of Prison Service*, 163.

38 Cleaver, *Soul on Ice*; Jackson, *Soledad Brother*; Carr, *Bad*; Abbott, *In the Belly of the Beast*; Williams, *Blue Rage, Black Redemption*; Senghor, *Writing My Wrongs*; Loya, *The Man Who Outgrew His Prison Cell*.

39 Malcolm X draws on his former life "in the streets as a hustler" to be a more effective minister. He also discusses how Nation of Islam proselytizers use "the same old junkie jungle language" to recruit addicts and cure their addiction. Malcolm X and Haley, *Autobiography*, 273, 299. For an excellent discussion of the ways that Malcolm X's past informed his identity as a Nation of Islam minister, see Walker, *The Trouble with Sauling Around*, 27–58.

40 Readers' lascivious, even erotic interests in prison life writing are well-known. As Ek writes, prison life writing is "a discursive site for satisfying voyeuristic pleasure." Ek, *Race and Masculinity*, 48.

41 Lejeune, *On Autobiography*.

42 Gilmore, *The Limits of Autobiography*, 3.

43 For a good illustration of the difficulties that imprisoned people face when publishing their work, see the discussion and analysis of Caryl Chessman's story in Cummins, *The Rise and Fall*, 33–62. In addition to prison regulations that can make publication difficult, laws have sometimes curtailed imprisoned people's capacities to read, write, and publish (an example being "Son of Sam" laws, which typically divert profits from imprisoned writers to victims of their crimes).

44 The notion of a "communications circuit" that links writers, publishers, booksellers, and readers comes from Darnton, "What Is the History of Books?," 30–31. For more about prison writing as a communications circuit, see Schorb, *Reading Prisoners*, 25–27.

45 Franklin, *The Victim as Criminal and Artist*, 233.

46 Dylan Rodríguez, who questions "the common aestheticization of [imprisoned people's] work into a 'genre' of literary text," provides the most eloquent critique of prison writing as a genre. *Forced Passages*, 82. See also idem, "Against the Discipline of 'Prison Writing.'"

47 Idem, *Forced Passages*, 83–94.

48 Frow, "Reproducibles, Rubrics, and Everything You Need," 1629.

49 Elizabeth Hinton argues that the roots of mass incarceration can be found in the Johnson administration, and Anne E. Parsons argues that the rise of mass incarceration coincided with the closing of asylums in the 1960s. Hinton, *From the War on Poverty to the War on Crime*; Parsons, *From Asylum to Prison*.

50 Senghor, *Writing My Wrongs*, Chapter 10.

51 Trounstine, *Shakespeare behind Bars*, 2.

52 "Changing Lives through Literature." See also Waxler and Trounstine, *Changing Lives through Literature*.

53 Bruchac, *The Light from another Country*, xiii.

54 BU Prison Education Program, "Welcome."

55 Cummins, *The Rise and Fall.* Books that provide alternative perspectives on the movement include Hames-García, *Fugitive Thought*; and Berger, *Captive Nation.*

56 Excellent analyses of *Soledad Brother* that nonetheless under-represent the significance of the prison in determining Jackson's autobiographical self include Berger, *Captive Nation*, 91–138; Bernstein, *America is the Prison*; Stanutz, "'Dying, but Fighting Back.'"

57 Abbott, *In the Belly of the Beast*; Gaddis and Long, *Killer.*

58 Jackson, *Soledad Brother*, 194.

59 Even in its inception, the prison was described as a gothic space. Caleb Smith writes that "in the language of [post-Revolutionary-era] reformers, inmates, and literary artists at large, the prison was represented as the dark house of ghosts and monsters." Smith, *The Prison and the American Imagination*, 29.

60 Dan Berger notes that the term "carceral state" is often used but rarely defined in studies of prisons. He writes: "Most historians have deployed the term in ways both temporally and conceptually limited: temporally, scholars have focused most heavily on either post-slavery convict leasing in the South or post-1945 explorations of carceral expansion, especially in the North and West." "Finding and Defining the Carceral State," 281. My use of the term differs temporally from Berger's examples and is perhaps more in line with Marie Gottschalk's use of the term in *The Prison and the Gallows.*

61 Olguín, *La Pinta*, 65.

62 Shaka Senghor acknowledges the influence of a black radical tradition throughout his work, but he emphasizes the role this tradition plays in his writing and life in a "Recommended Reading" section at the end of his book, where, among other authors, he includes the autobiographical work of Malcolm X, Angela Davis, Assata Shakur, and George Jackson. Senghor, *Writing My Wrongs*, 267.

63 Sawyer, "The Gender Divide."

64 Thompson, "Why Mass Incarceration Matters," 704.

65 http://sentencingproject.org/wp-content/uploads/2016/01/Trends-in-US-Corrections.pdf

66 Gottschalk, *The Prison and the Gallows*, 1.

67 Alexander, *The New Jim Crow*, 13.

68 Meyer et al., "Incarceration Rates and Traits."

CHAPTER 1: CONVERSION AND THE STORY OF THE US PRISON

1   Gumbel, "Paris Hilton Thanks God."

2   Franklin, *The Victim as Criminal and Artist*, 128.

3   There are many examples of religious conversions in prison life writing. The most famous are perhaps Colson, *Born Again*; and Cleaver, *Soul on Fire*.

4   Thomas, *Down these Mean Streets*; McCall, *Makes Me Wanna Holler*.

5   According to a census by the Bureau of Justice Statistics, "of the 272,111 persons released from prisons in 15 States in 1994, an estimated 67.5% were rearrested for a felony or serious misdemeanour within 3 years, 46.9% were reconvicted, and 25.4% resentenced to prison for a new crime." US Bureau of Justice, "Recidivism."

6   James, *The New Abolitionists*, xxii.

7   Caldwell, *The Puritan Conversion Narrative*, 2.

8   Meranze, "The Penitential Ideal," 440.

9   Morgan, *Visible Saints*, 101. See also Pettit, *The Heart Prepared*.

10 Caldwell, *The Puritan Conversion Narrative*, 1.

11 As Donatella Pallotti writes, "the 'truthfulness' and value of the spiritual experience and of the person who lived it are gauged by the degree of observance to a recognized, and sanctioned, model. The 'new birth' is indeed an experience of the heart, deeply personal and intimate, but it is also a process that is stimulated, nourished and directed by the assumptions and expectations of the religious community." "'Out of their Owne Mouths'?," 77.

12 Rowlandson, "The Captivity and Deliverance," 79–102.

NOTES

13   Castiglia, *Bound and Determined*, 1; Colley, *Captives*, 150; Smith, "Reading the Posthuman Backward," 142.

14   Caleb Smith suggests that perhaps captivity narratives, with their "tales of bondage, suffering, and redemption[,] may have been among the many ideological sources for the penitentiary." Smith, *The Prison and the American Imagination*, 11.

15   Slotkin, *Regeneration through Violence*, 441.

16   Douglass, *Narrative*, 107.

17   Douglass, *Narrative*, 113.

18   Sekora, "Black Message/White Envelope," 509.

19   Andrews, "The First Fifty Years," 8.

20   Fitzgerald, *The Evangelicals*.

21   For more on Quaker Spiritual journals, see Shea, *Spiritual Autobiography*, 3–84.

22   Bunyan, *Grace Abounding*.

23   A.A. World Services, "The Twelve Steps of Alcoholics Anonymous."

24   Crèvecoeur, *Letters*, 54.

25   Skotnicki, *Religion and the Development*, 39.

26   For an excellent discussion of this early genre of criminal literature and an explanation of how that literature developed into nineteenth-century "rogue narratives," a form of early criminal life writing, see Williams, "Rogues, Rascals, and Scoundrels." For more about the criminal conversion narrative, see Williams, "'Behold a Tragic Scene Strangely Changed into a Theater of Mercy.'"

27   Rogers et al., *Death the Certain Wages of Sin*, 135.

28   The continuity of the criminal conversion narrative from scaffold to penitentiary illustrates Colin Dayan's observation that "the social, economic, and even spiritual practices of remote times persist in legal forms and pronouncements." "Legal Terrors," 46.

29   Quoted in Skotnicki, *Religion and the Development*, 55.

30   Smith, *A Defence of the System*, 96.

31   Rush and the Society, "An Enquiry," 14.

32 Lehmann, "Challenges and Accomplishments," 491.

33 Sweeney, *Reading Is my Window*, 24.

34 Baxter, *A Call to the Unconverted*, x.

35 Rush, *Considerations*.

36 Cohen et al., *Eastern State Penitentiary*, 33; Lewis, *The Development of American Prisons*, 13, 43.

37 Reconfiguring Coleridge's "Life-in-Death," John Edgar Wideman writes: "Prison time must be hard time, a metaphorical death, a sustained, twilight condition of death-in-life." *Brothers and Keepers*, 35.

38 Hawkins and Alpert, *American Prison Systems*, 367.

39 For more on the decline of civil death laws and the re-emergence of unofficial forms of civil death toward the end of the twentieth century, see Chin, "The New Civil Death." See also Dayan, *The Law Is a White Dog*, 39–70. For an excellent discussion of civil death statutes and literary form, see Smith, *The Prison and the American Imagination*, 27–52. Smith also has a valuable essay on teaching civil death as a law and literature subject: "American Undead."

40 Tocqueville and Beaumont, *On the Penitentiary System*, 32.

41 Death remains one of the most commonly used metaphors for imprisonment. As Dylan Rodríguez writes, "a discourse of death and disappearance has become a common way for the currently and formerly imprisoned to describe both the social logic and the experience of incarceration." *Forced Passages*, 58.

42 Foucault, *Discipline and Punish*, 239.

43 Dayan, "Legal Terrors," 52.

44 Tocqueville and Beaumont, *On the Penitentiary System*, 6.

45 Tocqueville and Beaumont, *On the Penitentiary System*, 156.

46 It is worth noting that religious conversion remained important to the Auburn system in part because the person largely credited with the nationalization of the Auburn method, Louis Dwight, who was also the founder of and secretary for the influential Prison Discipline Society of Boston, wanted the Auburn system

to produce conversions: "His profound faith commitment came to be channelled and directed by means of a vow he made, that his life would be spent in seeking a form of 'prison discipline' that would promote religious conversion and remove inmates from the squalor in which they were forced to dwell." Skotnicki, *Religion and the Development*, 43–44.

47 Taylor, *Down on Parchman Farm*, 83. For more on the shift between these two institutions, see Mancini, *One Dies, Get another*; Oshinsky, *Worse than Slavery*; Blackmon, *Slavery by Another Name*. For a comparison between slaves and imprisoned people, see Sellin, *Slavery and the Penal System*. Also, for a slightly different analysis of this shift – one that questions the amount that plantation prisons or the work-lease program effectively took over where slavery left off – see Gottschalk, *The Prison and the Gallows*.

48 James, "Introduction," xxiii.

49 Hinton, *From the War on Poverty to the War on Crime*.

50 Murakawa, *The First Civil Right*.

51 Alexander, *The New Jim Crow*, 40–57. Alexander's argument that the War on Drugs caused the spike in prison numbers has been qualified by historians, including Murakawa and Hinton, who show that the roots of mass incarceration started much earlier.

52 Stuntz, *The Collapse*, 34.

53 Coates, "The Black Family," 60.

54 Davis, "From the Convict Lease System," 62.

55 Enoch Wines and Louis Dwight, *Report on the Prisons and Reformatories of the United States and Canada* (Albany: Van Benthuysen & Sons, 1867). Sullivan, *The Prison Reform Movement*, 17.

56 Sullivan, *The Prison Reform Movement*, 18. For more on the "new penology," see Pisciotta, "Scientific Reform."

57 Hawkins and Alpert, *American Prison Systems*, 186.

58 Hazelrigg, *Prison within Society*, 393.

59 *Struggle for Justice*, 44, 45, 46.

60 Hawkins and Alpert, *American Prison Systems*, 187.

61 Brockway, *Fifty Years of Prison Service*, 163.

62 Blomberg and Lucken, *American Penology*, 71.

63 Hawkins and Alpert, *American Prison Systems*, 190; MacNamara, "The Medical Model in Corrections," 440.

64 Sullivan, *The Prison Reform Movement*, 76. The authors of *Struggle for Justice* charge that replacing criminal values with values associated with free society amounted to "coerced cultural indoctrination" because the "values" that imprisoned people were supposed to accept were often white and middle-class (43).

65 "One survey found that 74 percent of prison facilities offered self-help programs of various types. Of those, AA had the strongest representation (in 95 percent of those facilities), followed by NA (in 85 percent). Less than one third offered other types of self-help programs." Peters and Wexler, *Substance Abuse Treatment*, 197.

66 Sullivan, *The Prison Reform Movement*, 70.

67 For more on these programs in the California prison system, see Cummins, *The Rise and Fall*.

68 *Struggle for Justice*, 45.

69 Sullivan and Vogel, "Reachin' behind Bars," 117.

70 Allen, "The Decline of the Rehabilitative Ideal," 154.

71 Rothman, *Conscience and Convenience*, 68.

72 Carr, *Bad*, 121.

73 Braly, *False Starts*, 360.

74 Jackson, *Soledad Brother*, 190.

75 Rothman, *Conscience and Convenience*, 44.

76 *Oxford English Dictionary*, "Parole."

77 Malcolm Braly, *False Starts*, 252.

78 Davis, *Are Prisons Obsolete?*, 69–70.

79 Nicole Hahn Rafter, *Partial Justice: Women, Prisons and Social Control* (London and New York: Routledge, 2017), xxvi.

80 Carby, "Policing the Black Woman's Body," *Critical* 739.

81 Gross, "African American Women," 29–30.

82 Welter, "The Cult of True Womanhood," 152.

83 Welter, "The Cult of True Womanhood," xxviii.

84   Davis, *An Autobiography*, 308–9.

85   Lindsey Linder, J.D., "An Unsupported Population: The Treatment of Women in Texas' Criminal Justice System," 17.

86   James, "Introduction," xxi–xlii.

CHAPTER 2: THE TREATMENT ERA

1   Guest, *Sentenced to Death*, xvi.

2   Bernstein, *America Is the Prison*, 51.

3   Rodríguez, *Forced Passages*, 121.

4   Buck and Whitehorn, "Cruel But Not Unusual," 261.

5   Jackson, *Soledad Brother*, 40.

6   "Dark Days, Bright Nights," Peneil's chapter on Black Power during the early 1970s, repeatedly returns to George Jackson, a "Black Power icon," because he played a critical role in the history of Black Power during this period. Peniel, *Waiting 'Til the Midnight Hour*, 241–75.

7   Caren Kaplan, "Resisting Autobiography: Out-Law Genres and Transnational Feminist Subjects," in *De/Colonizing the Subject: The Politics of Gender in Women's Autobiography*, eds. Sidonie Smith and Julia Watson (Minneapolis: University of Minneapolis Press, 1992), 120, 119.

8   Kaplan, "Resisting Autobiography," 119.

9   Clark, *The Brothers of Attica*; Woodfox, *Solitary*.

10   Liberatore, *The Road to Hell*, 8.

11   Liberatore, *The Road to Hell*, 16; Carr, *Bad*, 59.

12   Carr, *Bad*, 123.

13   James, *Imprisoned Intellectuals*, 85; Bernstein, *America Is the Prison*, 56–57.

14   Min Yee, "Death on the Yard: The Untold Killings at Soledad & San Quentin," *Ramparts*, April 1973, 35.

15   Yee, "Death on the Yard," 35.

16   Berger, *Captive Nation*, 101.

17   Berger, *Captive Nation*, 109.

18   Jackson, *Soledad Brother*, 290. There is some debate about what Jonathan Jackson actually said when he revealed his weapon to the court. Katherine Stanutz notes that "this quotation does not appear in the press reports of the situation." Stanutz, "'Dying, but Fighting Back.'"

19   For more on the trial, see Davis, *Autobiography*, 2.

20   Liberatore, *The Road to Hell*, 89–92.

21   Berger, *Captive Nation*, 124.

22   Jackson, *Soledad Brother*, 290.

23   Jackson, *Soledad Brother*, 290.

24   Jackson, *Blood in My Eye*, 12. For an interesting explanation of Jackson's use of the Cuban Revolution's theories of vanguardism, especially those of Che Guevara, see Corrigan, "Cross-Pollinating the Revolution."

25   Berger, *Captive Nation*, 96.

26   Foucault, *Discipline and Punish*, 251.

27   Duffy and Jennings, *The San Quentin Story*, 250.

28   Jackson, *Soledad Brother*, 200.

29   Jackson, *Soledad Brother*, 201.

30   Jackson, *Soledad Brother*, 63.

31   Jackson, *Soledad Brother*, 100.

32   Eric Cummins also notes that Jackson was deeply invested in the prison's criminal subculture and had, in addition, been allegedly involved in numerous acts of violence during the period when he was seeking parole. Cummins, *The Rise and Fall*, 156.

33   Jackson, *Blood in My Eye*, 181.

34   Jackson, *Soledad Brother*, 104.

35   Jackson, *Soledad Brother*, 106.

36   Jackson, *Soledad Brother*, 50.

37   Berger, *Captive Nation*, 119.

38   Berger, *Captive Nation*, 120.

39   Carr, *Bad*, 134.

40   Carr, *Bad*, 71.

41   Certeau, *The Practice of Everyday Life*, xvii.

42 Certeau, *The Practice of Everyday Life*, xiv.

43 Malewitz, "Regeneration through Misuse," 527.

44 Genet, "Introduction," 22.

45 Genet, "Introduction," 22.

46 Genet, "Introduction," 21.

47 *Oxford English Dictionary*, "Corrupt."

48 Jackson, *Soledad Brother*, 203.

49 Jackson, *Soledad Brother*, 267.

50 Jackson, *Soledad Brother*, 39–40.

51 Malcolm X and Haley, *Autobiography*, 195.

52 Jackson, *Soledad Brother*, 271. See also Bernstein, *America Is the Prison*, 57–58.

53 Jackson, *Soledad Brother*, 234.

54 Carmichael and Hamilton, *Black Power*, 5.

55 Liberatore, *The Road to Hell*, 19.

56 Jackson, *Soledad Brother*, 50.

57 Berger, *Captive Nation*, 166.

58 Carr, *Bad*, 192.

59 Berger, *Captive Nation*, 133, 305n148.

60 Hammer, "Introduction," 12.

61 Carr, *Bad*, 21.

62 Carr, *Bad*, 196.

63 Foucault, *Discipline and Punish*, 302–3.

64 Carr, *Bad*, 27.

65 Carr, *Bad*, 40.

66 Carr, *Bad*, 55.

67 Carr, *Bad*, 58.

68 Carr, *Bad*, 121.

69 Carr, *Bad*, 165.

70 Carr, *Bad*, 162.

71 Carr, *Bad*, 189.

72 Carr, *Bad*, 164.

73 Carr, *Bad*, 163.

74 Carr, *Bad*, 193.

75 Carr, *Bad*, 192.

76 Genet, "Introduction," 21.

77 Eakin, "Breaking Rules," 113–14.

78 Carr, *Bad*, 24.

79 Bryant, *Born in a Mighty Bad Land*, 2.

80 Bryant, *Born in a Mighty Bad Land*, 3.

81 Bryant, *Born in a Mighty Bad Land*, 2.

82 Bryant, *Born in a Mighty Bad Land*, 3.

83 Hammer, "Introduction," 17. Isaac Cronin, personal interview, 15 September 2008.

84 Ek, *Race and Masculinity*, 57.

85 Carr, *Bad*, 89–90.

86 Hammer, "Introduction," 16.

87 Gates, *The Signifying Monkey*, xviiii.

88 Hurston, *Dust Tracks*, 47.

89 Hurston, *Dust Tracks*, 47.

90 Brown, "Street Talk," 208.

91 Rymhs, *From the Iron House*, 14.

92 Bryant, *Born in a Mighty Bad Land*, 89.

93 Wepman, Newman, Binderman, *The Life*, 135–36.

94 Jackson, *"Get Your Ass in the Water"*, 51–52.

95 Jackson, *"Get Your Ass in the Water,"* 54–55.

96 Jackson, *"Get Your Ass in the Water,"* 47.

97 Jackson, *"Get Your Ass in the Water,"* 55.

98 Jackson, *"Get Your Ass in the Water,"* 91.

99 Carr, *Bad*, 37–38.

100 McCall, *Makes Me Wanna Holler*, 44.

101 Carr, *Bad*, 38.

102 Parsell, *Fish*; Ek, *Race and Masculinity*, 66.

103 Wepman, Newman, and Binderman, *The Life*, 137.

104 Carr, *Bad*, 64.

105 Carr, *Bad*, 122.

106 Carr, *Bad*, 57.

107 Carr, *Bad*, 161.

108 Rhodes, *Framing the Black Panthers*, 33.

109 Baldwin, "Many Thousands Gone," 34.

110 Sloop, *The Cultural Prison*, 16.

111 Rhodes, *Framing the Black Panthers*, 32.

112 Roberts, "Deviance, Resistance, and Love," 188.

113 Ek, *Race and Masculinity*, 71.

114 Jackson, *Soledad Brother*, 190.

115 Carr, *Bad*, 177, 172.

116 Carr, "Afterword," 201.

117 Burton and Lynn, *Becoming Ms. Burton*, 191.

118 Burton and Lynn, *Becoming Ms. Burton*, 233–34, 239.

119 Burton and Lynn, *Becoming Ms. Burton*, 239.

120 Burton and Lynn, *Becoming Ms. Burton*, 191.

CHAPTER 3: FROM THE TREATMENT ERA TO THE MONSTER FACTORY

1 For more about the history of the Attica uprising, see Thompson, *Blood in the Water*. An important primary source about the uprising is *Attica: The Official Report*. For a first-person account of the event, see Wicker, *A Time to Die*.

2 Heather Ann Thompson, *Blood in the Water*, 562.

3 "In America, support for rehabilitation clearly declined in the 1970s for a variety of reasons, not least of which was the belief that rehabilitation achieved little save for coddling criminals." Mears and Cochran, *Prisoner Reentry*, 94; see also Thompson, *Blood in the Water*, 561–64.

4 Lipton, Martinson, and Wilks, *The Effectiveness of Correctional Treatment*.

5 Sullivan, *The Prison Reform Movement*, 113–14; Sloop, *The Cultural Prison*, 139.

6 Foucault and Simon, "Michel Foucault on Attica," 27.

7 Jackson, *Soledad Brother*, 190.

8 Jackson, *Soledad Brother*, 49.

9 Jackson, *Soledad Brother*, 193.

10 George H.W. Bush's presidential campaign ad about Willie Horton is perhaps the most notorious use of the figure of the incorrigible prisoner for political purposes during this period.

11 Halberstam, *Skin Shows*, 6.

12 Alexander, *The New Jim Crow*, 181.

13 Alexander, *The New Jim Crow*, 94. Although Alexander is specifically discussing the post-1980s era of mass incarceration here, and while that period saw unique innovations in the curtailment of ex-convicts' rights, her terminology nonetheless still applies to the experiences of ex-convicts of earlier periods.

14 Gaddis and Long, *Killer*, 25.

15 Gaddis and Long, *Killer*, 144.

16 Gaddis and Long, *Killer*, 221.

17 Gaddis and Long, *Killer*, 200.

18 Gaddis and Long, *Killer*, 326.

19 Henry Lesser donated Panzram's handwritten confession to San Diego State University. A scanned copy of the work can be found here: Karl Panzram, "Panzram's Autobiographical Manuscript," Box 1, Virtual Folder, Carl Panzram Papers, Special Collections and University Archives, San Diego State University.

20 Gaddis and Long, *Killer*, 16.

21 Wilson and Seaman, *The Serial Killers*, 44.

22 Desmond, "Flannery O'Connor's Misfit," 136.

23 O'Connor, "A Good Man is Hard to Find," 18.

24 O'Connor, "A Good Man is Hard to Find," 21.

25 A reprint of *Killer*, renamed *Panzram: A Journal of Murder*, similarly notes a connection between The Misfit and Panzram but does not address how the prison is central to both The Misfit's and Panzram's identities. Gaddis and Long, *Panzram*.

26 Gaddis and Long, *Killer*, 25.

27 Gaddis and Long, *Killer*, 372.

28 Gaddis and Long, *Killer*, 210.

29 Gaddis and Long, *Killer*, 31.

30 Gaddis and Long, *Killer*, 74, 166, 236.

31 Osborne quoted in Rothman, *Conscience and Convenience*, 119.

32 Best and Marcus, "Surface Reading," 1.

33 Gaddis and Long, *Killer*, 216.

34 Rothman, *Conscience and Convenience*, 5.

35 Gaddis and Long, *Killer*, 227.

36 Gaddis and Long, *Killer*, 228.

37 Gaddis and Long, *Killer*, 229.

38 Gaddis and Long, *Killer*, 230.

39 Gaddis and Long, *Killer*, 231.

40 Gaddis and Long, *Killer*, 170.

41 Gaddis and Long, *Killer*, 230. The "mind of a murderer" metaphor is surprisingly ubiquitous in discussions of imprisoned people and prison life writing. When Caryl Chessman's *Cell 2455* was published, reviewers used a similar metaphor as Gaddis and Long to explain the value of Chessman's work. For example, the *New York Herald Tribune Book Review* congratulated Chessman for providing "a great deal of insight into a criminal's mind." Qtd in Cummins, *The Rise and Fall*, 39.

42 In this way, life writing interlocks with biopower, with the state's use of data to expand its surveillance powers over vast bodies of people.

43 Gaddis and Long, *Killer*, 265.

44 Gaddis and Long, *Killer*, 220.

45 Gaddis and Long, *Killer*, 221.

46 Gaddis and Long, *Killer*, 241.

47 Gaddis and Long, *Killer*, 240.

48 In *My Return*, Abbott contends that "Mailer's letter [to the parole board] did not result in [his] parole." Mailer certainly did play a role in Abbott's early release; but it is also quite likely that Abbott would have been released anyway, since he was due (even, past due) for parole. Abbott with Zack, *My Return*, 1987.

49 Des Pres, "A Child of the State."

50 Abbott, *In the Belly of the Beast*, 22.

51 Qtd in Dearborn, *Mailer*, 360.

52 Abbott, *In the Belly of the Beast*, 13.

53 Critical analyses that link the gothic with the US prison are so common that they can even be distilled to studies of the gothic, the prison, and Edgar Allan Poe: Smith, *The Prison and the American Imagination*, 56–57; Dayan, "Poe, Persons, and Property"; Haslam, "Pits, Pendulums, and Penitentiaries."

54 Abbott, *In the Belly of the Beast*, 197–98.

55 Halberstam, *Skin Shows*, 27.

56 Here, I consider representations of affect as gothic in the book rather than the production of affect for readers, as Reyes discusses in "Gothic Affect," 11–23.

57 Abbott, *In the Belly of the Beast*, 61.

58 Abbott, *In the Belly of the Beast*, 5.

59 Sedgwick, "The Character in the Veil," 255.

60 Halberstam, *Skin Shows*, 108.

61 For more about the psychological and emotional effects of solitary confinement, see Grassian, "Psychopathological Effects."

62 Abbott, *In the Belly of the Beast*, 114, 143.

63 Rodríguez, *Forced Passages,* 85.

64 Jackson, *Soledad Brother*, 39-40.

65 Abbott, *In the Belly of the Beast*, 118.

66 Jackson, *Blood in my Eye.* 108.

67 Abbott, *In the Belly of the Beast*, 196.

68 Abbott, *In the Belly of the Beast*, 196.

69 Mailer, "The White Negro."

70 Rollyson, *The Lives of Norman Mailer*, 305.

71 Dearborn, *Mailer*, 357.

72 In a September 1981 front-page article in the *New York Times Book Review* that was printed in reaction to Richard Adan's murder, Michiko Kakutani also suggests that Abbott modelled himself on Mailer's writings. She emphasizes Mailer's fictional characters rather than the "white negro," however: "Like Lieutenant Hearn in 'The Naked and the Dead,' Mr. Abbott asserted his own

identity in the face of an arbitrary system of officially regulated morality; like Sergius O'Shaugnessy in 'The Deer Park,' he was self-educated and self-made; like Stephen Rojack in 'An American Dream,' he had killed without apology." Kakutani, "The Strange Case," BR1.

73 Mailer, "The White Negro," 214, 211.

74 Susan Gubar defines racechanges as the intentional transgression of racial boundaries, whether to parody the other (like blackface minstrelsy) or to "'learn about the other by being the other,'" as Deavere Smith suggests in Gubar's book. Gubar, *Racechanges*, xxi.

75 Melville, *Letters from Attica*, 57.

76 Abbott, *In the Belly of the Beast*, 176.

77 Abbott, *In the Belly of the Beast*, 171, 173–75, 175–76.

78 Abbott, *In the Belly of the Beast*, 171–73.

79 Abbott, *In the Belly of the Beast*, 172.

80 Golub, "History Died for Our Sins," 23.

81 Abbott, *In the Belly of the Beast*, 176.

82 Abbott, *In the Belly of the Beast*, 182. For a discussion of the class paradigm of race, see Michael Omi and Howard Winant, *Racial Formation in the United States: From the 1960s to the 1980s* (New York: Routledge & Kegan Paul, 1986), 24–35.

83 Abbott, *In the Belly of the Beast*, 183.

84 Abbott, *In the Belly of the Beast*, 183.

85 Wiegman, "Whiteness Studies and the Paradox of Particularity," 123.

86 Abbott, *In the Belly of the Beast*, 175.

87 Abbott, *In the Belly of the Beast*, 176.

88 Abbott, *In the Belly of the Beast*, 176.

89 Wiegman, "Whiteness Studies and the Paradox of Particularity," 139.

90 Wiegman, "Whiteness Studies and the Paradox of Particularity," 121.

91 Abbott, *In the Belly of the Beast*, 176.

92 hooks, *Black Looks*, 25.

93 Carroll, *Affirmative Reaction*, 21.

94 For more on the white abolitionist argument, see Roediger, *Towards the Abolition of Whiteness*; or Ignatiev and Garvey, *Race Traitor*.

95 Jenkins, *Decade of Nightmares*, 239, 238.

96 Dilulio, "The Coming of the Super-Predators," 23. As I noted earlier, historians like Naomi Murakawa and Elizabeth Hinton have emphasized that the forces of mass incarceration and the criminalization of black masculinity started much earlier than Dilulio's work and the Reagan-era War on Drugs. See also Muhammad, *The Condemnation of Blackness*.

97 Sloop, *The Cultural Prison*, 136.

CHAPTER 4: LIFE WRITING IN
THE CONTEMPORARY CARCERAL STATE

1 Gottschalk, *The Prison and the Gallows*, 1. Eric Schlosser, in an influential 1998 article in *The Atlantic*, famously calls the public/ private partnerships, the "set of bureaucratic, political, and economic interests that encourage increased spending on imprisonment," "the prison-industrial complex." Eric Schlosser, "The Prison-Industrial Complex," *The Atlantic Monthly*, 1 December 1998.

2 Gramlich, *Federal Prison Population Fell*.

3 Baca is typically celebrated for transcending the conditions of his imprisonment in his life writings. See, for example, Franklin, "Can the Penitentiary Teach."

4 Senghor, shakasenghor.com, 2016.

5 See, for example, Loïc Wacquant's argument that mass incarceration "is one component of a more comprehensive restructuring of the American state to suit the requirements of neoliberalism." "Deadly Symbiosis."

6 Fraser, "Etheridge Knight Is Dead," 24.

7 BLAK Fintech, Twitter Profile.

8   Spencer, "Unlocked Potential."

9   "Cedar Tree, inc. Jimmy Santiago Baca.com; "The Atonement
     Project," *Detroit Soup*, 2015. Many thanks to an early reader of this
     book, who clarified that The Atonement Project was a University
     of Michigan course.

10   Baca, *A Place to Stand*, 6; Franklin, *Autobiography*.

11   Absent and/or abusive fathers are a frequent theme in prison life
     writing. For example, like Baca's *A Place to Stand*, Tom Runyon's
     In for Life (1953) begins by discussing how Runyon's father abuses
     and eventually abandons him. Runyon, *In for Life*.

12   Olguín, *La Pinta*, 66.

13   Senghor's story is a small piece of a much larger story about the
     effects of mass incarceration on his Detroit neighborhood. As
     Heather Ann Thompson writes, "Of all the prisoners released
     to Wayne County, Michigan, in the year 2000, a full 41 percent
     returned to only eight particularly devastated zip codes in the city
     of Detroit." "Why Mass Incarceration Matters," 715.

14   Baca, *A Place to Stand*, 4.

15   Baca, *A Place to Stand*, 244.

16   Senghor, *Writing My Wrongs*, 1.

17   Senghor, *Writing My Wrongs*, 106, 151.

18   For example, in *A brief Account of the Life and Abominable Thefts of
     the Notorious Isaac Frazier,* the eponymous Frazier concludes that
     "the love of money, the ruling principle of my mind, has brought
     me to the grave in the flower of life, when my sun is scarce risen;
     at the age of 28, I am going down into the house of silence, to be
     numbered with the dead." Frasier, *A brife [sic] account of the life.*
     For a fascinating explanation of how Frasier's confession fits into
     the history of the criminal confession, see Williams, "Rogues,
     Rascals, and Scoundrels."

19   Baca, *A Place to Stand*, 5.

20   Baca, *A Place to Stand*, 185.

21   Senghor, *Writing My Wrongs*, 191.

22   Tocqueville and Beaumont, *On the Penitentiary System*, 3.

23 Cohen et al., *Eastern State Penitentiary*, 38.

24 Baca, *A Place to Stand*, 184, 188, 186.

25 Senghor, *Writing My Wrongs*, 2, 58.

26 Senghor, *Writing My Wrongs*, 61.

27 Senghor, *Writing My Wrongs*, 177.

28 Senghor, *Writing My Wrongs*, 192.

29 Senghor, *Writing My Wrongs*, 22, 195, 240.

30 Slaughter, *Human Rights, Inc*, 4.

31 Slaughter, *Human Rights, Inc.*, 279, 274.

32 Slaughter, *Human Rights, Inc.*, 279.

33 Smith, *The Prison and the American Imagination*, 13–14.

34 Smith, *The Prison and the American Imagination*, 49.

35 Smith, *The Prison and the American Imagination*, 192.

36 Baca, *A Place to Stand*, 209.

37 Baca, *A Place to Stand*, 206.

38 Rousseau, *On the Social Contract*, 56.

39 Rousseau, *On the Social Contract*, 56.

40 Baca, *A Place to Stand*, 167.

41 Lowell, "In the Cage," 53.

42 Clarke, "'Only Man is Miserable,'" 135.

43 *OED Online*, "Hyena."

44 Baca, *A Place to Stand*, 167.

45 Baca, *A Place to Stand*, 167–168.

46 Lombroso, *Criminal Man*, 51.

47 Lombroso, *Criminal Man*, 49.

48 Lombroso, *Criminal Man*, 91.

49 Lombroso, *Criminal Man*, 175.

50 Lombroso, *Criminal Man*, 175.

51 Stoddard, *The Revolt against Civilization*, 5. In *The Great Gatsby*, Tom Buchanan misidentifies Stoddard (confusing him with psychologist and eugenicist Henry H. Goddard) when he explains that Stoddard's *The Rise of the Colored Empires* details how "the white race will be – will be utterly submerged" by "these other races." *The Great Gatsby*, 13.

52 Stoddard, *The Revolt Against Civilization*, 23.

53 Stoddard, *The Revolt Against Civilization*, 25.

54 Sloop, *The Cultural Prison*, 142.

55 Baca, *Working in the Dark*, 88; idem, *A Place to Stand*, 244.

56 Bender, *Imagining the Penitentiary*, 4.

57 Smith, "Autobiographical Discourse," x.

58 Senghor, *Writing My Wrongs*, 203–4.

59 shakasenghor.com.

60 shakasenghor.com.

61 Shorters, "Introduction," xxiv.

62 Moynihan, *The Negro Family*. For more on the Moynihan Report, see Moynihan and Rainwater, *The Moynihan Report*; Patterson, *Freedom Is Not Enough*; Geary, *Beyond Civil Rights*; Ibrahim, *Troubling the Family*, 48–52. For more on the Moynihan Report and its role in criminalizing blackness, see Murakawa, *The First Civil Right*, 77–78; Hinton, *From the War on Poverty to the War on Crime*, 20–21, 58–61, 74–77.

63 Bourdieu uses "cultural capital" in a number of his works, most notably in *Distinction*.

64 Thornton, *Club Cultures*, 26.

65 Danny Trejo's success in Hollywood has often been ascribed to his "authenticity." For example, in a *Guardian* review of Trejo's film, *Machete*, John Patterson writes: "But it is Trejo's first life [as an imprisoned person], truly *una vida loca*, that demonstrates why his first 20 bit parts on the big screen were all no-name 'thug,' 'boxer,' 'gangbanger,' and 'hoodlum' roles – and why he brings such authenticity when he arrives on set." Patterson, "The Face that Launched a Thousand Bit Parts." See also *Scared Straight!*; "ConBody."

66 Ito, "Foreword," x.

67 Senghor, *Writing My Wrongs*, 257.

68 Senghor, *Writing My Wrongs*, 257.

69 Senghor, *Writing My Wrongs*, 259.

70 Browne, *Dark Matters*, 6; Fanon, *Black Skin, White Masks*, 84.

71   For an example of Detroit ruin tourism, see Boileau, "Tour Detroit." For more about ruin tourism in Detroit, see Binelli, "How Detroit Became"; Steinmetz, "Harrowed Landscapes"; Scarbrough, "Visiting the Ruins of Detroit."

CHAPTER 5: "LOVE IS CONTRABAND IN HELL"

1   Foucault, *The History of Sexuality*, 101.

2   Goldman, *Living My Life*.

3   Collins, *Black Feminist Thought*, 18.

4   For a helpful explanation of the category of the "political prisoner," see James, *Imprisoned Intellectuals*, 11–14.

5   Rafter, *Partial Justice*, 58.

6   Rafter, *Partial Justice*, 61.

7   Rafter, *Partial Justice*, 54.

8   Gross, "African American Women," 27–28.

9   Gross, *Colored Amazons*, 105–6.

10   For more on the policing of black women, and how a caricature of black womanhood as "incoherent" stabilized white womanhood as a "coherent" juridical category, see Haley, *No Mercy Here*, 8.

11   Rashad Shabazz also makes use of Foucault's theory of the carceral continuum to identify the "mechanisms of constraint" that are built into black communities in Chicago that create "a prison-like environment." *Spatializing Blackness*, 2.

12   Johnson, *Inner Lives*, 7.

13   Davis, *Are Prisons Obsolete?*, 77.

14   Sarah Haley, *No Mercy Here*, 4.

15   Shakur, *Assata*, 102–4.

16   Shakur, *Assata*, 113–16.

17   Shakur, *Assata*, 113.

18   Cleaver, *Soul on Ice*, 26.

19   Shakur, *Assata*, 106.

20   Shakur, *Assata*, 109.

21   Shakur, *Assata*, 83–84.

NOTES

22 Barbara Deming, *Prisons That Could Not Hold* (San Francisco: Spinsters Ink, 1985), 4.

23 Goffman, *Asylums*, 14.

24 Shakur, *Assata*, 83.

25 Shakur, *Assata*, 92.

26 Shakur, *Assata*, 125.

27 Collins, *Black Feminist Thought*, 81, 83.

28 Shakur, *Assata*, 123.

29 See also Collins, *Black Feminist Thought*, 69–96.

30 Moynihan, *The Negro Family*, 29.

31 Shakur, *Assata*, 92.

32 Margo V. Perkins, *Autobiography As Activism: Three Black Women of the Sixties*, 108.

33 Perkins, *Autobiography As Activism*, 109.

34 Collins, *Black Feminist Thought*, 53.

35 Davis, *Autobiography*, 199, 239, 162, 63, 396.

36 Davis, *Autobiography*, 293.

37 Rosenberg, *An American Radical*, 161.

38 Rosenberg, *An American Radical*, 69.

39 Cover, "Violence and the Word," 1601.

40 Rosenberg, *An American Radical*, 70.

41 Silvan Tomkins, *Shame and Its Sisters: A Silvan Tomkins Reader*, 136.

42 Elspeth Probyn, "Writing Shame," 72.

43 Rosenberg, *An American Radical*, 70.

44 Karlene Faith, *Unruly Women: The Politics of Confinement and Resistance* (Vancouver: Press Gang, 1993), 242.

45 Shakur, *Assata*, 47; Davis, *Autobiography*, 32–33.

46 Elaine Scarry, *The Body in Pain*, 41.

47 Scarry, *The Body in Pain*, 42.

48 Scarry, *The Body in Pain*, 42.

49 Rosenberg, *An American Radical*, 314.

50 Rosenberg, *An American Radical*, 314.

51 Rosenberg, *An American Radical*, 156.

52 Rosenberg, *An American Radical*, 291.

53 Davis, *Autobiography*, 53.

54 Davis, *Autobiography*, 54.

55 Rosenberg, *An American Radical*, 291.

56 Rosenberg, *An American Radical*, 306.

57 Rosenberg, *An American Radical*, 307–8.

58 Hersch and Meyers, "The Gendered Burdens," 179.

59 Gaines, *Laughing in the Dark*, 110.

CONCLUSION: "THESE WOMEN, LIKE MYSELF"

1 Baca, *A Place to Stand*, back cover.

2 The growing awareness of the prison crisis can be seen in the recent rise of bipartisan efforts to address mass incarceration, such as the proposed Smarter Sentencing Act (S. 1933), which is sponsored by Senators Richard Durbin (D-IL) and Mike Lee (R-UT).

3 Davis et al., *Evaluating the Effectiveness*.

4 Wideman, *Brothers and Keepers*, 189.

5 Burton and Lynn, *Becoming Ms. Burton*, 94.

6 Burton and Lynn, *Becoming Ms. Burton*, 246.

7 Burton and Lynn, *Becoming Ms. Burton*, 245.

8 Burton and Lynn, *Becoming Ms. Burton*, 245, 146–47, 148.

9 Burton and Lynn, *Becoming Ms. Burton*, 147–48.

10 Kerman, *Orange Is the New Black*; Harris, *They Always Call Us Ladies*.

11 In this regard, Kerman's book is comparable to Harris's *They Always Call Us Ladies*.

12 Fludernik, "'Stone Walls,'" 155–56.

13 Burton and Lynn, *Becoming Ms. Burton*, 245.

14 Jackson, *Soledad Brother*, 40.

15 Baca, *A Place to Stand*, 225.

BIBLIOGRAPHY

A.A. World Services, Inc. "The Twelve Steps of Alcoholics Anonymous." https://www.aa.org/assets/en_US/service-material -from-the-gso/smf-121-the-twelve-steps-of-alcoholics-anonymous.

Abbott, Jack Henry. *In the Belly of the Beast: Letters from Prison*. New York: Vintage Books, 1982.

Abbott, Jack Henry, with Naomi Zack. *My Return*. Buffalo: Prometheus Books, 1987.

Alexander, Michelle. *The New Jim Crow: Mass Incarceration in the Age of Colorblindness*. New York: New Press, 2010.

Allen, Francis. "The Decline of the Rehabilitative Ideal in American Criminal Justice." *Cleveland State Law Review* 27 (1978): 147–56.

Andrews, William L. "The First Fifty Years of the Slave Narrative." In *The Art of the Slave Narrative: Original Essays in Criticism and Theory*, edited by John Sekora and Darwin T. Turner, 6–24. Macomb: Western Illinois University Press, 1982.

"The Atonement Project: Ponyride SOUP Winner – September 2013." *Detroit Soup*, 2015. https://detroitsoup.com/the-atonement -project.

Attica: The Official Report of the New York State Special Commission on Attica. New York: Praeger, 1972.

Baca, Jimmy Santiago. *A Place to Stand: The Making of a Poet*. New York: Grove Press, 2001.

———. *Working in the Dark: Reflections of a Poet of the Barrio*. Santa Fe: Red Crane, 1992.

Baldwin, James. "Many Thousands Gone." In *Notes of a Native Son*, 24–25. Boston: Beacon, 1984.

Baxter, Richard. *A Call to the Unconverted. To Which Are Added, Several Valuable Essays*. Boston: Lincoln and Edmands, 1831.

Bender, John. *Imagining the Penitentiary: Fiction and the Architecture of Mind in Eighteenth-Century England*. Chicago: University of Chicago Press, 1987.

Berger, Dan. *Captive Nation: Black Prison Organizing in the Civil Rights Era*. Chapel Hill: University of North Carolina Press, 2014.

———. "Finding and Defining the Carceral State." *Reviews in American History* 47, no. 2 (June 2019): 279–85.

Bernstein, Lee. *America Is the Prison: Arts and Politics in Prison in the 1970s*. Chapel Hill: University of North Carolina Press, 2016.

Berthoff, Warner. "Witness and Testament: Two Contemporary Classics." *New Literary History* 2, no. 2 (1971): 311–27.

Best, Stephen, and Sharon Marcus. "Surface Reading: An Introduction." *Representations* 108, no. 1 (2009): 1–21. https://www.jstor.org/stable/10.1525/rep.2009.108.1.1.

Binelli, Mark. "How Detroit Became the World Capital of Staring at Abandoned Old Buildings." *New York Times Magazine*, 9 November 2012.

Blackmon, Douglas. *Slavery by Another Name: The Re-Enslavement of Black Americans from the Civil War to World War II*. New York: Doubleday, 2008.

BLAK Fintech. Twitter Profile. https://twitter.com/blakfintech?lang=en.

Blomberg, Thomas G., and Karol Lucken. *American Penology*. New York: Aldine de Gruyter, 2000.

Blunk, Tim, and Raymond Luc Levasseur. *Hauling Up the Morning (Izando La Manana): Writings and Art by Political Prisoners and Prisoners of War in the U.S.* Trenton: Red Sea Press, 1990.

Boileau, Lowell. "Tour Detroit: Web Journeys into the Heart of Detroit." https://www.detroityes.com/tour-detroit.php.

Bourdieu, Pierre. *Distinction: A Social Critique of the Judgement of Taste*. Cambridge, MA: Harvard University Press, 1984.

Braly, Malcolm. *False Starts: A Memoir of San Quentin and Other Prisons*. Boston: Little, Brown, 1976.

Brockway, Z.R. *Fifty Years of Prison Service: An Autobiography*. New York: Charities Publication Committee, 1912. https://ia601406.us.archive.org/30/items/fiftyyearsprisooobrocgoog/fiftyyearsprisooobrocgoog.pdf.

Brown, H. Rap. "Street Talk." In *Rappin' and Stylin' Out: Communication in Urban Black America*, edited by Thomas Kochman, 205–8. Urbana: University of Illinois Press, 1972.

Browne, Simone. *Dark Matters: On the Surveillance of Blackness*. Durham: Duke University Press, 2015.

Bruchac, Joseph. *The Light from Another Country: Poetry from American Prisons*. Greenfield Center: Greenfield Review Press, 1984.

Bryant, Jerry H. *Born in a Mighty Bad Land: The Violent Man in African American Folklore and Fiction*. Bloomington: Indiana University Press, 2003.

Buck, Marilyn, and Laura Whitehorn (with Susie Day). "Cruel but Not Unusual – the Punishment of Women in U.S. Prisons." In *The New Abolitionists: (Neo)Slave Narratives and Contemporary Prison Writings*, edited by Joy James, 261–73. Albany: SUNY Press, 2005.

Bunyan, John. *Grace Abounding to the Chief of Sinners*. London: Larkin, 1666.

BU Prison Education Program. "Welcome to the BU Prison Education Program." Boston University. http://sites.bu.edu/pep.

Burton, Susan, and Cari Lynn. *Becoming Ms. Burton: From Prison to Leading the Fight for Incarcerated Women*. New York: The New Press, 2017.

Caldwell, Patricia. *The Puritan Conversion Narrative: The Beginnings of an American Expression*. Cambridge: Cambridge University Press, 1983.

Carby, Hazel. "Policing the Black Woman's Body in an Urban Context." *Critical Inquiry* 18, no. 4 (Summer 1992): 738–55.

Carmichael, Stokely, and George V. Hamilton. *Black Power: The Politics of Liberation*. New York: Vintage, 1992.

Carr, Betsy. "Afterword." In *Bad: The Autobiography of James Carr* by James Carr, edited by Dan Hammer and Isaac Cronin. Edinburgh, London, and Oakland: AK Press/Nabat, 2002.

Carr, James. *Bad: The Autobiography of James Carr*, edited by Dan Hammer and Isaac Cronin. Edinburgh, London, and Oakland: AK Press/Nabat, 2002.

Carroll, Hamilton. *Affirmative Reaction: New Formations of White Masculinity*. Durham: Duke University Press, 2011.

Caster, Peter. *Prisons, Race, and Masculinity in Twentieth-Century US Literature and Film*. Columbus: Ohio State University Press, 2008.

Castiglia, Christopher. *Bound and Determined: Captivity, Culture-Crossing, and White Womanhood from Mary Rowlandson to Patty Hearst*. Chicago: University of Chicago Press, 1996.

"Cedar Tree, inc.: A 501(c)(3) Non-Profit Organization." 2016. *JimmySantiagoBaca.com*. https://www.jimmysantiagobaca.com/cedar-tree.

Certeau, Michel de. *The Practice of Everyday Life*. Translated by Steven Rendall. Berkeley: University of California Press, 1988.

"Changing Lives through Literature: An Alternative Sentencing Program." UMass Dartmouth. http://cltl.umassd.edu/home-html.cfm.

Chessman, Caryl. *Cell 2455, Death Row: A Condemned Man's Own Story*. New York: Carroll and Graf, 2006.

Chevigny, Bell Gale, ed. *Doing Time: 25 Years of Prison Writing*. New York: Arcade, 1999.

Chin, Gabriel J. "The New Civil Death: Rethinking Punishment in the Era of Mass Conviction." *University of Pennsylvania Law Review* 160, no. 6 (2012): 1789–833.

Clark, Richard X. *The Brothers of Attica*. New York: Links Books, 1973.

Clarke, Colin A. "'Only Man Is Miserable': The Evolving View of Imprisonment in Robert Lowell's Poetry." In *Prose and Cons: Essays on Prison Literature in the United States*, edited by D. Quentin Miller, 131–46. Jefferson: McFarland, 2005.

Cleaver, Eldridge. *Soul on Fire*. Waco: Word Books, 1978.

———. *Soul on Ice*. New York: Dell, 1991.

Coates, Ta-Nehisi. "The Black Family in the Age of Mass Incarceration." *The Atlantic* 316, no. 3 (2015). https://www

.theatlantic.com/magazine/archive/2015/10/the-black-family-in
-the-age-of-mass-incarceration/403246.

Cohen, Jeffrey A., et al. *Eastern State Penitentiary Historic Structures
Report*, vol. 1. Philadelphia, 1994.

Coletu, Ebony. "Biographic Mediation." *A/B: Auto/Biography Studies* 32
no. 2 (2017): 384.

Colley, Linda. *Captives: Britain, Empire, and the World, 1600–1850*. New
York: Anchor Books, 2004.

Collins, Patricia Hill. *Black Feminist Thought: Knowledge, Consciousness,
and the Politics of Empowerment*, 2nd ed. New York and London:
Routledge, 2000.

Colson, Charles W. *Born Again*. Lincoln: Chosen Books, 1976.

"ConBody." https://conbody.com.

Corrigan, Lisa M. "Cross-Pollinating the Revolution: From Havana to
Oakland and Back Again." *Journal of Postcolonial Writing* 50, no. 4
(2014): 452–65.

Cover, Robert M. "Violence and the Word." *Yale Law Journal* 95, no. 8
(1986): 1601–29.

Crèvecoeur, Michel Guillaume Jean de. *Letters from an American
Farmer*. Repr. ed. New York: Fox, Duffield, 1904.

Cronin, Isaac. Interviewed by Simon Rolston, 15 September 2008.

Cummins, Eric. *The Rise and Fall of California's Radical Prison
Movement*. Stanford: Stanford University Press, 1994.

Darnton, Robert. "What Is the History of Books?" In *Reading in
America*, edited by Cathy N. Davidson, 30–31. Baltimore: Johns
Hopkins University Press, 1989.

Davies, Ioan. *Writers in Prison*. Oxford: Blackwell, 1990.

Davis, Angela. *Are Prisons Obsolete?* New York: Seven Stories Press,
2003.

———. "From the Convict Lease System to the Super-Max Prison."
In *States of Confinement: Policing, Detention, and Prisons*, edited by
Joy James, 60–74. New York: St. Martin's Press, 2000.

Davis, Angela Y. *Angela Davis: An Autobiography*. New York: Random
House, 1974.

Davis, Lois M., Robert Bozick, Jennifer L. Steele, Jessica Saunders, and Jeremy Miles. *Evaluating the Effectiveness of Correctional Education: A Meta-Analysis of Programs That Provide Education to Incarcerated Adults.* Santa Monica: RAND Corporation, 2013.

Dayan, Colin. *The Law Is a White Dog: How Legal Rituals Make and Unmake Persons.* Princeton: Princeton University Press, 2011.

———. "Legal Terrors." *Representations* 92, no. 92 (2005): 42–80. http://gateway.proquest.com/openurl?ctx_ver=Z39.88 -2003&xri:pqil:res_ver=0.2&res_id=xri:ilcs-us&rft_id=xri:ilcs:rec: abell:R03842384.

Dayan, Joan. "Poe, Persons, and Property." *American Literary History* 11, no. 3 (1999): 405–25. http://gateway.proquest.com/openurl?ctx_ ver=Z39.88-2003&xri:pqil:res_ver=0.2&res_id=xri:ilcs-us&rft_id= xri:ilcs:rec:abell:R01759416.

Dearborn, Mary V. *Mailer: A Biography.* Boston: Houghton Mifflin, 1999.

Deming, Barbara. *Prisons That Could Not Hold.* San Francisco: Spinsters Ink, 1985.

Desmond, John. "Flannery O'Connor's Misfit and the Mystery of Evil." *Renascence: Essays on Values in Literature* 56, no.2 (2004): 129–37. http://gateway.proquest.com/openurl?ctx_ver=Z39.88 -2003&xri:pqil:res_ver=0.2&res_id=xri:ilcs-us&rft_id=xri:ilcs:rec: abell:R03533550.

Des Pres, Terrence. "A Child of the State." *New York Times,* 19 July 1981, BR1.

Dilulio, John J. Jr. "The Coming of the Super-Predators." *The Weekly Standard,* 27 November 1995.

Dorsey, Peter A., *Sacred Estrangement: The Rhetoric of Conversion in Modern American Autobiography.* University Park: Pennsylvania State University Press, 1993.

Douglass, Frederick. *Narrative of the Life of Frederick Douglass, an American Slave,* edited by Houston A. Baker. New York: Penguin Books, 1986.

Duffy, Clinton T., and Dean Jennings. *The San Quentin Story*. New York: Doubleday, 1950.

Eakin, Paul John. "Breaking Rules: The Consequences of Self-Narration." *Biography* 24, no. 1 (2001): 113–27. http://www.jstor.org/stable/23540312.

Ek, Auli. *Race and Masculinity in Contemporary American Prison Narratives*. New York: Routledge, 2005.

Faith, Karlene. *Unruly Women: The Politics of Confinement and Resistance*. Vancouver: Press Gang, 1993.

Fanon, Frantz. *Black Skin, White Masks*. Translated by Charles Lam Markmann. New York: Grove Press, 1967.

Fitzgerald, F. Scott. *The Great Gatsby*. New York: Scribner, 2004.

Fitzgerald, Frances. *The Evangelicals: The Struggle to Shape America*. New York: Simon and Schuster, 2017.

Fludernik, Monika. "'Stone Walls Do (Not) a Prison Make': Rhetorical Strategies and Sentimentalism in the Representation of the Victorian Prison Experience." In *Captivating Subjects: Writing Confinement, Citizenship, and Nationhood in the Nineteenth Century*, 144–74. Toronto: University of Toronto Press, 2016.

Foucault, Michel. *Discipline and Punish: The Birth of the Prison*. Translated by Alan Sheridan. New York: Vintage Books, 1995.

———. *The History of Sexuality: An Introduction*, vol. 1. Translated by Robert Hurley. New York: Vintage Books, 1990.

Foucault, Michel, and John K. Simon. "Michel Foucault on Attica: An Interview." *Telos* 19 (1974): 154–61. http://journal.telospress.com/content/1974/19/154.abstract.

Faith, Karlene. *Unruly Women: The Politics of Confinement and Resistance*. New York: Seven Stories Press, 2011.

Franklin, Benjamin. *The Autobiography of Benjamin Franklin*. New York: Vintage Books/The Library of America, 1990.

Franklin, H. Bruce. "Can the Penitentiary Teach the Academy How to Read?" *PMLA* 123, no. 3 (2008): 643–650. https://www.jstor.org/stable/25501882.

———. *Prison Writing in 20th-Century America*. New York: Penguin Books, 1998.

———. *The Victim as Criminal and Artist: Literature from the American Prison*. New York: Oxford University Press, 1978.

Fraser, C. Gerald. "Etheridge Knight Is Dead at 57; Began Writing Poetry in Prison." *New York Times*, 14 March 1991, 24. https://www.nytimes.com/1991/03/14/obituaries/etheridge-knight-is-dead-at-57-began-writing-poetry-in-prison.html.

Frasier, Isaac. *A Brife [sic] Account of the Life, and Abominable Thefts, of the Notorious Isaac Frasier, Under Sentance [sic] of Death, for Burglary*. Early American Imprints, Series 1, no. 41823 ed. New Haven: Printed by T. & S. Green, 1768.

Frow, John. "'Reproducibles, Rubrics, and Everything You Need': Genre Theory Today." *PMLA* 122, no. 5 (Oct. 2007): 1626–34.

Gaddis, Thomas E., and James O. Long. 1970. *Killer: A Journal of Murder*. New York: Macmillan.

———. *Panzram: A Journal of Murder*. Los Angeles: Amok Books, 2002.

Gaines, Patricia. *Laughing in the Dark: From Colored Girl to Woman of Color – a Journey from Prison to Power*. New York: First Anchor Books, 1994.

Galt Harpham, Geoffrey. "Conversion and the Language of Autobiography." In *Studies in Autobiography*, edited by James Olney, 42–50. New York and Oxford: Oxford University Press, 1988.

Gates, Henry Louis, Jr. *The Signifying Monkey: A Theory of Afro-American Literary Criticism*. New York: Oxford University Press, 1988.

Geary, Daniel. *Beyond Civil Rights: The Moynihan Report and Its Legacy*. Philadelphia: University of Pennsylvania Press, 2015.

Genet, Jean. "Introduction." In *Soledad Brother: The Prison Letters of George Jackson* by George Jackson, 17–24. New York: Penguin Books, 1971.

Gilmore, Leigh. *The Limits of Autobiography: Trauma and Testimony*. Ithaca: Cornell University Press, 2001.

Goffman, Erving. *Asylums: Essays on the Social Situation of Mental Patients and Other Inmates*. Chicago: Aldine, 1962.

Goldman, Emma. *Living My Life*. New York: Penguin Classics, 2006.

Golub, Mark. "History Died for our Sins: Guilt and Responsibility in Hollywood Redemption Histories." *Journal of American Culture* 21, no. 3 (1998): 23–45. http://gateway.proquest.com/openurl?ctx_ver=Z39.88-2003&xri:pqil:res_ver=0.2&res_id=xri:ilcs-us&rft_id=xri:ilcs:rec:abell:R01249199.

Gottschalk, Maria. *The Prison and the Gallows: The Politics of Mass Incarceration in America*. Cambridge and New York: Cambridge University Press, 2006.

Gramlich, John. *Federal Prison Population Fell during Obama's Term, Reversing Recent Trend*: Pew Research Center, 2017. http://www.pewresearch.org/fact-tank/2017/01/05/federal-prison-population-fell-during-obamas-term-reversing-recent-trend.

Grassian, Stuart. "Psychopathological Effects of Solitary Confinement." *American Journal of Psychiatry* 140, no. 11 (1983): 1450–54. http://dx.doi.org/10.1176/ajp.140.11.1450.

Gready, Paul. "Autobiography and the 'Power of Writing': Political Prison Writing in the Apartheid Era." *Journal of Southern African Studies* 19, no. 3 (1993): 489–523. http://www.jstor.org/stable/2636913.

Green, Tara T. "Introduction." In *From the Plantation to the Prison: African American Confinement Literature*, 1–8. Macon: Mercer University Press, 2008.

Gross, Kali Nicole. "African American Women, Mass Incarceration, and the Politics of Protection." *Journal of American History* 102, no. 1 (2015): 25–33.

———. *Colored Amazons: Crime, Violence, and Black Women in the City of Brotherly Love, 1880–1910*. Durham: Duke University Press, 2006.

Gubar, Susan. *Racechanges: White Skin, Black Face in American Culture.* New York: Oxford University Press, 1997.

Guest, David. *Sentenced to Death: The American Novel and Capital Punishment.* Jackson: University Press of Mississippi, 1997.

Gumbel, Andrew. "Paris Hilton Thanks God for Her Prison Sentence." *The Independent,* 12 June 2007.

Halberstam, Judith. *Skin Shows: Gothic Horror and the Technology of Monsters.* Durham: Duke University Press, 1995.

Haley, Sarah. *No Mercy Here: Gender, Punishment, and the Making of Jim Crow Modernity.* Chapel Hill: University of North Carolina Press, 2016.

Hames-García, Michael. *Fugitive Thought: Prison Movements, Race, and the Meaning of Justice.* Minneapolis: University of Minnesota Press, 2004.

Hammer, Dan. "Introduction." In *Bad: The Autobiography of James Carr,* by James Carr. Edited by Dan Hammer and Isaac Cronin, 9–20. Edinburgh, London, and Oakland: AK Press/Nabat, 2002.

Harris, Jean. *They Always Call Us Ladies: Stories from Prison.* New York: Scribner, 1988.

Haslam, Jason W. 2005. *Fitting Sentences: Identity in Nineteenth- and Twentieth-Century Prison Narratives.* Toronto: University of Toronto Press.

———. "Pits, Pendulums, and Penitentiaries: Reframing the Detained Subject." *Texas Studies in Literature and Language* 50, no. 3 (2008): 268–84. http://muse.jhu.edu/journals/texas_studies_in_literature_and_language/v050/50.3.haslam.html.

Hawkins, Richard, and Geoffrey P. Alpert. *American Prison Systems: Punishment and Justice.* Englewood Cliffs: Prentice Hall, 1989.

Hazelrigg, Lawrence E. *Prison within Society: A Reader in Penology.* Garden City: Doubleday, 1968.

Hersch, Joni, and Erin E. Meyers. "The Gendered Burdens of Conviction and Collateral Consequences on Employment." *Journal of Legislation* 45, no. 2 (2018): 171–93.

Hinton, Elizabeth. *From the War on Poverty to the War on Crime: The Making of Mass Incarceration in America*. Cambridge, MA: Harvard University Press, 2016.

hooks, bell. *Black Looks: Race and Representation*. Boston: South End Press, 1992.

Hurston, Zora Neale. *Dust Tracks on a Road*. New York: HarperPerennial, 1991.

Ibrahim, Habiba. *Troubling the Family: The Promise of Personhood and the Rise of Multiracialism*. Minneapolis: University of Minnesota Press, 2012.

Ignatiev, Noel, and John Garvey. *Race Traitor*. New York: Routledge, 1996.

Ito, Joi. "Foreword." In *Writing My Wrongs: Life, Death, and Redemption in an American Prison*, xi–xv. New York: Convergent Books, 2016.

Jackson, Bruce. *"Get Your Ass in the Water and Swim Like Me": Narrative Poetry from Black Oral Tradition*. Cambridge, MA: Harvard University Press, 1974.

Jackson, George. *Blood in My Eye*. New York: Random House, 1972.
———. *Soledad Brother: The Prison Letters of George Jackson*. New York: Penguin Books, 1971.

James, Joy. "Introduction: Democracy and Captivity." In *The New Abolitionists: (Neo)Slave Narratives and Contemporary Prison Writing*, edited by Joy James, xxi–xlii. Albany: SUNY Press, 2005.

James, Joy, ed. *Imprisoned Intellectuals: America's Political Prisoners Write on Life, Liberation, and Rebellion*. Transformative Politics Series. Lanham: Rowman and Littlefield, 2003.

———. *The New Abolitionists: (Neo)Slave Narratives and Contemporary Prison Writing*. Albany: SUNY Press, 2005.

———. *States of Confinement: Policing, Detention, and Prisons*. New York: St. Martin's Press, 2000.

———. *Warfare in the American Homeland: Policing and Prison in a Penal Democracy*. Durham: Duke University Press, 2007.

James, William. 2003. *The Varieties of Religious Experience: A Study in Human Nature*. London and New York: Routledge.

Jenkins, Philip. *Decade of Nightmares: The End of the Sixties and the Making of Eighties America*. Oxford: Oxford University Press, 2006.

Johnson, Paula C. *Inner Lives: Voices of African American Women in Prison*. New York: New York University Press, 2003.

Kadar, Marlene. *Essays on Life Writing: From Genre to Critical Practice*. Toronto: University of Toronto Press, 1992.

Kakutani, Michiko. "The Strange Case of the Writer and the Criminal." *New York Times*, 20 September 1981.

Kaplan, Caren. "Resisting Autobiography: Out-Law Genres and Transnational Feminist Subjects." In *De/Colonizing the Subject: The Politics of Gender in Women's Autobiography*, edited by Sidonie Smith and Julia Watson, 115–38. Minneapolis: University of Minnesota Press, 1992.

Kerman, Piper. *Orange Is the New Black*. New York: Spiegel and Grau, 2015.

Lehmann, Vibeke. "Challenges and Accomplishments in U.S. Prison Libraries." *Library Trends* 59, no. 3 (2011): 490–508. doi:10.1353/lib.2011.0001.

Lejeune, Philippe. *On Autobiography*. Translated by Katherine Leary, edited by Paul John Eakin. Minneapolis: University of Minnesota Press, 1989.

Lewis, Orlando Faulkland. *The Development of American Prisons and Prison Customs, 1776–1845*. Albany: Prison Association of New York, 1922.

Liberatore, Paul. *The Road to Hell: The True Story of George Jackson, Stephen Bingham, and the San Quentin Massacre*. New York: Atlantic Monthly Press, 1996.

Lieson Brereton, Virginia. *From Sin to Salvation: Stories of Women's Conversions, 1800 to the Present*. Bloomington: Indiana University Press, 1991.

Linder, Lindsey. "An Unsupported Population: The Treatment of Women in Texas' Criminal Justice System." The Texas Criminal Justice Coalition. 2018. http://www.texascjc.org/unsupported-population-treatment-women-texas%E2%80%99-criminal-justice-system

Lipton, Douglas, Robert Martinson, and Judith Wilks. *The Effectiveness of Correctional Treatment: A Survey of Treatment Evaluation Studies.* New York: Praeger, 1975.

Lombroso, Cesare. *Criminal Man.* Translated by Mary Gibson and Nicole Hahn Rafter. Durham: Duke University Press, 2006.

Lowell, Robert. "In the Cage." In *Lord Weary's Castle and the Mills of the Kavanaughs*, 53. New York: Meridian Books, 1966.

Loya, Joe. *The Man Who Outgrew His Prison Cell: Confessions of a Bank Robber.* New York: HarperCollins, 2004.

MacNamara, Donal E.J. "The Medical Model in Corrections." *Criminology* 14, no. 4 (1977): 439–48.

Mailer, Norman. "The White Negro." In *The Long Patrol: 25 Years of Writing from the Work of Norman Mailer*, edited by Robert F. Lucid, 209–28. New York: World, 1971.

Malcolm X, and Alex Haley. *The Autobiography of Malcolm X.* New York: Ballantine Books, 1992.

Malewitz, Raymond. "Regeneration through Misuse: Rugged Consumerism in Contemporary American Culture." *PMLA* 127, no. 3 (2012): 526–41.

Mancini, Matthew. *One Dies, Get Another: Convict Leasing in the American South, 1866–1928.* Columbia: University of South Carolina Press, 1996.

Mandel, Barrett J. "The Didactic Achievement of Malcolm X's Autobiography." *Afro-American Studies: An Interdisciplinary Journal* 2 (1972): 269–74. http://ezproxy.library.ubc.ca/login?url=http://search.ebscohost.com/login.aspx?direct=true&db=mzh&AN=1972110064&login.asp&site=ehost-live&scope=site.

Marable, Manning. *Malcolm X: A Life of Reinvention.* London: Penguin, 2012.

McCall, Nathan. *Makes Me Wanna Holler: A Young Black Man in America*. New York: Vintage Books, 1995.

McHugh, Kathleen, and Catherine Komisaruk. "Something Other Than Autobiography: Collaborative Life-Narratives in the Americas – an Introduction." *Biography* 31, no. 3 (2008): vii–xii.

Mears, Daniel P., and Joshua C. Cochran. *Prisoner Reentry in the Era of Mass Incarceration*. Los Angeles: Sage, 2015.

Melville, Sam. *Letters from Attica*. New York: Morrow, 1972.

Meranze, Michael. "The Penitential Ideal in Late Eighteenth-Century Philadelphia." *Pennsylvania Magazine of History and Biography*, 1 October 1984. 419–50.

Meyer, Ilan H., Andrew R. Flores, Lara Stemple, Adam P. Romero, Bianca D.M. Wilson, and Jody L. Herman. "Incarceration Rates and Traits of Sexual Minorities in the United States: National Inmate Survey, 2011–2012." *American Journal of Public Health* 107, no. 2 (2017): 267–73. https://search.proquest.com/docview/1865707993.

Morgan, Edmund Sears. *Visible Saints: The History of a Puritan Idea*. New York: NYU Press, 1963.

Moynihan, Daniel Patrick. *The Negro Family: The Case for National Action*. Washington, 1965.

Moynihan, Daniel Patrick, and Lee Rainwater. *The Moynihan Report and the Politics of Controversy*. Cambridge, MA: MIT Press, 1978.

Muhammad, Khalil Gibran. *The Condemnation of Blackness: Race, Crime, and the Making of Modern Urban America*. Cambridge, MA: Harvard University Press, 2010.

Murakawa, Naomi. *The First Civil Right: How Liberals Built Prison America*. New York: Oxford University Press, 2014.

O'Connor, Flannery. "A Good Man Is Hard to Find." In *A Good Man Is Hard to Find and Other Stories*, 1–24. New York: Mariner Books, 2001.

Ohmann, Carol. "The Autobiography of Malcolm X: A Revolutionary Use of the Franklin Tradition." *American Quarterly* 22, no. 2 (1970): 131–49. http://ezproxy.library.ubc.ca/login?url=http://

search.ebscohost.com/login.aspx?direct=true&db=mzh&AN=1970
107903&login.asp&site=ehost-live&scope=site.

Olguín, B.V. *La Pinta: Chicana/O Prisoner Literature, Culture, and Politics*. Austin: University of Texas Press, 2010.

Olney, James. "'I was born': Slave Narratives, Their Status as Autobiography and as Literature." In *The Slave's Narrative*, edited by Charles T. Davis and Henry Louis Gates, Jr., 148–75. Oxford: Oxford University Press, 1985.

Omi, Michael, and Howard Winant. *Racial Formation in the United States: From the 1960s to the 1980s*. New York: Routledge and Kegan Paul, 1986.

Oshinsky, David M. *Worse Than Slavery: Parchman Farm and the Ordeal of Jim Crow Justice*. New York: Free Press, 1997.

Oxford English Dictionary, 2nd ed. "Parole." 1989.

OED Online. "Hyena | Hyaena, N." 2018.

Pallotti, Donatella. "'Out of their Owne Mouths'? Conversion Narratives and English Radical Religious Practice in the Seventeenth Century." *Journal of Early Modern Studies* 1, no. 1 (2012): 73–95. http://gateway.proquest.com/openurl?ctx_ver=Z39.88-2003&xri:pqil:res_ver=0.2&res_id=xri:ilcs-us&rft_id=xri:ilcs:rec:abell:R05118391.

Panzram, Carl. "Panzram's Autobiographical Manuscript, Box 1, Virtual Folder 1." Special Collections & University Archives, San Diego State University.

Parsell, T.J. *Fish: A Memoir of a Boy in a Man's Prison*. New York: Carroll and Graf, 2006.

Parsons, Anne E. *From Asylum to Prison: Deinstitutionalization and the Rise of Mass Incarceration after 1945*. Chapel Hill: University of North Carolina Press, 2019.

Patterson, James T. *Freedom Is Not Enough: The Moynihan Report and America's Struggle over Black Family Life from LBJ to Obama*. New York: Basic Books, 2010.

Patterson, John. "The Face That Launched a Thousand Bit Parts: From Junkie Thief to Innumerable Character Roles, the Man with the Most Striking Mug in Hollywood Is Finally Getting His Chance to Star." *The Guardian*, 18 November 2010. https://www.theguardian.com/film/2010/nov/18/danny-trejo-machete.

Peniel, Joseph. *Waiting 'Til the Midnight Hour: A Narrative History of Black Power in America*. New York: Holt Paperbacks, 2007.

Perkins, Margo V. *Autobiography as Activism: Three Black Women of the Sixties*. Jackson: University Press of Mississippi, 2000.

Peters, Roger H., and Harry K. Wexler. 2005. *Substance Abuse Treatment for Adults in the Criminal Justice System: A Treatment Improvement Protocol (TIP 44)*. Rockville: Substance Abuse and Mental Health Services Administration, 2005.

Pettit, Norman. *The Heart Prepared: Grace and Conversion in Puritan Spiritual Life*. New Haven: Yale University Press, 1966.

Pisciotta, Alexander W. "Scientific Reform: The 'New Penology' at Elmira, 1876–1900." *Crime and Delinquency* 29, no. 4 (1983): 613–30. http://journals.sagepub.com/doi/full/10.1177/0011128783 02900408.

Probyn, Elspeth. "Writing Shame." In *The Affect Theory Reader*, edited by Melissa Gregg and Gregory J. Seigworth, 71–90. Durham: Duke University Press.

Rafter, Nicole Hahn. *Partial Justice: Women, Prisons and Social Control*. London and New York: Routledge, 2017.

Reyes, Xavier Aldana. "Gothic Affect: An Alternative Approach to Critical Models of the Contemporary Gothic." In *New Directions in 21st Century Gothic: The Gothic Compass*, edited by Lorna Piatti-Farnell and Donna Lee Brien, 11–23. London and New York: Routledge, 2015.

Rhodes, Jane. *Framing the Black Panthers: The Spectacular Rise of a Black Power Icon*. Urbana: University of Illinois Press, 2007.

Roberts, Dorothy E. "Deviance, Resistance, and Love." *Utah Law Review* 1 (1994): 179–91.

Rodríguez, Dylan. "Against the Discipline of 'Prison Writing': Toward a Theoretical Conception of Contemporary Radical Prison

Praxis." *Genre: Forms of Discourse and Culture* 35, nos. 3–4 (2002): 407–28. http://dx.doi.org/10.1215/00166928-35-3-4-407.

———. *Forced Passages: Imprisoned Radical Intellectuals and the US Prison Regime.* Minneapolis: University of Minnesota Press, 2004.

Roediger, David R. *Towards the Abolition of Whiteness: Essays on Race, Politics, and Working Class History.* London: Verso, 1994.

Rogers, John, Joseph Gerrish, Nicholas Noyes, William Hubbard, Bartholomew Green, John Allen, Samuel Phillips, Benjamin Eliot, and Esther Rodgers. *Death the Certain Wages of Sin to the Impenitent: Life the Sure Reward of Grace to the Penitent [...].* Early American Imprints. Boston: Printed by B. Green, and J. Allen, for Samuel Phillips at the brick shop, 1701. http://find.galegroup.com/ecco/infomark.do?contentSet=ECCOArticles&docType=ECCOArticles&bookId=1474100400&type=getFullCitation&tabID=T001&prodId=ECCO&docLevel=TEXT_GRAPHICS&version=1.0&source=library&userGroupName=waseda.

Rollyson, Carl. *The Lives of Norman Mailer: A Biography.* New York: Paragon House, 1991.

Rosenberg, Susan. *An American Radical: A Political Prisoner in My Own Country.* New York: Citadel, 2011.

Rothman, David J. *Conscience and Convenience: The Asylum and Its Alternatives in Progressive America.* Boston: Little, Brown, 1980.

Rousseau, Jean-Jacques. *The Confessions.* Translated by J.M. Cohen. Harmondsworth: Penguin Books, 1953.

———. *On the Social Contract; with Geneva Manuscript and Political Economy.* Translated by Judith R. Masters, edited by Roger D. Masters. New York: St. Martin's Press, 1978.

Rowlandson, Mary. "The Captivity and Deliverance of Mrs. Mary Rowlandson of Lancaster, Who was Taken by the French and Indians." In *American Colonial Prose: John Smith to Thomas Jefferson*, edited by Mary Ann Radzinowicz, 79–102. New York: Cambridge University Press, 1984.

Runyon, Tom. *In for Life, a Convict's Story.* New York: W.W. Norton, 1953.

Rush, Benjamin. *Considerations on the Injustice and Impolicy of Punishing Murder by Death*. Philadelphia: From the press of Mathew Carey, 1792.

Rush, Benjamin, and the Society for Promoting Political Enquiries. "An Enquiry into the Effects of Public Punishments upon Criminals and upon Society. Read in the Society for Promoting Political Enquiries, Convened at the House of His Excellency Benjamin Franklin, Esquire, in Philadelphia, March 9th, 1787." Ann Arbor: University of Michigan Library. https://quod.lib .umich.edu/e/evans/N16141.0001.001?view=toc.

Rymhs, Deena. *From the Iron House: Imprisonment in First Nations Writing*. Waterloo: Wilfrid Laurier University Press, 2008.

Sawyer, Wendy. "The Gender Divide: Tracking Women's State Prison Growth." *Prison Policy Initiative*, 9 January 2018. https://www .prisonpolicy.org/reports/women_overtime.html.

Scarbrough, Elizabeth. "Visiting the Ruins of Detroit: Exploitation or Cultural Tourism?" *Journal of Applied Philosophy* (2016): 1–18.

Scared Straight! Directed by Arnold Shapiro. Los Angeles: Golden West Television, 1978.

Scarry, Elaine. *The Body in Pain: The Making and Unmaking of the World*. Oxford: Oxford University Press, 1985.

Schlosser, Eric. "The Prison-Industrial Complex." *The Atlantic Monthly*, 1 December 1998. https://www.theatlantic.com/magazine/ archive/1998/12/the-prison-industrial-complex/304669.

Schorb, Jodi. *Reading Prisoners: Literature, Literacy, and the Transformation of American Punishment, 1700–1845*. New Brunswick: Rutgers University Press, 2014.

Sedgwick, Eve Kosofsky. "The Character in the Veil: Imagery of the Surface in the Gothic Novel." *PMLA* 96, no. 2 (1981): 255–70. http://gateway.proquest.com/openurl?ctx_ver=Z39.88 -2003&xri:pqil:res_ver=0.2&res_id=xri:ilcs-us&rft_id=xri:ilcs:rec: abell:R01762553.

Sekora, John. "Black Message/White Envelope: Genre, Authenticity, and Authority in the Antebellum Slave Narrative." *Callaloo: A*

Journal of African American and African Arts and Letters 10, no. 3 (1987): 482–515. http://gateway.proquest.com/openurl?ctx_ver=Z39.88-2003&xri:pqil:res_ver=0.2&res_id=xri:ilcs-us&rft_id=xri:ilcs:rec:abell:R01769649.

Sellin, J. Thorsten. *Slavery and the Penal System.* New York: Elsevier, 1976.

Senghor, Shaka. shakasenghor.com.

———. *Writing My Wrongs: Life, Death, and Redemption in an American Prison.* New York: Convergent Books, 2016.

The Sentencing Project. *Trends in US Corrections: US State and Federal Prison Population, 1925–2015.* Washington, D.C., 2017. https://sentencingproject.org/wp-content/uploads/2016/01/Trends-in-US-Corrections.pdf

Shabazz, Rashad. *Spatializing Blackness: Architectures of Confinement and Black Masculinity in Chicago.* Champaign: University of Illinois Press, 2015. muse.jhu.edu/book/41570.

Shakur, Assata. *Assata: An Autobiography.* Chicago: Chicago Review Press, 1999.

Shea, Daniel B., Jr. *Spiritual Autobiography in Early America.* Princeton: Princeton University Press, 1968.

Shorters, Trabian. "Introduction." In *Reach: 40 Black Men Speak on Living, Leading, and Succeeding.* Edited by Ben Jealous and Trabian Shorters, xxiii–xxv. New York: Atria Books, 2015.

Skotnicki, Andrew. *Religion and the Development of the American Penal System.* Lanham: University Press of America, 2000.

Slaughter, Joseph R. *Human Rights, Inc: The World Novel, Narrative Form, and International Law.* New York: Fordham University Press, 2007.

Sloop, John M. *The Cultural Prison: Discourse, Prisoners, and Punishment.* Tuscaloosa: University of Alabama Press, 1996.

Slotkin, Richard. *Regeneration through Violence: The Mythology of the American Frontier, 1600–1860.* Middletown: Wesleyan University Press, 1973.

Smith, Caleb. "American Undead: Teaching the Cultural Life of Civil Death." In *Teaching Law and Literature*, edited by Austin Sarat, Cathrine O. Frank, and Matthew Daniel Anderson, 147–154. New York: Modern Language Association of America, 2011.

———. *The Prison and the American Imagination*. New Haven: Yale University Press, 2009.

Smith, George W. *A Defence of the System of Solitary Confinement of Prisoners Adopted by the State of Pennsylvania, with Remarks on the Origin, Progress and Extension of this Species of Prison Discipline*. Philadelphia: Philadelphia Society for Alleviating the Miseries of Public Prisons, 1833. https://archive.org/details/gri_33125013775586.

Smith, Sidonie. "Autobiographical Discourse in the Theaters of Politics." *Biography* 33, no. 1 (2010): v–xxvi. https://www.jstor.org/stable/23541045.

———. "Reading the Posthuman Backward: Mary Rowlandson's Doubled Witnessing." *Biography* 35, no. 1 (2012): 137–52. http://www.jstor.org/stable/23540937.

Smith, Sidonie, and Julia Watson. *Reading Autobiography: A Guide for Interpreting Life Narratives*. Minneapolis: University of Minnesota Press, 2001.

Spencer, Jennifer. "Unlocked Potential: From Incarceration to Entrepreneurship." *Entrepreneur*, 13 March 2017. https://www.entrepreneur.com/article/290097.

Stanutz, Katherine. "'Dying, but Fighting Back': George Jackson's Modes of Mourning." *MELUS: Multi-Ethnic Literature of the United States* 42, no. 1 (2017): 32–52. http://ezproxy.library.ubc.ca/login?url=http://search.ebscohost.com/login.aspx?direct=true&db=mzh&AN=2017381367&login.asp&site=ehost-live&scope=site http://muse.jhu.edu/article/658261.

Steinmetz, George. "Harrowed Landscapes: White Ruingazers in Namibia and Detroit and the Cultivation of Memory." *Visual Studies* 23, no. 3 (2008): 211–37.

Stoddard, Lothrop. *The Revolt against Civilization: The Menace of the Under Man*. New York: Charles Scribner's Sons, 1922.

Struggle for Justice. A Report on Crime and Punishment in America, Prepared for the American Friends Service Committee. New York: Hill and Wang, 1971.

Stuntz, William J. *The Collapse of American Criminal Justice.* Cambridge. MA: Harvard University Press, 2011.

Sullivan, Larry E. *The Prison Reform Movement: Forlorn Hope.* Boston: Twayne, 1990.

Sullivan, Larry E., and Brenda Vogel. "Reachin' behind Bars: Library Outreach to Prisoners, 1798–2000." In *Libraries to the People: Histories of Outreach*, edited by Robert S. Freeman and David M. Hovde, 113–27. Jefferson: McFarland, 2003.

Sweeney, Megan. *Reading Is My Window: Books and the Art of Reading in Women's Prisons.* Chapel Hill: University of North Carolina Press, 2010.

Taylor, Williams Banks. *Down on Parchman Farm: The Great Prison in the Mississippi Delta.* Columbus: Ohio State University Press, 1999.

Thomas, Piri. *Down These Mean Streets.* New York: A.A. Knopf, 1967.

Thompson, Heather Ann. *Blood in the Water: The Attica Prison Uprising of 1971 and Its Legacy.* New York: Knopf Doubleday, 2016.

———. "Why Mass Incarceration Matters: Rethinking Crisis, Decline, and Transformation in Postwar American History." *Journal of American History* 97, no. 3 (2010): 703–34. http://www .jstor.org/stable/40959940.

Thornton, Sarah. *Club Cultures: Music, Media, and Subcultural Capital.* Hanover: University Press of New England, 1996.

Tocqueville, Alexis de, and Gustave Beaumont. *On the Penitentiary System in the United States and its Application in France: With an Appendix on Penal Colonies, and also, Statistical Notes.* Translated by Francis Lieber. Philadelphia: Carey, Lea & Blanchard, 1833.

Tomkins, Silvan. *Shame and Its Sisters: A Silvan Tomkins Reader.* Edited by Eve Kosofsky Sedgwick and Adam Frank. Durham: Duke University Press, 1995.

Trounstine, Jean. *Shakespeare behind Bars: The Power of Drama in a Women's Prison.* New York: St. Martin's Press, 2014.

US Bureau of Justice. "Recidivism." Bureau of Justice Statistics, Office of Justice Programs. http://bjs.ojp.usdoj.gov/index. cfm?ty=tp&tid=17.

Viswanathan, Gauri. *Outside the Fold: Conversion, Modernity, and Belief.* Princeton: Princeton University Press, 1998.

Wacquant, Loïc. "Deadly Symbiosis." *Punishment and Society* 3, no. 1 (2001): 95–133. http://journals.sagepub.com/doi/full/10.1177/14624740122228276.

Walker, Madeline Ruth. *The Trouble with Sauling Around: Conversion in Ethnic American Autobiography, 1965–2002.* Iowa City: University Of Iowa Press, 2011.

Waxler, Robert P., and Jean R. Trounstine, eds. *Changing Lives through Literature.* Notre Dame: University of Notre Dame Press, 1999.

Welter, Barbara. "The Cult of True Womanhood: 1820–1860." *American Quarterly* 18, No. 2 (Summer 1966): 151–74.

Wepman, Dennis, Ronald B. Newman, and Murray B. Binderman. *The Life: The Lore and Folk Poetry of the Black Hustler.* Philadelphia: University of Pennsylvania Press, 1976.

Wicker, Tom. *A Time to Die: The Attica Prison Revolt.* Lincoln: University of Nebraska Press, 1994.

Wideman, John Edgar. *Brothers and Keepers.* New York: Holt Rinehart and Winston, 1984.

Wiegman, Robyn. "Whiteness Studies and the Paradox of Particularity," *Boundary 2* 26, no. 3 (1999): 131.

Williams, Daniel E. "'Behold a Tragic Scene Strangely Changed into a Theater of Mercy': The Structure and Significance of Criminal Conversion Narratives in Early New England." *American Quarterly* 38, no. 5 (1986): 827–47.

———. "Rogues, Rascals, and Scoundrels: The Underworld Literature of Early America." *American Studies* 24, no. 2 (1983): 5–19. http://www.jstor.org/stable/40641771.

Williams, Stanley Tookie. *Blue Rage, Black Redemption: A Memoir.* New York: Simon and Schuster, 2007.

Wilson, Colin, and Donald Seaman. *The Serial Killers: A Study in the Psychology of Violence*. London: W.H. Allen, 1990.

Wines, Enoch, and Louis Dwight. *Report on the Prisons and Reformatories of the United States and Canada*. Albany: Van Benthuysen & Sons, 1867.

Woodfox, Albert, with Leslie George. *Solitary: My Story of Transformation and Hope*. Toronto: HarperCollins, 2019.

Yee, Min. "Death on the Yard: The Untold Killings at Soledad and San Quentin." *Ramparts*, April 1973, 35–40.

Young, Sandra. "The Dynamic of Interrogation in Prison Narratives: The Position of the Reader in the Reconstruction of the Subject." *Inter Action* 3 (1995): 16–26. http://gateway.proquest.com/openurl?ctx_ver=Z39.88-2003&xri:pqil:res_ver=0.2&res_id=xri:ilcs-us&rft_id=xri:ilcs:rec:abell:R03214173.

BIBLIOGRAPHY

INDEX

INDEX

BOOKS IN
THE LIFE WRITING SERIES

PUBLISHED BY

WILFRID LAURIER UNIVERSITY PRESS

Haven't Any News: Ruby's Letters from the Fifties edited by Edna Staebler
with an Afterword by Marlene Kadar • 1995 / x + 172 pp. / ISBN
978-0-88920-248-1

"I Want to Join Your Club": Letters from Rural Children, 1900–1920
edited by Norah L. Lewis with a Preface by Neil Sutherland • 1996
/ xii + 250 pp. (30 b&w photos) / ISBN 978-0-88920-260-3

And Peace Never Came by Elisabeth M. Raab with Historical Notes by
Marlene Kadar • 1996 / x + 196 pp. (12 b&w photos, map) / ISBN
978-0-88920-292-4

*Dear Editor and Friends: Letters from Rural Women of the North-West,
1900–1920* edited by Norah L. Lewis • 1998 / xvi + 166 pp. (20
b&w photos) / ISBN 978-0-88920-287-0

The Surprise of My Life: An Autobiography by Claire Drainie Taylor
with a Foreword by Marlene Kadar • 1998 / xii + 268 pp. (8 colour
photos and 92 b&w photos) / ISBN 978-0-88920-302-0

Memoirs from Away: A New Found Land Girlhood by Helen M. Buss /
Margaret Clarke • 1998 / xvi + 154 pp. / ISBN 978-0-88920-350-1

The Life and Letters of Annie Leake Tuttle: Working for the Best by
Marilyn Färdig Whiteley • 1999 / xviii + 150 pp. / ISBN 978-0-
88920-330-3

Marian Engel's Notebooks: "Ah, mon cahier, écoute" edited by Christl
Verduyn • 1999 / viii + 576 pp. / ISBN 978-0-88920-333-4 cloth /
ISBN 978-0-88920-349-5 paper

Be Good, Sweet Maid: The Trials of Dorothy Joudrie by Audrey Andrews
• 1999 / vi + 276 pp. / ISBN 978-0-88920-334-1

Working in Women's Archives: Researching Women's Private Literature and Archival Documents edited by Helen M. Buss and Marlene Kadar • 2001 / vi + 120 pp. / ISBN 978-0-88920-341-9

Repossessing the World: Reading Memoirs by Contemporary Women by Helen M. Buss • 2002 / xxvi + 206 pp. / ISBN 978-0-88920-408-9 cloth / ISBN 978-0-88920-409-6 paper

Chasing the Comet: A Scottish-Canadian Life by Patricia Koretchuk • 2002 / xx + 244 pp. / ISBN 978-0-88920-407-2

The Queen of Peace Room by Magie Dominic • 2002 / xiv + 114 pp. / ISBN 978-0-88920-417-1

China Diary: The Life of Mary Austin Endicott by Shirley Jane Endicott • 2002 / xvi + 254 pp. / ISBN 978-0-88920-412-6

The Curtain: Witness and Memory in Wartime Holland by Henry G. Schogt • 2003 / xii + 132 pp. / ISBN 978-0-88920-396-9

Teaching Places by Audrey J. Whitson • 2003 / xiv + 182 pp. (9 colour photos) / ISBN 978-0-88920-425-6

Through the Hitler Line by Laurence F. Wilmot, M.C. • 2003 / xvi + 152 pp. / ISBN 978-0-88920-426-3 cloth / ISBN 978-0-88920-448-5 paper

Where I Come From by Vijay Agnew • 2003 / xiv + 298 pp. / ISBN 978-0-88920-414-0

The Water Lily Pond by Han Z. Li • 2004 / x + 254 pp. / ISBN 978-0-88920-431-7

The Life Writings of Mary Baker McQuesten: Victorian Matriarch edited by Mary J. Anderson • 2004 / xxii + 338 pp. / ISBN 978-0-88920-437-9

Seven Eggs Today: The Diaries of Mary Armstrong, 1859 and 1869 edited by Jackson W. Armstrong • 2004 / xvi + 228 pp. / ISBN 978-0-88920-440-9 cloth / ISBN 978-0-55458-439-0 paper

Incorrigible by Velma Demerson • 2004 / vi + 178 pp. / ISBN 978-0-88920-444-7

Love and War in London: A Woman's Diary 1939–1942 by Olivia Cockett; edited by Robert W. Malcolmson • 2005 / xvi + 208 pp. / ISBN 978-0-88920-458-4

I Have a Story to Tell You by Seemah C. Berson • 2010 / xx + 288 pp. (24 b&w photos) / ISBN 978-1-55458-219-8

We All Giggled: A Bourgeois Family Memoir by Thomas O. Hueglin • 2010 / xiv + 232 pp. (20 b&w photos) / ISBN 978-1-55458-262-4

Just a Larger Family: Letters of Marie Williamson from the Canadian Home Front, 1940–1944 edited by Mary F. Williamson and Tom Sharp • 2011 / xxiv + 378 pp. (16 b&w photos) / ISBN 978-1-55458-323-2

Burdens of Proof: Faith, Doubt, and Identity in Autobiography by Susanna Egan • 2011 / x + 200 pp. / ISBN 978-1-55458-333-1

Accident of Fate: A Personal Account 1938–1945 by Imre Rochlitz with Joseph Rochlitz • 2011 / xiv + 226 pp. (50 b&w photos, 5 maps) / ISBN 978-1-55458-267-9

The Green Sofa by Natascha Würzbach, translated by Raleigh Whitinger • 2012 / xiv + 240 pp. (5 b&w photos) / ISBN 978-1-55458-334-8

Unheard Of: Memoirs of a Canadian Composer by John Beckwith • 2012 / x + 393 pp. (74 illus., 8 musical examples) / ISBN 978-1-55458-358-4

Borrowed Tongues: Life Writing, Migration, and Translation by Eva C. Karpinski • 2012 / viii + 274 pp. / ISBN 978-1-55458-357-7

Basements and Attics, Closets and Cyberspace: Explorations in Canadian Women's Archives edited by Linda M. Morra and Jessica Schagerl • 2012 / x + 338 pp. / ISBN 978-1-55458-632-5

The Memory of Water by Allen Smutylo • 2013 / x + 262 pp. (65 colour illus.) / ISBN 978-1-55458-842-8

The Unwritten Diary of Israel Unger, Revised Edition by Carolyn Gammon and Israel Unger • 2013 / x + 230 pp. (90 b&w illus.) / ISBN 978-1-77112-011-1

Boom! Manufacturing Memoir for the Popular Market by Julie Rak • 2013 / viii + 250 pp. (7 b&w illus.) / ISBN 978-1-55458-939-5

Motherlode: A Mosaic of Dutch Wartime Experience by Carolyne Van Der Meer • 2014 / xiv + 132 pp. (6 b&w illus.) / ISBN 978-1-77112-005-0

Not the Whole Story: Challenging the Single Mother Narrative edited by Lea Caragata and Judit Alcalde • 2014 / x + 222 pp. / ISBN 978-1-55458-624-0

Street Angel by Magie Dominc • 2014 / vii + 154 pp. / ISBN 978-1-77112-026-5

In the Unlikeliest of Places: How Nachman Libeskind Survived the Nazis, Gulags, and Soviet Communism by Annette Libeskind Berkovits • 2014 / xiv + 282 pp. (6 colour illus.) / ISBN 978-1-77112-066-1

Kinds of Winter: Four Solo Journeys by Dogteam in Canada's Northwest Territories by Dave Olesen • 2014 / xii + 256 pp. (17 b&w illus., 6 maps) / ISBN 978-1-77112-118-7

Working Memory: Women and Work in World War II edited by Marlene Kadar and Jeanne Perreault • 2015 / viii + 246 pp. (46 b&w and colour illus.) / ISBN 978-1-77112-035-7

Wait Time: A Memoir of Cancer by Kenneth Sherman • 2016 / xiv + 138 pp. / ISBN 978-1-77112-188-0

Canadian Graphic: Picturing Life Narratives edited by Candida Rifkind and Linda Warley • 2016 / viii + 310 pp. (59 colour and b&w illus.) / ISBN 978-1-77112-179-8

Travels and Identities: Elizabeth and Adam Shortt in Europe, 1911 edited by Peter E. Paul Dembski • 2017 / xxii + 272 pp. (9 b&w illus.) / ISBN 978-1-77112-225-2

Bird-Bent Grass: A Memoir, in Pieces by Kathleen Venema • 2018 • viii + 346 pp. / ISBN 978-1-77112-290-0

My Basilian Priesthood, 1961–1967 by Michael Quealey • 2019 • viii + 222 pp. / ISBN 978-1-77112-242-9

What the Oceans Remember: Searching for Belonging and Home by Sonja Boon • 2019 • xvi + 320 pp. (8 b&w illus.) / ISBN 978-1-77112-423-2

Rough and Plenty: A Memorial by Raymond A. Rogers • 2020 • x + 316 pp. (9 b&w photos) / ISBN 978-1-77112-436-2

Limelight: Canadian Women and the Rise of Celebrity Autobiography • 2020 • viii + 360 pp. (6 colour images) / ISBN 978-1-77112-429-4

Prison Life Writing: Conversion and the Literary Roots of the U.S. Prison System by Simon Rolston • 2021 • x + 316 pp. / ISBN 978-1-77115-517-8